Beyond Empire

POSTCOLONIALISM & MISSION IN A GLOBAL CONTEXT

Jonathan Ingleby

AuthorHouse™ UK Ltd.
500 Avebury Boulevard
Central Milton Keynes, MK9 2BE
www.authorhouse.co.uk
Phone: 08001974150

© 2010 Jonathan Ingleby. All rights reserved.

No part of this book may be reproduced, stored in a retrieval system, or transmitted by any means without the written permission of the author.

First published by AuthorHouse 3/1/2010

ISBN: 978-1-4490-8230-7 (sc)

This book is printed on acid-free paper.

Critical comment on *Beyond Empire*

"Jonathan Ingleby fills a gaping void in the literature with his postcolonial approach to a theology of mission. His wide-ranging survey touches upon the pressing issues facing our churches, with helpful biblical reflections woven throughout. Moreover, his apocalyptic tenor is appropriate to both the Jesus tradition and our own times."

Ched Myers
Bartimaeus Cooperative Ministries (www.bcm-net.org)

"This book is a challenging and disturbing read. It challenges many superficial assumptions of 'received wisdom' about world mission and its history, and it disturbs some of the equally superficial optimism that greets the rise of majority world Christianity. Writing from long personal experience and remarkably wide reading, Jonathan Ingleby exposes the dark and depressingly long legacy of colonialism and the distortions it has wreaked (and continues to wreak) in Christian life, faith and mission. The book brings together, in a conversation that is rarely heard, postcolonialist, biblical and missional perspectives, along with personal analysis and comment on a wide range of contemporary political, economic and religious realities in the international sphere. But its uncomfortable realism about our present world order (Christian or otherwise) does not omit the ultimately greater biblical reality - the hope of God's kingdom and the new beginning that comes with Christ."

Christopher J. H. Wright
International Director, Langham Partnership International

"In a world where mission is still done from the perspectives of Christendom and worldly power, the church needs a prophet whose penetrating analysis befits the vision of the kingdom of God.

Mission studies have tended to be based on historical studies, cultural anthropology, or contemporary strategic concerns. This book is an original and challenging contribution that integrates postcolonial and mission studies and addresses wide ranging issues - global poverty, consumerism, social transformation, war on terrorism, neo-colonialism, migration and personal discipleship. The result is some refreshing but deeply disturbing insights deserving serious attention by all, particularly among Christians accustomed to doing mission from the position of power. Dr Ingleby is a prophet of our times, and this publication should become an essential reading not only for the classroom but for all concerned Christians."

Kang San Tan
Head of Mission Studies, Redcliffe College

"In this wide-ranging and passionately argued book Jonathan Ingleby shows how the legacy of empire and the continuing realities of neo-colonialism impact theology, mission and human well-being. 'Beyond Empire' brings into sharp focus many crucial challenges and opportunities. It should establish 'post-colonial' as a vital category for missiological reflection alongside the more familiar categories of post-modern and post-Christendom."

Stuart Murray Williams
Chair, Anabaptist Network

Beyond Empire

Postcolonialism & Mission in a Global Context

To my son, David, who kept me at it!

Acknowledgements

This book owes a great deal to my students at Redcliffe College with whom I shared my thoughts on much of the material that follows. Teaching them forced me to be a little less obscure than I usually am! I found the voices from the Global South particularly enlivening.

I enjoyed regular help and stimulation from my colleagues and ex-colleagues, especially Rob Cook, Kang San Tan, Simon Steer and Andy and Carol Kingston-Smith. Not all of them saw eye to eye with me, and that was also a great help.

My thanks to the editors of the Redcliffe College journal, *Encounters*, for agreeing to my use of material first published there. My quite numerous contributions to the early editions of the journal meant that I had a useful archive of my own thinking.

I have also used, with permission, articles (considerably revised) previously published in *Transformation*. My thanks to David Singh and the Oxford Centre for Mission Studies for that help.

My wife, Sue, and the other members of the family, have all encouraged me to go on writing, and provided me with the time and space to do it. I am most grateful.

Contents

INTRODUCTION
Why postcolonialism? xvii

CHAPTER ONE
Defining mission in the light of postcolonialism 1
- A narrow discourse 2
- A missiological contribution 4
- Looking at postcolonialism theologically 5
- Wrong connections 8
- Connecting: some practical examples 9
- The failure of the church 11
- So what must we do? 12

CHAPTER TWO
Struggling free from the colonial past 14

Imperialism revisited 14
- The Domination System 14
- Resisting the Empire – a consistent Biblical theme 17
- 'He was given a mouth' 19
- More from Revelation 13 25
- Jesus and the Domination System 27
- More Biblical exegesis 29
- Examples from history 31
- The imperial inheritance 35
- Some intellectual tools 37

Postcolonialism and the politics of dispossession 40

Postcolonial Resistance 46
- Interpolation 48
- Mimicry 50
- Archaeology and Magic Realism 52
- Palimpsest 54
- Representation 55

- What about the church? 60

Postcolonialism and the global culture **62**
- A global culture? 62
- The effects of globalisation on traditional culture:
  three possibilities 66
- Responding to cultural change: some examples 67
- Leaving the local 70
- Destroying local communities 73
- The global youth culture 77
- The destruction of 'life-worlds' 78
- Western secularism 79
- The local fights back 80
- Global and local: an ecclesiological perspective 84
- How to hang on to the local 86

Postcolonialism and Development **88**
- Did we start at the wrong place? 88
- Are we part of the problem rather than part of the solution? .. 91
- Can you contextualise into the Empire or do you need
  to fight it? 93
- What about power? 94
- What about community? 95
- Have we got the right perspective? 97
- Have we a prophetic word for today? 98

CHAPTER THREE

New Formations **100**

Hybridity or The Third Space **100**
- Strangers 101
- Identity 104
- Confusion 106
- How Shall We Describe the Kingdom of God? 111

Migration and Diaspora **115**
- People on the move 117
- Identity issues 118
- Diaspora 121

Fate of the indigenous peoples **125**
- The postcolonial approach 125

- Traditional and modern: taking sides 126
- Questions about survival 130

The Postcolonial City **136**
- Are we really in that much trouble? 137
- How did it happen? 137
- What can we do? 140

What About Zion? **144**

The New Authoritarianism **151**

Pedagogical and performative **159**

CHAPTER FOUR

What next for mission? **164**

The modern missionary movement **165**

The South and the West **173**
- The Churches in the South 173
- Hierarchical 175
- Patriarchal 176
- Territorial 176
- Insufficiently contextualised and overly culturally determined 177
- Legalistic 179
- Membership not discipleship 179
- Western retention of power 182
- Southern alternatives 184
- Conclusion 191

CHAPTER FIVE

The Great Economy **192**

Three preliminary considerations **192**

Government **195**
- A Just Society? 196
- An alternative to capitalism: the politics of security 197
- Responding to insecurity 199
- Advocacy 202

- Government close up 204
- Two models 206
- Consequences and conclusions 207

The Biblical Witness **210**
- The testimony of Deuteronomy 210
- Utopian imaginations and the Song of Songs 211
- Isaiah's testimony 213

Apocalypse Now **215**
- (a) Edge of Darkness 217
- (b) Where Satan has his throne 218
- (c) The Great War 218
- (d) Walter Benjamin 221
- (e) Two recent films: apocalyptic and the nature of 'failure' . 222
- (f) Puddleglum and The Silver Chair 224

CHAPTER 6

Postcolonialism: a gift from the sponsor of world mission 226

Conclusion: Time to Wake Up 228

APPENDIX 1

Israel and the land 236

APPENDIX 2

Eschatology and mission 244

BIBLIOGRAPHY

INDEX

Introduction

WHY POSTCOLONIALISM?

Why postcolonialism? What, if anything, does it have to do with the mission of the Church today?

It seems to me that most of us Western Christians do not understand what our non-Western brothers and sisters really think about their history. It is not in their interest to tell us and we do not really want to know; a secret which we ought to be able to share but seldom bring into the open. In fact, if we only knew, they see us as blindly overlooking some of the great follies and evils of the past (such as colonialism and slavery) and making a determined attempt to re-write history to our advantage. They suspect that even our Christian history all too readily celebrates the West's supposed successes and triumphs, while tidying over its failures and mistakes. They have an uncomfortable feeling that we really do not mean to give up our colonial ways, that in this respect our usual business is 'business as usual'.

Yet, surely, this is fundamental to mission. If our Christian discourse is riddled with notions of success, of growth, of prosperity and the like, when are we going to notice that the Kingdom of God simply cannot be described in these terms? If our Christian history fails to convey the truth about the past, how can we live truthfully in the present?

Postcolonial thought has devoted itself to understanding the colonial past and to describing its ongoing effects. In other words – given that Western colonialism has until quite recently 'filled the world'[1] – it is re-writing the universal history of our times. Also, it is writing it from a particular point of view: that of the people who were and are history's losers. Is this not where we Christians should be standing?

To regain a just perspective we must begin with this history; not in any academic or theoretical spirit, rather out of the conviction that unless we write history, history will write us. Westerners tend to view the history of the recent past primarily in terms of a rather triumphalistic celebration of the defeat of Fascism and Communism. We feel that history is on our side. What we may not have noticed is that the events of the twentieth century, taken as a whole, suggest that very big questions need to be placed against the myth of Western progress. The defeat of the twentieth century dictators, good in itself, masks the wider issues of colonial exploitation, world war, genocide, and weapons of mass destruction. The very fact that Fascism arose in two of Europe's most 'civilised' nations and was a widespread phenomenon demands explanation. The failure of the so-called Enlightenment Project raises questions we have largely failed to answer.

Fortunately, I would argue, the postcolonial discourse helps us to do so. It involves a fundamental critique of our Western history and its Enlightenment assumptions. The long, sad story of the failure of secularism as a response to sacralism is, in many respects, a *colonial* question. 'New totalist and instrumentalist theories of the universe, society and the human being were now legitimating colonial projects and advancing military technologies and industrial profiteering', says the social critic and New Testament scholar, Ched Myers speaking of the dawn of the Age of Reason (Myers 1994, 31). We might add that the 'military technologies' and 'industrial profiteering' were not simply different aspects of the Enlightenment Project along with the search for colonies, but they were 'colonial' in themselves. As Wendell Berry has put it: 'Industrialism prescribes an economy that is placeless and displacing. It does not distinguish one place from another…It thus continues the economy of colonialism. The shift of colonial power from European monarchy to global corporation is perhaps the dominant theme of modern history' (Berry 2002). In Britain, for example, as part of the nation's imperial project, the working class was being successfully 'colonised' at the same time as foreigners in distant lands, and for the same reason: so that it could be commercially exploited. It is no coincidence that radical thought in Britain at the time was staunchly anti-imperialist, just as it was naturally opposed to industrial profiteering. Most

---

[1] If we take Africa as an example, within living memory virtually the whole of Africa was under European control.

British wars from the seventeenth century onwards were colonial wars fought to acquire and/or defend colonial possessions. Britain's industrial strength, at its peak in the nineteenth century, was based on control of material resources, exclusion of potential commercial rivals and exploitation of labour. For this a number of 'arrangements' were necessary: colonial acquisitions, the building of a strong navy, and cheap labour (slaves in the West Indies, miners and factory workers etc. in Britain).

What has this to do with us in the twenty first century? Well, firstly, the Enlightenment thinking which underpins the Enlightenment project is still with us. We in the West have by no means renounced our 'civilising' (read 'colonising') mission, based on the supposed inherent superiority of our language, laws, science, and technology, and our vaunted freedom from irrationality and superstition. Also we have tacitly agreed that force may be used to attain our ends if necessary. Colonial wars are still being fought; nations are still not genuinely independent: they have struggled free from colonial status only to be subject to neo-colonialism; the workers of the world still labour impossible hours in harsh conditions and for little pay.

And, we Western Christians are complicit – not all of us, of course, and not everywhere, but the majority. Going back perhaps as far as Constantine and the Christendom project, most of us have sided with power and the political establishment. A little Christian postcolonialism is called for.

Chapter One

DEFINING MISSION IN THE LIGHT OF POSTCOLONIALISM

In the twenty-first century it is not possible to treat the word 'mission' as if it stood for something quite obvious and explicable, something which stands alone without needing any context. When people say that they have 'a heart for mission' I am always inclined to think – 'good, but what does that mean?' After all the word 'mission' simply implies that someone is about to be sent somewhere. But where are we being sent and to what purpose?

The Apostle Paul had a strongly developed sense of purpose! He talked about 'fighting the fight' and 'finishing the race'. He thought there was a prize waiting for him (2 Timothy 4:7-8). He wanted to 'achieve' the resurrection (Philippians 3:11). He spoke, in Ephesians 6, about a struggle which is not against human enemies but against spiritual forces. He realised that he was up against 'powers' that were much stronger than he was. So this *defined* the struggle. My hope is that understanding postcolonialism may help us to identify the powers that are threatening us, and that thereby we may define our struggle. Paul had a vision of a man from Macedonia who said 'come over and help us' (Acts 16:9). He had, at least for the time being, a Macedonian context. What did that Macedonian context demand from him? Well, there was a fortune telling girl and she needed delivering from her masters (Acts 16:16f.). (And how many people are kept in slavery today by ruthless and money grabbing owners and need some help to get free?) There was also a group of Jewish women who met 'outside the city gate' (you had to have *men* if you were going to form a synagogue) and they needed to be incorporated into the people of God (Acts 16:13-15). Again, there was a town gaoler who needed to be 'saved' but did not really know what that meant, though he probably guessed that the men he was dealing with had been unjustly imprisoned (Acts 16:30). Immediately Paul answers the call, mission begins and immediately he is in the battle, a battle which involves exploitive labour, discrimination against women, and unjust practices, along with what we would call today 'church planting'.

Has this got anything to do with postcolonialism? It certainly has. Look about you. What do you see? You do not have to look very hard to see a world in turmoil, a world where there are 150 million street children, where a billion people every morning wake up hungry, where we are daily beating our ploughshares into swords and our pruning hooks into spears in the name of the false god 'security'. It is into *this* world that we are sent. A study of postcolonialism is worth doing if it reminds us that we are in a battle, indeed a struggle for survival. It is worth doing if it tunes us into the world's suffering and our part in it as followers of the 'suffering servant'. It is worth doing if it gives us a new sense of urgency. 'The end of all things is near' as the Apostle Peter says, 'be serious and discipline yourselves' (1 Peter 4:7). Above all, it will have served its purpose if it challenges us to be better disciples of Jesus 'in this present age'.

A narrow discourse

The truth is that there are too many matters, and the study of postcolonialism is one of them, that we treat as outside of our concern as Christian people. The discourse of the church is too narrow. There are a number of ways in which this works out.

Firstly, we do not use the resources that we have. We have people in our church congregations with a whole range of useful disciplines such as the modern social sciences, yet we seldom if ever consult them.

Secondly and paradoxically, we are too quickly overawed by those who claim to be experts. Here is Arundhati Roy:

> Speaking for myself I have no personal or ideological axe to grind. I have no professional stakes to protect. I'm prepared

> to be persuaded. I'm prepared to change my mind. But instead of an argument, or an explanation, or a disputing of the facts, one gets insults, invective and the Experts' Anthem: You don't understand and it's too complicated to explain. The subtext of course is: Don't worry your little head about it. Go and play with your toys. Leave the *real* world to us (Roy 2003, 187).

Would that more Christians had Roy's anger at this sort of patronising response to our questions.

Thirdly, we need to widen the possibilities of choice by systematically reviewing those aspects of our public life that we have relegated to the realm of 'no choice'. How many times do you hear somebody say 'there is no alternative'? On the lips of the powerful this almost always means that there is some sort of power game going on. Spoken by the weak it usually represents a weary defeatism. Zygmunt Bauman suggests that one role of sociology (that detailed examination of 'the way of the world') is essentially to keep us from falling into this sort of situation. He puts it this way:

> The calling of sociology is nowadays to enlarge and to keep the width of that part of the human world which is subject to incessant discursive scrutiny and so to keep it saved from ossification into the 'no-choice' condition (Bauman 2001, 13).

Yes, but it is also the calling of those of us who proclaim the good news of God's rule. Christians are involved in this proclamation when they refuse to allow uncomfortable realities such as world poverty to slip off the world's agenda.

One way of taking up this responsibility has been described by John Stott in his book *The Contemporary Christian* (1992) as 'double listening' ('listening to the world' and 'listening to the Word'). Stott is drawing here on one of the key insights of Liberation Theology, namely that we cannot do our thinking about God abstracted from the world, and that effective learning begins with experience, goes on to reflection on that experience, and then proceeds to action based on experience and reflection together. This creates a discourse which uses Scripture and science, especially the social sciences, together. Scripture gives us our 'message' ('the rule of God is near') and models for us a community which connects us to others, reminding us that we need each other, and that we need to learn to serve each other. Social science helps us to see the world in a more complex way and, as we have seen, to attack the natural fatalism that constantly disempowers us. Clearly, what is needed here is some sort of marriage between our understanding of God and his purposes – Divine revelation, if you like – and history, the world of human interactions which make up our context.

In a sense, that is what Christians are trying to do all the time. We are trying to connect what we understand as 'the will of God' with our daily circumstances. That is why we are rightly so concerned about such personal issues as guidance and discipleship. Here, however, I am trying to describe the bigger picture. How can we interpret the sweep of history, to see it from God's point of view, so to speak?

A missiological contribution

In this vital task – what I call 'interpreting the sweep of history' – missiologists and theologians might do worse than to spend some time sitting humbly at the feet of our 'materialist' fellow pilgrims and learning to read history from their script. The sheer volume of careful research into many aspects of our world's history and society is amazing. We can take advantage of it. When we have done this perhaps we can contribute to the debate a few truths of our own. What can we say for ourselves?

First, we Christians are people who are constituted by history, by memory. ('Do this' said Jesus, 'to remember me'.) We are in danger of forgetting this! Jewish folk are less inclined to forget than we are. They have always stressed that the critical issue was *remembrance*. One of the most depressing features of the current theological scene is that in many quarters the recounting of present experience and speculation about the future have taken the place of serious Biblical exegesis. Let me give just one example: the Synoptic Gospels contain messages (I am thinking of the Olivet discourse – Matthew 24, Mark 13, Luke 17) intended to minister to the experience of a small persecuted group of believers, at odds with both the Jewish and Roman authorities, but who are beginning to understand the teaching of their leader that his death (and perhaps also the destruction of Jerusalem in 70 CE[2]) is something which has already inaugurated the Kingdom of God with all that that means. Their responsibility is now the preaching of the good news about the advent of that Kingdom. What sort of description do we have today from our exegetes. Instead of a patient and faithful identification with Jesus and his

---

[2] This is the position of N.T.Wright. See Wright 1996, 339ff.

discipline (and the 'mustard seed Kingdom' that Jesus proclaimed) we have a triumphalistic and speculative account of the progress of the Kingdom, characterised by a constant re-invention of the future and a disregard for the serious historical investigation that the New Testament requires. No wonder we are in a muddle.

Second, we need to remember that Jesus was on the side of the poor. The Kingdom of God as proclaimed by Jesus was a 'place' where those who had been marginalised and forgotten and 'written out of history' could be reconstituted. Jesus saw this, above all, as his work (Luke 4:18,19). It was, as we say nowadays, 'an upside down Kingdom', where the first would be last and the last first. This leaves us with a very down to earth challenge. The mission of the church, I believe, is fundamentally to do with 'the lost'. The great issues are those to do with identity, or, if you prefer, with the alienation and amnesia that lead to loss of identity. As we have seen, history and theology together speak to us powerfully in these very areas. Is it not time that we who are called to mission begin to see that our (neglected) task is precisely this 'calling forth' through all the means at our disposal, including scholarly study, those who have been consigned to 'the rubbish heap of history' but who in the Lord's eyes are 'chosen and precious'?

Third, nobody and nothing fall outside the scope of God's redemption. Any interpretation of history which excludes people from God's desire to be 'their God' is wrong. The gospel word is 'whosoever will may come'.

Fourth, the revealer of history is Jesus himself, who takes the scroll of history and undoes the seals, who calls forth the New Jerusalem, and who plants in it the tree of life by which the nations are healed.

Looking at postcolonialism theologically

Those of us who are Christians and live in the West have, I suggest, a very ambivalent attitude to our own culture. There is much that we want to affirm – perhaps because of its Christian origins, but also much that we feel instinctively is the enemy of the values for which Christians stand. Also, we are not sure whether we are prepared to stand with others, for example Islamic or Jewish thinkers, who are similarly involved in looking for a different basis on which to conduct their lives in a postcolonial society. How many bases are there? In this paragraph I have already mentioned the Christian, Jewish and Islamic world views, and there are no doubt many others. Do we simply accept this pluralist approach? Yet most of us understandably still feel that we need an overarching framework within which to live. We know that if society admits to no 'rule of law' or global ethic, it may appeal increasingly to power and violence to settle its differences (an example would be the Palestinian-Israeli dispute). Even a secularist like David Harvey finds this a difficult situation. He complains that this 'overarching framework' has not as yet made an appearance, that there is a 'lack of visionary ideals with which to combat the desolation' (Harvey 2000,156). His hope is that if society is 'made and imagined' it can also be 'remade and reimagined' (159). Christians might want to ask whether there is indeed some 'universal aspiration' that can be put to the gospel's account? Is it possible that society can be 'remade and reimagined' according to the rule of God?

So, to say it again, what about an adequate *theological* description of postcolonialism? Let me try an example.In a fascinating section in his essay on *sati* (widow immolation) in Bengal, Ashis Nandy makes the general point that a series of famines and major epidemics had created a suspicion that the maternal deity, Chandi, previously a symbol of nurture and protection, was now an 'unpredictable punitive mother' (Nandy 1990, 8ff.). So great was the ambiguity that Chandi had become two goddesses. On the one hand there was generous life-giving Durga, and on the other Kali, 'a treacherous cosmic mother, eager to betray and prone to aggression'. Kali was particularly popular in Calcutta (Kolkata). There it was not so much harsh economic circumstances as the confusion that many felt at the way that colonialism had introduced new and unpredictable ways which created new devotees for the goddess.

Drawing on this account I would like to suggest, firstly, that Kali had become what the New Testament calls a 'power'. She had been invested with authority by the fearful experience of her worshippers. Their experience of a 'satanic' world – famine, disease, confusion, death – created and fed into an idea of the deity which accurately reflected that experience. They worshipped (gave worth to) Kali and did what they could in order to win her favour or at least placate her. They were 'carried away' (1 Corinthians 12:2) by fear of her. The springs of evil in this situation were human, but they flowed into a lake that inundated the whole city; out of individual sin and rebellion a power grew that enslaved even those who had not contributed to it.

Secondly, what were the causes of famine and anomia (absence of recognised law) in Bengal and Calcutta? The answer again is that they were *human* causes. The anomia stemmed directly from the colonial incursion which overthrew traditional authorities and introduced new sources of patronage. Equally, the most severe Bengal famines had to do with the destruction by human agencies of peasant societies and their means of defending themselves against harsh conditions. This is the argument, made with irresistible power by Mike Davis in his book *Late Victorian Holocausts*. According to Davis mass starvation in the nineteenth century in India was 'avoidable political tragedy' rather than 'natural disaster' (2001, 8 and *passim*).

We might then draw up this equation. A people can be ruined spiritually by actions which are (apparently) purely 'materialist'. Economic exploitation and the quest for political power may lead not only to physical decline but to spiritual degradation as well. Perhaps the often remarked upon spiritual oppressiveness of Calcutta, with its worship of Kali and its dark ritualism, has its origin not in the halls of some demon lord, but in the brightly lit council chambers of the East India Company and the India Office. The directors of the Company and the Victorian civil servants were not, one suspects, addicted to the occult. They were not worshippers of Kali, indeed they despised 'that sort of thing'. They were simply intent on making money and keeping order (so that they might make more money). They could be ruthless if necessary, but few would have called them 'wicked'. For all that they were demonic forces in a system of evil. This is the sequence.

Colonial, exploitive practises

Food-insecurity, famine, disruption of traditional practices

Loss of confidence in 'divine' providence, creation of vengeful deities

Worship of Kali, ritual practices

Calcutta – hopelessness, oppression, fear

Defining mission in the light of postcolonialism

The connection with colonialism today can readily be made. The present disastrous conditions which exist in parts of sub-Saharan Africa, for example – famine, disease, civil war, corruption, genocide – is certainly a call to confront spiritual powers in the spirit of Ephesians 6:12. But we are mistaken if we think that the battle is primarily to be won in Africa. That may have been the case once upon a time, but we are now living in a postcolonial society. The great battles for the soul of humanity are going on above all in Washington, Brussels, London and Geneva. And these battles are being lost, or rather we Christians are not fighting them. Worse still, some of us are firing in the wrong direction. How easily we deceive ourselves! The whole sad parade of so-called 'spiritual warfare' is a massive transference of meanings away from the reality of our greed, economism, consumerism, desire for comfort, racism, national pride, misuse of power and the like, to a fictitious world where we can indulge our fantasies about 'other worlds' and 'the end of the age', while disclaiming any responsibility for the world's ills.

Wrong connections

We must refuse to allow our discourses to be polarised. This can happen from both ends. If it is true that Christians have all too often tried to 'shut out' the material world and its politics, it is also true that generations of intellectuals from the Enlightenment onwards have attempted to *substitute* politics for religion. 'In our time the destiny of man presents its meanings in political terms' says Thomas Mann.[3] Really? Is that *all* we can say about the destiny of man? Or again, Michael Oakeshott commenting on Hobbes' *Leviathan* connects politics directly with salvation.

> It is characteristic of political philosophers that they take a sombre view of the human situation; they deal in darkness. Human life in their writings appears, generally, not as a feast or even as a journey, but as a predicament, and the link between politics and eternity is the contribution that the political order is conceived as making to the deliverance of mankind (Oakeshott 1960, x).

This is by no means a small issue. 'The children of Christians make good Marxists' as somebody said. In his biography of John Maynard Keynes, Robert Skidelsky meditates on the way that a whole generation of Cambridge students

---

[3] This is the quotation used by W.B.Yeats at the head of his poem 'Politics'. He also protests against the reductionism of Mann's statement.

turned to Marxism in the 1930s (1992, 514-23). Skidelsky recognised that the attraction of Marx to the young men of Keynes's generation was not really intellectual but a mixture of 'personal and social salvation'. In this sense he felt that Marxism was rather like the Moral Rearmament movement! Keynes understood this, says Skidelsky, and took Marxism seriously as 'a sickness of the soul'. He saw that Marx and Freud had 'invaded the spaces left vacant by his own generation's demolition of Christianity' (Skidelsky 1992, 518).

And whose fault is this, this flight from faith? We have already noted how Christians too often want nothing to do with politics, or as little to do with them as possible, and we should not be surprised if this creates its own nemesis. Young people, and some older people too, are looking for something that will change the world. Churches that do not connect with what these young people see as the 'real' world will lose them, particularly if those same churches seem to have sold out to the establishment.

Connecting: some practical examples

Am I describing all this in a too confrontational way? Perhaps so. The chief point is that we need to connect. So how does this work out in practice? Let me try to explain by a couple of examples from my own experience. They are examples of areas of concern that are very high on the agendas of young people going into mission today and have been selected for that reason.

Working with street children

There appears to be widespread concern among Christian people at the state of the world's children. Indeed 'children at risk' is a hot topic for many people today, whether Christians or not. 'Street children' (more than 150,000,000 worldwide by some definitions[4]) are a particular focus of attention. Rightly this is an issue which Christians feel that they cannot ignore. It is a theological concern and a political, social and economic concern as well. If we pause to consider the *causes* of the phenomenon (before we rush to treat the symptoms) it seems evident that rootless societies produce rootless children. The problems no doubt relate to the homes where the children were born, and behind these problems lie deeper structural problems of poverty and marginalisation. Also

---

[4] This might be on the high side. New Internationalist (April, 2005) agree that estimates vary a great deal, between 30 million and 170 million in fact.

it has been suggested that there are forces in society today that are powerfully effective in detaching us from our roots. We need to ask how and why does this happen? So there is much social, political and economic analysis that needs to be done. But we must not forget theology. One of the great Biblical themes according to Walter Brueggemann is 'rootedness' (Brueggemann 1977). In all sorts of ways we must resist those forces that make us 'chaff', blown about by every wind that comes along. If you work in the slums of our great cities you may find that avaricious land developers are seeking to destroy the small communities that, against all the odds, have begun to grow and claim an identity. Protecting and fostering those communities, and encouraging their leaders, will be part of mission work. It may be one way, and a very important way, in which families can retain enough strength and cohesion to hold onto their children.

What I am saying is that the street children phenomenon cannot be understood in isolation and therefore political, economic and sociological insights must be added to theological and Biblical ones. I am also suggesting that some aspects of society are not neutral and value free but act as a domination system which needs to be resisted.

Working in the Muslim world (issues to do with Islamic fundamentalism)

Many Christians today are intrigued and confused by the phenomenon of Islamic fundamentalism and believe that the events of September 11, 2001 have brought these issues into sharp focus. It has long been clear that fundamentalism is in part a response to globalisation, and that we cannot understand what is going on in, say, the Middle East or Afghanistan and Pakistan, without some insight into this dialectic. Contemporary Islam is often deeply threatened by the culture of modernity, conveyed to it on a global scale through the modern media, especially satellite television. Al Qaeda gave as its main reasons for the bombings of September 11, firstly the presence of U.S. troops on Saudi Arabian soil (that is their proximity to the holy sites of Islam), secondly the present status of the Israeli-Palestinian conflict and thirdly the ongoing bombing of Iraq. The given motive for terrorism is a political/theological mix. Consider this brief response by Osama Bin Laden to the post 9/11 situation.

> Our duty, which we have fulfilled, is to incite the *umma* to take up a holy war in the name of God, against America, Israel, and their allies...It is time for the Muslim people to

> realise…that the countries of the region have no sovereignty. Our enemies move about freely and merrily in our seas, land and air. They hit without asking permission from anyone…I say that there are two sides in the conflict: the international crusade movement allied with Jewish Zionism and led by America, Britain, and Israel. And the other side is the Muslim world. It is unacceptable in such a conflict that he [sic] commits an aggression, enters my land and holy places, and robs the oil of the Muslims and then when he is confronted by any form of resistance from the Muslim he says: they are terrorists. This is either sheer stupidity, or assuming that others are stupid. We believe that it is our legitimate duty to resist this occupation with all the strength we have got and punish the enemy with the same means that it uses against us. Osama bin Laden, interview on Al Jazeera News Network, September 20, 2001 (translated from Arabic) (Castells 2004, 108).

It is time for some politics if we are to understand these frustrations. But there are some big theological issues as well. Where is the enemy for those of us in mission? Is it the 'pluralists' (Western culture and its long arm) or is it those who are fiercely defending their still-rooted cultures (Muslim fundamentalists, so called)? Once again we find ourselves in the middle of a battle, perhaps rather uncomfortably occupying a sort of no-man's-land. In this unfamiliar territory we need the tools of theological as well as political and cultural analysis.

I am not, the reader must understand, trying to 'solve' or even properly discuss these issues to do with street children or Islamic fundamentalism – not at this point anyway. I am simply saying that any proper involvement with these issues requires a bringing together of the appropriate social sciences and the relevant theological insights.

The failure of the church

All this prompts a meditation on the failure of the church to respond adequately to this situation. I would judge that at one level in society today there is an encouragingly large amount of comment and protest about world trends, such as postcolonialism. People want to get involved. Though the interest and involvement in traditional politics seems to be declining, at other levels there is a flurry of activity. People are organising mass mail protests; the media is being regularly supplied with critiques of government policies and trade rules; violations of people's rights or damage to the environment are given prominence; huge crowds turn up for mass demonstrations; alternative social fora attract large numbers – these are just some examples. I have in the past worked with two organisations, the World Development Movement and a local organisation called Gloucestershire Network Against the War , and we were engaged in most of the things mentioned above, as well as organising public meetings. I note, however, that there were not many Christians involved. Indeed when I campaigned in local elections for the Christian Peoples Alliance, a small Christian party, I found that there was a good deal of indifference, not to mention actual opposition, from *Christians*. Is this a general trend? Is it true that Christians are largely silent on these issues, and if so why? Does this silence come from our churches and theological institutions?

Christians on the whole have been much more interested in cultural change than political or economic change. Of course, there is nothing wrong with studying cultural movements; indeed it can be essential, particularly when defining and defending communities. Nevertheless the Bible consistently sees the political realm as profoundly important. It is not a coincidence that Jesus refers to the *Kingdom* of God. Economic studies are equally important. Much of our 'religion' has to do with the worship of the great god PROFIT and obeying the laws of his temple, aka the MARKET. But even this is a political question. You will find that economic hegemony is usually backed up before long by missiles and bombs. The key questions remain questions of power and loyalty. Who rules here? Who is Lord?

So what must we do?

Firstly, we need to warn people about the coming trouble. I hope this is what this book is partly about. In an attempt to be faithful to the teaching of Jesus and especially the apocalyptic passages in the New Testament the central themes are: the inevitability of the crisis, its unexpectedness, and our need to be alert. We simply cannot afford to ignore issues to do with economic recession, ecological crisis, the arms race, the growing alienation of the poor, fundamentalist resistance to Western cultural imperialism, and the like.

Secondly, there is no suggestion in the Biblical texts that any human situation, however apparently disastrous, is hopeless and that nothing can be done.

Indeed because of the crisis we need to build secure foundations. So we must not only be fully aware of the crisis we are in, or to which we are heading, but be doing everything we can to offer alternatives. Christians should be promoting better economic behaviour, thinking through positive 'green' politics, opposing the arms trade, working for fair trade, and addressing neo-colonialism. This would be in the spirit of Jesus himself, who, side by side with the warnings he issued, offered the people of his day a way out, namely the rule of God.

Of course we are often simply unable to offer alternatives because we are too deeply implicated in the world order that is ripe for destruction. 'Come out from her [Babylon], my people, lest you have any part in her sins, and share in her plagues' (Revelation 18:4) is a warning for all of us in the wealthy West. Can a Christian really work with a good conscience for a company like Shell in the light of what happened in the Ongoni delta (Maier 2000, 125)? The illustration Jesus uses (in Luke's account) is Lot's wife. She found it impossible wholly to leave Sodom and ended up sharing its destruction. When we link this with the sin of Sodom as described in Ezekiel – 'now this was the sin of your sister Sodom: She and her daughters were arrogant, overfed and unconcerned; they did not help the poor and needy' (Ezekiel 16:49) – it could be that we in the wealthy West are all potentially in trouble.

Chapter Two

STRUGGLING FREE FROM THE COLONIAL PAST

Imperialism revisited

If we are to understand how we are 'to struggle free from the colonial past' then we need a better understanding of colonialism (or we could use the more comprehensive word 'imperialism') and in particular its relation to what the New Testament calls 'the world'.

The Domination System

'World' as a Biblical term can be ambiguous and some scholars, Walter Wink is the prime example, have preferred the usage 'Domination System'. Wink also claims that Scripture describes a fundamental conflict between the forces of evil – the Domination System – and the rule of God. Here is a typical passage:

> For John, in the book of Revelation, 'the Kingdom of the world' (11.15) is not a geographical or planetary term. It refers to the alienated and alienating reality that seduces humanity into idolatry: the worship of political power as

> divine. The Roman Empire had made itself the highest value and the ultimate concern, arrogating to itself the place of God. Whether it be the Pax Romana, or the Pax Britannica or the Pax Americana, empires can maintain cohesion across racial, ethnic, linguistic and national lines only by creating a bogus solidarity. This they achieve by demanding the worship of the spirituality of empire. (Wink 1992, 300)

This means that far more serious than individual rebellion is the way that human sin has created structures of evil – lords, ideologies, institutions, identities and the like – that are too strong for us. It is their strength that often prevents us from 'seeing' the rule of God. One of the reasons why we believe that 'things never change', that resistance is futile, for example, is because, in Paul's telling phrase 'we have been carried away by dumb idols' (1 Corinthians 12:2). It is clearly time that we proclaim that 'Jesus is Lord' (12:3) and mean it! In one sense it is all in the mind. (Where else would it be?) We simply cannot *think* the rule of God.

Yet we are surrounded by these 'powers'. It only takes a little imagination to see how many and how deadly they are. Dying to them, not admitting that they have any legitimate power, not giving them any space, is how they are defeated. They are defeated on a grand scale by communities of God's rule, that openly demonstrate alternative values. For those of us, and it is most of us, who feel that on our own we have not the power to resist, then immersion in these communities is essential.

The powers that are attempting to subvert and destroy the rule of God, are defeated powers. What does this mean? Here we have to struggle with the double emphasis of the New Testament which boldly proclaims that the powers are indeed defeated (Colossians 2:13-15, Ephesians 1:20-23) but also looks forward to the day when they will be finally defeated (1 Corinthians 15:24-6). We are certainly here in the 'now but not yet' of New Testament eschatology. However, we do need a definite sense of what has been accomplished at the cross. Walter Wink is clearly troubled by his feeling that in practical terms the cross did not much alter power relationships there and then (Wink 1984, 60) and there is certainly a difficulty here. Was the cross merely exemplary – it demonstrated how the powers might be defeated – or was it, as one might say, performative? Perhaps we should not make a great distinction between the two. The demonstration of power in weakness was in fact what disarmed the powers. Though they continued to be operative their secret was out, and those who understood that, could defeat them. In terms of Revelation 12, the war in heaven has been successfully concluded but the defeated and displaced enemy is still able to cause trouble on earth. He *can* be overcome though the warfare remains costly (11). It is also true that the devil's time is short, though that makes the conflict even more furious (12). In the Colossians passage (see above) the context of Christ's victory over the powers is forgiveness, cancellation of debt and freedom from the past. This links powerfully with the way that we are 'bound' by the powers of our world today. It is guilt and fear and past failure that give the powers their foothold in our lives and ultimately which bring us under their control. The Colossians passage also speaks of demonstration. The powers are openly stripped of their force and are held up to public example as defeated. People see them for what they are. Just as the cross demonstrates power in weakness, the powers are now seen to be weak in their power. For example, the corporate financial collapses that the commercial world has recently experienced in a dramatic way, show us that financial institutions, once apparently so secure and impressive, are not necessarily the safe investment we thought them. By contrast, the rule of God, no bigger than a mustard seed, seems insignificant, but is infinitely worth investing in. So it is that the powers seem formidable, and unbeatable, but the cross demonstrates that love is stronger than fear, mercy triumphs over judgement, life comes out of death, and that embracing the enemy renders his weapons powerless. I am far from suggesting that this exhausts the significance of the cross. I am saying, however, that in our struggles with the powers we have found the way to victory, and that way is the way of the cross.

To the very last, Jesus demonstrated that he would not accept the seductive offers of the powers. ('You who would destroy the temple and build it in three days, save yourself! If you are the Son of God, come down from the cross.' Matthew 27:40) The voice of temptation never left Jesus from the moment he took up his mission to its very end. 'We are the real powers' it said. 'You have great potential, and together we can do much, indeed together we can rule the world (Matthew 4:8,9).' But seductive voices need somebody to listen to them. When seducers find that their offers are rejected they begin to see that their power is being diminished. Their confidence ('I have an offer that you can't refuse') turns to despair ('this is your last chance; this offer cannot be repeated'). To take a modern political example, the British administration in India was helpless in the face of Gandhi because ultimately they could not offer him anything that he wanted. It is this which makes people who will die for a cause (Revelation 12:11 again) so invulnerable.

Resisting the Empire – a consistent Biblical theme

It is a recurrent theme in Scripture that the Biblical authors are against *empires* (which might be just another way of describing the Domination System). By contrast, they are in favour of *cities* in that they express true community, though not cities that express imperial demands on their subjects, as the city of Babel in the book of Genesis did. So we have the New Jerusalem, the true community, which is described by John of Patmos as 'always coming down like a bride out of heaven' (Revelation 3:12, 21:2. G. B. Caird points out the continuous present tense in 1966, 270-1). From the very beginning of human history even until now God is at work to create these health giving communities. God is also a lover of human diversity and culture and 'the nations' have a positive relationship with New Jerusalem. They are invited to bring their 'glory' into the city (Revelation 21:26); they will be healed (Revelation 22:2); they provide representatives who praise God, and, we can assume, it is the very diversity of that praise which brings him special pleasure (Revelation 5:9). It should be added that the 'nations' in Revelation, are cultures and peoples, not nations in the late European sense, which, as in the case of Britain above with its imperialist pretensions, may be part of the problem rather than the solution.

The third player, the Empire (Babylon or Rome) is seen, as we have said, as the enemy of God, always tending towards the persecution of God's people, deceiving the nations, always riding for a fall because always overstretching itself. It reminds us of all the great empires of history, with their tendency to 'gobble up' the nations, to unify religion and culture, to use their military might for economic gain. Small nations, like Israel, were constantly threatened by this process to the point where they might simply cease to exist. Their territory could be overrun, their national treasures confiscated, their culture subverted, their gods relegated to anonymity. Assyrians, Babylonians, Persians, Greeks, Romans one way or another they were all at the same game. Empire is a threat both to nations in the more general sense, and in particular to God's purpose to 'call out a people for himself'. In the Old Testament this means a threat to Israel. In the New Testament it poses the question: who is Lord, Jesus or Caesar? Thus to come back to the book of Revelation, the Empire deceives the nations and persecutes the church (New Jerusalem).

We need to *teach* this as integrally to do with the mission of the church. Those who are proclaiming the good news of God's rule, who will be engaged in spiritual warfare (so pitifully relegated nowadays to a fitful demonology) who are equipped with a Biblical understanding of 'the signs of the times', need this fundamental insight. Indeed they need these weapons more than ever because the Empire has raised its ugly head in a new and more insidious way in our day than ever before. We are not simply living in a world where economic and political arrangements and their cultural consequences are value free, as some would have us believe. Of course it is difficult for those who have lost the spiritual dimension of life to understand the spiritual battle, and the idea of 'value-free' is still one of the dreams of modernity. But we Christians should know better. If we fail to make clear that we are still in the battle against 'the Empire', then we have not equipped our people as we should have.

This equipment will come, in part, through new Biblical exegesis, new theological models, new methods of historical investigation. Let me illustrate something of what I have in mind by going back again to the book of Revelation. As I have said, this book is fundamentally about Christians living under imperialism and the dangers of not making a stand against it. The seven letters of chapters two and three are full of references to this conflict: for example the letter to Pergamum 'where Satan has his throne'. I want to concentrate however on the struggle described in Revelation 12 and 13. The triumph of the male child (Jesus) in 12:5 leads to the expulsion of Satan from heaven (12:9) and to a renewed and fiercer onslaught against believers on earth. This is how it must have seemed to the recipients of this apocalyptic tract. Jesus had triumphed, but was no longer with them as a physical presence. Satan had been defeated, but his persecuting power was more evident than ever. The situation is, perhaps, analogous to that in the book of Job where the Satan is getting nowhere in his attempts to persuade God to turn against Job, but he is given permission to attack him through illness and misfortune.

Particularly evident and particularly ominous is the Beast, first introduced in 13:1b, who stands for the immediate foe, in this case the Roman Empire, 'the domination system' of the author's day. So impressive was this enemy, so powerful, that the game seemed to be up. Resistance was futile. 'Who is like the Beast and who can fight against it?' (13:4). The Beast is no mean enemy. It is genuinely powerful and invested with worldly authority and it is 'worshipful'. We read that 'the whole earth followed the Beast and worshipped it' (13:4) particularly after it had demonstrated apparently miraculous powers (13:3). Its authority extends to 'every tribe and people and language and nation' (13:7) and this echoes in a sinister way the famous universal ascription of praise to the Lamb in Revelation 7:9. Let me pause to suggest that the Domination System in our day is like the Beast in another way, in that the Beast appeared to be at death's door but miraculously revived (13:3). When times are bad as they are now – there is increasing unemployment, the market is falling, debt seems uncontrollable, or whatever the symptoms – people await, often with amazing confidence, the resurrection of their fortunes. They are convinced that things will get better. The one thing they cannot countenance is that the system they 'worship' may be fundamentally flawed.

Even for Christians, the Beast (imperial power) sometimes seems to be 'on the side of the angels', especially as it is quite good at manipulating our fears. Take, for example, the second Iraq war. It is natural to condemn international terrorism and Saddam Hussein's regime in Iraq, and we feel that anybody who deals with such a threat demands our support and gratitude. However, what is really going on here? There are many injustices in the world. Why choose this one? The truth is that *selective* action against 'evil' is a longstanding imperialist strategy. In the Roman Empire the *pax romana* meant a 'quiet' world, easily managed, and there were without doubt some blessings that accrued. Certainly you would expect imperial powers to explain matters in these terms.But those, like the Jewish people, who had been assimilated to Roman power in a series of bloody wars, might have described the situation differently. Essentially, the new world order is also portrayed in this way. The United States and its allies describe themselves as 'spreading democracy and freedom', even as they drop their bombs on unsuspecting victims. Culturally and economically, too, imperialism is presented as a boon, and of course there are plenty of people who are prepared to see it in this light, particularly if they are the ones who are becoming wealthy. Again, we can see parallels with the Roman Empire, indeed with the behaviour of all empires.

'He was given a mouth'

One of the features of this Beast (in Revelation) is that 'he was given a mouth' (13:5). Most of its power then, and it is the same today, lies in the *word*, that is to say in propaganda, image, reputation, hype, logos, spin, media manipulation, advertising and the whole process of cultural hegemony. The question we need to ask is: 'Who controls the truth?' The power and sophistication of the media provide ever more effective ways of influencing how people think, and what they believe. Michael Hardt and Antonio Negri in their book *Empire* (2000) have some valuable material on the way in which the new imperial order *controls* its subjects, and they put the use of communications at the head of the list. They actually speak of 'the linguistic production of reality' (34) and cite as an example the reaction to September 11, 2001. Thus the 'war against terrorism' has been 'produced' by the media, in such a way as to legitimate the imperialism of the new world order. In a similar vein they contend that '[I]n the society of the spectacle only what appears exists, and the major media have something of a monopoly on what appears to the general population' (322). The media coverage of the Second Gulf war is another instance of this.

With regard to control methods more generally, Hardt and Negri believe that the imperial system depends on 'interventions'. Obviously this applies to the cultural or communications field, but also to financial intervention and the use of force. Under this system, intervention has been 'internalised and universalised' (35). It begins with the use of moral instruments such as NGOs, very useful because they appear to be ethical, and leads on to the conduct of 'just wars' (without weapons initially e.g. the war on AIDS). Moral crusades then lead to military intervention. In such cases military action is portrayed as 'an internationally sanctioned police action' (thus continuing the myth of redemptive violence). The enemy is usually portrayed as 'terrorists', 'war-lords', 'an international mafia' or the like. Notice that 'armies and police anticipate the courts and preconstitute the rules of justice that the courts must then apply'. This is 'an inversion of the conventional order of constitutional logic' (38). This can be described as 'a state of permanent exception' i.e. every case is a special case (39). Under this system every imperial war is a civil war. Try distinguishing the role of the army, the police, the CIA and the FBI under these circumstances (189). You may well ask: what does the imperial machine appeal to for its legitimation? Michael Hardt and Antonio Negri have some good insights here also. Their answer is that the machine appeals to itself. Its authenticity comes from its 'languages of self-validation' which are inextricably part of the communication industry. As we have seen, the 'war against terrorism' has been 'produced' (think about the way the hero's life is 'produced' in the film *The Truman Show*) by the media, in such a way as to legitimate the imperialism of the new world order. The communications industry continually validates and re-validates the imperial machine. It produces its own authority which rests on nothing outside of itself.

We Christians today (the author included) are very feeble in this area. We know that we are being subverted and controlled but we are slow to take a stand. The last thing that most of us want is to be labelled 'fanatics', in any way threatening the *status quo*. We like to think of ourselves as reasonable people, not at all argumentative or aggressive, and we are very quick to disassociate ourselves from anyone *we* think is like that. When we do 'come on strong' we immediately feel guilty. All in all we are happy to be considered 'nice' people, indeed that is sometimes our definition of what true Christians are like. I suggest that this is a dangerous position in which to be. Our foes are well aware of these attitudes and have developed a technique to take advantage of it, which might be described as 'defensive attack'. This amounts to the skilful labelling of all those who are 'disturbing the peace' as mavericks and troublemakers. After all, they say, everything was all right until these people came along, and in any case we all know that the *status quo* is the natural order of things.

Of course this does not only happen to Christians. Naomi Klein in her book *Fences and Windows* has demonstrated how governments and authorities are very quick to use this tactic of 'defensive attack' against anybody they take to be a threat. As Klein says, 'Most dissent deterrence takes place when we accept the stories in newspapers, filled with anonymous sources and unattributed statements, about how some of the activists are actually 'agitators' who are 'planning to use violence' (2002, 134). Notice that this description is given *before* anything has happened. She has an example from Italy: 'Before a single activist had taken to the streets, a pre-emptive state of emergency had been essentially declared [in Genoa]; airports were closed off and much of the city was cordoned off' (150). Klein remarks about this that on her initial visit to Italy – we are still in the period before the demonstration in Genoa – she found that most people were talking about the alleged threat posed by the activists while there was little discussion of the violations of civil liberties that had already taken place.

Antonio Gramsci understood very well what a powerful weapon was available to 'the authorities' in labelling their opponents as abnormal or deviant. Gramsci came up with the very interesting idea of cultural hegemony. It is an idea which I have found hugely useful ever since I first came across it. Gramsci's idea was that one group (he would have said 'class') could exercise effective control over another, not only by economic and political means, but also by a cultural dominance or 'hegemony'. The dominating group is so skilful and successful in projecting its own view of the world at large that these ideas are accepted by everybody else, even by those who are being dominated, as a 'common sense' account of affairs, as the way things are 'naturally'. Only somebody fundamentally misguided or deceived, would seek to challenge the *status quo*. We may well ask, how does all this happen? How does 'cultural hegemony' of this sort come about? The answer is a rather bad joke. In effect it comes about because the existing power structures are able to shout loudest. Their claims are often spurious, amounting very often to little more than 'the king's new clothes'. Certainly they often lack, as the saying goes 'external verification'. However, the very confidence of their assertions (together with the control they exercise over the media) often gives them instant public credence.

Gramsci's conclusion was that successful change will only be brought about when those who have been subjected to cultural hegemony are introduced to a new vision of how things really are, when they see that the existing order is not 'natural' or 'common sense' at all. Thus we need to demonstrate in as many ways as possible that we Christians (indeed, we citizens) are simply not prepared to accept that 'the way things are' is the way that they will always be. Nor are we prepared to accept our valuation as mavericks, pessimists, eccentrics, lefties, fanatics and the like. Quite the reverse. We stand in the tradition of the Old Testament prophets, Jesus himself, St Francis, the Radical Reformers, Gandhi, Martin Luther King and Nelson Mandela. If we think only of the last three and the history of the twentieth century it is clear that Gandhi, King and Mandela were treated in the first instance as dangerous outsiders. If not, why were they vilified and imprisoned? The very people who praise them now have inherited the mantle of the establishment that bitterly opposed them in their day. We Christians cannot expect the world to be any less of an enemy today. Jesus warned us about this. What is often more troubling, indeed shameful, is that Christians themselves claim that they can get by without accepting Jesus' radical call to discipleship. When this happens we know that something is seriously awry.

Visible protests such as street demonstrations have been one of the most successful ways of drawing the attention of the world at large to perceived wrongs. However in recent times protest has been linked, by the establishment and for their own reasons, with *security* issues. TIME magazine (February 18, 2002), just to mention one source, attributed the muted response of protesters at both the Davos forum in New York and the Munich Conference on Security Policy (Josef Joffe, *Open Societies, Closed Minds* p.60) to this dilemma. It suggested that since September 11 protestors were rightly anxious that they would be tarred with the same brush as terrorists. This has continued up to the present. The same article, however, has to admit that this whole debate reveals a concern over the failure of the democratic process. There is something rather disconcerting about the way that the good and the great have to withdraw behind a huge and expensive police presence, largely to avoid the most concerned and politically articulate members of their constituency.

In fact this hiding away sends another message about modern democracy. What is the point of the ballot box and the referendum, the opinion poll and the letters page? People exercise their democratic rights but it does not seem to make any difference. And when they do identify a true focus of power it is surrounded by armed guards. Thus it is that the System, or one manifestation of it, presides over a world of politics in which the power slips away to global forums, conferences, summits and the like. This disempowers everyone. Here we have another example, small but significant, of the way that security issues are undermining democracy. The thesis of a number of hard-liners at the moment seems to be that you do not have to enter the democratic debate as long as you can characterise the enemy (Bin Laden, Al Qaeda, and perhaps the Taliban) as 'essentially evil' – a 'fundamentalist' argument used by supposedly non-fundamentalist people. Members of Al Qaeda must be wiped out because they cannot be redeemed. This allows a distinction to be made between (possibly) good terrorists – those who have a political agenda and may end up being the sort of people you have to work with (e.g. ETA or the IRA) and who are seen already by some as 'freedom-fighters', and bad terrorists, those who are pure irrational evil. Which of course makes them devils rather than humans, a position which no Christian can take. In fact this is a distinction which does not bear much examination. Are these people 'essentially evil' because they think that everybody else is wrong? On that basis you are going to have to wipe out a great number of people. In any case what evidence is there that Osama Bin Laden and his followers are not open to debate? Listening to the man himself, you get the usual political mixture of things that are plainly false, things that are debatable and things that anybody might agree with. He claims, for example, that the ongoing major issue between the West and the Muslim world is the Arab-Israeli conflict. I think that there are many people who agree with this. Is it that Al Qaeda uses suicide bombers? So have many other organisations (Hamas, Tamil Tigers, Kashmiri separatists). Do they target innocent civilians? That has been a terrorist stock-in-trade for a long time now, and was the overt policy of the British government in the bombing of Germany in the Second World War. No, this crude dualism – we are good, they are evil; we are rational they are irrational; you are either for us or against us – simply allows us to legitimise our actions even when they are illegal, salve our consciences when we resort to violence, and worst of all, excuses us from asking what might be the causes of the enemy's enmity. Christians should have nothing to do with this for ethical reasons, but those who design policy in the West need equally to beware of these attitudes. Failure to understand your 'enemy' is not a clever way to wage a war.

There are, of course, those who are critical of the powerful (and I must say that the internet has helped us out in this respect) but what an uneven contest it is! Here is a 'sermon' I preached quite soon before the invasion of Iraq. I hope it illustrates my point.

Imagine me a week ago at the monthly meeting of the Gloucestershire Network Against the War in Cheltenham. Rather a small untidy room; somebody has forgotten to turn on the heating. There are four of us. We are planning a public meeting to protest about the possibility of war against Iraq. We agree that what we really need is a 'big name'. The secretary says rather defensively that he has tried Tony Benn and John Simpson of the BBC but they were not prepared to come. A day of action is also proposed. One suggestion is a protest outside General Command Headquarters (GCHQ). Our banner maker is concerned that she does not have time to make one – she is working this Saturday. Somebody volunteers that they have seen a little shop just off the Stroud Road where they do a special offer on banners at £22.50. Can we afford to buy one? The treasurer thinks that perhaps we can.

Four anxious, rather scruffy, somewhat impoverished middle aged plotters planning to take on the might of GCHQ with its millions of pounds invested in impressive buildings, ultra high-tech equipment and salaries to suit sophisticated and intelligent minds. Quite apart from the nature of the work, so much wealth providing jobs, security and status. So many people with so much to lose. All hail the great military industrial complex – the bountiful provider of these inestimable benefits!

Of course that is probably not how those who work there see it. They are, after all, the defenders of the realm, doing important work ('the official secrets act' has a certain ring about it) or just earning an honest living and caring for their families. Protesters are disturbers of the peace (needing a little attention from the local police force, perhaps), vaguely unpatriotic, a lunatic fringe, even a threat to decent people.

As a Christian I like to think that I am relatively untroubled by this uneven contest. Christians do not expect to be on the side of wealth and power, to prostrate themselves before the gods of security and status, certainly not to work for the military industrial complex. Christians expect to be among the impoverished, fighting losing battles against impossible odds – or have I got that wrong?

I find, in fact, that many of my fellow Christians are not all that convinced by this argument. They have theological, pragmatic, political and personal reasons for siding with the establishment. Translated into real life situations all of these reasons mean much the same thing – Christians are as interested in preserving their own privileged life-styles as anybody else. It follows that they see no mileage in challenging the structures of society, indeed they feel it is not something that Christians ought to do. Christians should be going to Alpha courses not protest meetings. Also, what about all those Christians who are already in the defence establishment, all honest folk? In any case, Christians have always felt that war was acceptable under some circumstances. Doesn't terrorism threaten us all? We need to remember September 11, though admittedly up to that date we weren't much bothered, because terrorism usually meant somebody else getting blown up in distant places. And then there is the more secret argument, the one I only admit to myself: this job has the pay, perks and status that my intelligence and education deserve.

You see, that is the trouble. The discourse of most Christians is no different from anybody else's. Of course we want a good job; of course we want security in whatever form we can get it; of course we are attracted by status and power; of course we just want to get on with our lives and avoid trouble. Which one of us has not felt the tug of these things? The difficulty is, to say it again, Christians are supposed to be different. Jesus is Lord means that Caesar is not. In the Empire of his day Paul expected to be in prison 'for the sake of the gospel'; he expected to be treated, to use his own phrase as the 'rubbish of the world' (1 Corinthians 4:13). And don't even mention Jesus! All that business of foxes and holes, and crosses and denying oneself.

The writer of the book of Revelation must have had similar thoughts. Why even bother to write to tiny congregations in Asia Minor when what you were encouraging them to do was to take on the might of the Roman Empire. Why lead them to a battle you know they are going to lose?

More from Revelation 13

To return to Revelation 13, we read that the beast makes 'war on the saints' (13:7) and is allowed *to conquer them*. This seems rather dire, though there is some good news first. This is the second time we have come across the phrase 'it is allowed…' in the book of Revelation. The beast's authority is 'by permission' and it is only for a short time (42 months). We must not lose sight that we do *not* live in a dualist universe. Good is real; evil is only the shadow. However, there is no room for triumphalism either. Final victory has been postponed (we are between D Day and V Day as the analogy goes) and certainly that is often what it feels like.

The second beast we meet in chapter 13 is more of the same (13:11). The beast 'causes those who do not worship the image of the beast to be killed' (13:15). So, if you do not join the system, you perish. And of course people do. Another way of putting this is that you have to have the mark of the Beast in order to buy and sell. In Communist Russia the mark of the Beast was probably membership of the communist party. But that is not *our* Beast. Our Beast is a different expression of imperialism – most likely 'free trade', the market, the IMF and 'structural adjustment'.

Let me attempt to sum up 'the system' (or should I say 'the System') as I see it in a series of questions.

What, as far as our society is concerned:

(1) commands universal worship? (13:12)
(2) performs great signs and deceives the inhabitants of the earth? (13:13)
(3) creates a system of visible membership? (13:16)
(4) excludes commercially those who are not in the club? (13:17)

Despite the commercial aspects of the system they are not fundamental. Fundamental, rather, is the ethos, the 'demon' of the System. 'Small and great, rich and poor, free and slave' all receive the mark of the beast (13:16). It does not matter whether you are on the board of a company listed in Fortune 100 or struggling on the minimum wage, whether you live in fashionable part of town or the run-down inner city; whether you live a wealthy free-wheeling life style or work long hours in a sweatshop, the question remains: have you placed your ambitions, your highest values, your long term hopes, your ultimate aspirations in the care of the System? Spiritual warfare may be what I am in, but I may not *see* this, I may not recognise the mark of the Beast, because my consciousness has been formed by the material constraints of life. 'I've got to earn a living, haven't I?' 'Do you call this luxury, you should see the fat cats on the other side of town.' 'Just another twenty pounds a week, and I could really make a go of things?' and so on.

I realise that all this is too dramatic by far for our post-modern, post Christian, post evangelical, post Catholic, post everything age, living under the sign of a globalising world, belonging to the network society, enjoying the benefits of consumer choice, buying into a flexible lifestyle. One of our difficulties with Revelation 13 (indeed the whole of the Book of Revelation) is that it is too dramatic, too stark, too realistic. We have defended ourselves (successfully, alas) against the fierce imagery by thinking of it as a product of some antique mind set. (To be fair we have been encouraged in this by generations of crazed exegetes who have made such a nonsense of the Book that we have been able to turn away from its message with the minimum of bad conscience.) We feel that we are more sophisticated today. We do not see things in such lurid colours; our palette includes more shades and tones. Perhaps so. But what we must not miss is that the Book is describing a deadly struggle in which the Empire has its hands round the throat, so to speak, of the church, and something needs to happen quickly or the Empire will win. And…we are in the same situation today.

The book of Revelation is an anti-imperialist tract for a heedless people. As the authors of *Unveiling Empire* insist, 'John did not write his book to manufacture a crisis for a people who had become complacent about the empire. Rather he tried to reveal that complacency *was* the crisis…The primary struggle in which the *ekklesiai* was urged to participate was resisting assimilation into the dominant Roman imperialist ethos' (Howard-Brook & Gwyther 1999, 116). The religion and culture (they were interchangeable) of the Empire were offered as the only viable reality and as such became for Christians a direct challenge to their vision of the reign of God. The book of Revelation does not primarily offer a vision of the future so much as an alternative value system. This claim to live by another, different, set of values affects every part of life. From the viewpoint of present day imperialism it is particularly noteworthy that there is a good deal of emphasis, as we have seen in Revelation 13:16,17, on economics. The free gift of the water of life in Revelation contrasts the economy of God with the economy of Empire. Sharing is the rule as against exploitation. The kings of the earth voluntarily bring their treasures into the New Jerusalem in sharp contrast to the merchants of Babylon who bewail their commercial losses (Howard-Brook & Gwyther 1999, 90-91). Does all this connect with today's imperialism? It certainly does. Here is *Unveiling Empire* again. 'Just as the Roman elite lived in sumptuous luxury in cities in which poverty, crime, and violence were endemic, so, too, do the lords of Empire today' (251). As far as our response is concerned: 'We cannot stop the Empire being Empire. Christians must leave Babylon to become citizens of the New Jerusalem' (242).

Jesus and the Domination System

It is encouraging to think that Jesus experienced the threat of the Domination System – and resisted it. The news of the arrest of John the Baptist (Matthew 4:12) for example, must have been intended as a warning to keep quiet. Less dramatically there was the day to day pressure to conform to the Empire's standards, described in paradigmatic form through the temptations in the wilderness (Matthew 4:1-11). His response was to form a new and alternative community – not, on the surface, a very impressive rejoinder to a Tempter who claimed to have 'all the kingdoms of the world' in his gift. The outcome of this move was a period of extensive *healing*, firstly by Jesus, but then by the community at large (Matthew 10:1). Healing included exorcism. In the gospels exorcism stands for a revelation of the powerless nature of imperial myths. Those who were delivered from the power of 'the strong man' could begin to think straight. In Mark 1:27 we read that the synagogue attendees recognised the authority of Jesus as a teacher and that it delivered them from the authority of the scribes who were trying to control them by means of their purity and debt codes (Myers 1988, 141-3). At Gadara the people found the demoniac 'clothed and in his right mind' (Mark 5:15). A woman (Luke 10:13-17) who had had a 'sickness spirit' for eighteen years and who was bent double, stood up straight and looked Jesus in the eye. Those who had previously been 'carried off by idols' (1 Corinthians 12:2) now stood their ground as they confessed Jesus as Lord. People who were 'all their lives held in slavery by the fear of death' (Hebrews 2:15) were delivered.

In every age the false Empire also claims to be a healer, but this is a blasphemous lie. In fact the Empire is characterised by disease. Interesting examples of these diseases are identified by Warren Carter in his commentary on Matthew's Gospel (Carter 2000, 126-7). There the terms for sickness used (in 4:23-5) are quite specific in designating the effects of imperial rule. *Pains* (v. 24) have to do with torture and wounds received in war. *Demoniacs* are those under Satan's control, and it is Satan who claims to control 'all the empires of the world' (Matthew 4:8-9). As Carter points out: 'A number of scholars relate demon possession to circumstances of oppression and colonialism, 'social tensions...class antagonisms rooted in economic exploitation, conflicts between traditions...colonial domination and revolution' (126). *Epileptics* (verse 24 , thus in most translations) are literally the 'moonstruck'. Vespasian set up a monument to the moon god, Selene, outside Antioch (where Matthew's readers probably lived) because allegedly the capture of Jerusalem was aided by bright moonlight. Matthew is saying that God's Empire is the real ruler of the moon, and evidence is provided by the deliverance of the moonstruck. The last word used is *paralytics* and of course paralysis may be a psychosomatic response to trauma or a subconscious form of resistance.

What is important is that the true therapeutic impulse lies within the Kingdom and not elsewhere. I do not have to tell you how sick and diseased we are today because of the System. We are, for a start, quite literally being poisoned by the products of our industry and our transport systems. Respiratory diseases, such as asthma, are on the increase because the System depends on motorised transport. Obesity, heart disease, cancers and the like abound because of our unhealthy lifestyle which is a product not only of our lack of self discipline but also of our avaricious multinational food corporations and their mendacious advertising. Millions of children die every year because companies refuse to give up their aggressive marketing of breast milk substitutes. We are bombarded with images, icons, logos. The car is that reliable, sexy, absolutely necessary status symbol that we all love. Nobody, apparently, is going to tell us that it is destroying us. (I challenge my readers to play the deconstruction game as a defence against this bombardment. All you have to do is to take a well-known logo and work out what it really means. An obvious example is Nike's 'Just Do It' which is, of course, a threat against complaining sweat shop workers. DuPont's 'Solutions for a small planet', might be thought of as a *final* solution given that they are into GM food. Microsoft's 'Tell me where do you want to go today' should have the additional information: 'Anywhere, as long as you don't expect to get out from behind your computer.') Deliverance from these lies and their injurious effects, is, in part at least, the 'healing' that the gospel brings.

More Biblical exegesis

Anti-imperialist exegesis is also available from the Old Testament, the Apocalyptic writing in the Gospels and from Paul's letters. Isaiah 56-66 and Zechariah 9-14 speak in opposition to the then ruling consensus, the Persian empire, just as the book of Daniel challenges the Seleucid empire (Howard-Brook & Gwyther 1999, 61-2). In Jesus' teaching the 'coming of the Son of Man' (the death, resurrection, and ascension of Jesus) and the 'gathering of the elect' (the preaching world-wide of the gospel) result in the overthrow of the 'celestial powers' (Mark 13:24-6). 'Stars falling from heaven, the sun (associated almost always with the Emperor) refusing to shine, the moon turning to blood, is assaulting the cosmic imagery (and undermining the symbolic universe) invoked in legitimating Roman rule.' 'Plagues, famines and earthquakes meant that the earth no longer consented to the "peace of Rome" which had been fortified by appeals to the fruitfulness of the earth and the security of its peoples.' These are quotes from Herzog (Howard-Brook & Gwyther 1999, 132).

Again, 'what happens when we line up Paul's gospel and Caesar's Empire?' asks N. T. Wright (Wright 2000, 160). By the time of Paul's mission the imperial cult had become the *means* by which the Romans controlled huge areas, often without an overt military presence. Paul's mission was a direct challenge to this. It was not Caesar who was Lord but Jesus. 'His missionary work must be conceived not simply in terms of a travelling evangelist offering people a new religious experience, but of an ambassador of a king-in-waiting, establishing cells of people loyal to this new king, and ordering their lives according to his story, his symbols, and his praxis, and their minds according to his truth.' This was a direct challenge to the Empire. After all, 'gospel' in the Roman world was usually associated with the good news of the birth, accession, arrival, special favour etc. of the Emperor. Paul's gospel is 'the announcement that the crucified and risen Jesus of Nazareth is Israel's Messiah and the world's Lord' (165). It is the fulfilment of the message of Isaiah 52 (where there is also an appeal, by the way, to quit Babylon). It might also link with Isaiah 49:6 and the promise that the Servant will be given as a light to the nations. Paul describes this in Romans 1:5 as bringing all nations into the 'obedience of faith'. The truth is that Israel's king was always supposed to be the world's true king (Psalm 72:8, Isaiah 11:10). Paul's argument about the gospel, begun in Romans 1:5, comes full circle in Romans 15:8-12 where the hope of the nations is that God will provide 'the root of Jesse' to rule over them (167). So the main challenge here is to Caesar and the imperial cult. 'Caesar, by being a servant of the state, had provided justice and peace to the whole world. He was therefore to be hailed as Lord and trusted as Saviour. This is the world in which Paul announced that Jesus, the Jewish Messiah, was Saviour and Lord' (168).

Wright has a similar exegesis of Philippians 3. Being 'citizens of heaven' (3:20) does not mean here that one day we shall go to a better place. The Philippians did not expect to retire to Rome. It meant that Rome set their standards for them and was there to help them if they needed it. In the same way New Testament apocalyptic describes a parallel reality – the heavenly court and the throne of God – where true values were to be found and resources for those in the conflict were stored. The central point of the chapter is that Paul is appealing to the Philippians to rethink their allegiance to Caesar in the same way as he has rethought his allegiance to Judaism and also in the spirit of Christ (chapter 2) who gave up his 'rights' (179).

Neil Elliott's interpretation of Paul does not simply line up Paul against the Roman Empire but against the whole array of cosmic powers (of which, of course, the Empire is one representative). As he says: 'We should marvel not that Paul can speak of his 'word of the cross' without specifically identifying Pilate, but that his indictment goes beyond Pilate to include all the powers of heaven and earth together that stand hostile to God' (Elliott 1995, 113). He continues, 'Paul interprets Jesus' death as the *beginning of God's final 'war of liberation' against all the Powers that hold creation in thrall* through the instruments of earthly oppression (123). Notice that Jesus' death is just the beginning of the last battle. It continues to this day, though victory is certain.

Examples from history

Since the Romans there have been many attempts at Empire (not just in the Middle East and Europe) and the rise of the West culminated in the British Empire, the biggest of them all. Standing against this trend in every era there have been those who resisted imperial attitudes and actions. In Reformation times it was the Anabaptists. In the United States a whole tradition stemmed from the Quakers and their kin, producing people like Thoreau and Hawthorne. Bishop Bell and Dietrich Bonhöffer opposed imperialism during World War Two; Mohandas Gandhi and Martin Luther King were other recent anti-imperialists, now with a worldwide reputation.

Let me illustrate this further with the well known story of the rise and fall of fascism. We do not really have to argue about whether fascism was an evil (these thoughts are being put together on Holocaust Day). There is some danger in this, of course, in that everything we disagree with can be labelled 'fascism' and we can then disassociate ourselves from it and pretend it has nothing to do with us. Despite this danger I want to argue that today's experience of poverty and wealth, of immigration, of race discrimination and state violence are really quite close to the European experience in the 1930s. Hitler's treatment of the Jews seems so irrationally fanatical, that we feel that there is nothing equivalent in our own experience. Yet we need to bring the history of fascism down to earth, *our* earth. There was a good deal of calculation as well as fanaticism in Hitler's policies. The attitude of many ordinary Europeans was by no means exceptional in its mixture of fear, greed and racial superiority. The point is that they have their counterparts today. Consider the attitudes commonly adopted by many citizens particularly, but not exclusively, in the West. They display a residual racism against fellow citizens who are different in colour from themselves, a preference for violence, and a mistrust of developing nations as the source of disease, terrorism, cheap labour, corrupt governments, and unwanted immigrants. All this on the back of an aggressive capitalism that insists that their way of life (which in this case means their standard of living) gives them, or at least their nations' businesses, the right to exploit weaker and poorer nations. Many of these folk are Christians, at least nominally, good to their families and friends, generous in terms of charities, people you would like to meet. I have no doubt the same could have been said of many Germans in the 1930s.

The fact is that today's imperialism demonstrates all the typical features of fascist imperialism, indeed of imperialism more widely, including its promise to benefit those it has subjected, while in reality exploiting them. Here we see an imperial technique. As we have seen, the Romans were past masters at this sort of thing, ruling vast tracts of territory, often more by convincing people of the advent of a new golden age than by simple military might. However in practice the Roman army, the source of Rome's initial strength and the supposed guarantor of its civilisation, ruined Rome. Similarly, the knights of the Middle ages, intended originally to protect society, ended up by laying the countryside waste (Weil 2001, 72-3). The British in their heyday convinced others that they were offering a superior civilisation, and that this justified their expansionist policies.

The United States, as the new imperial power at large in the world today, does the same. I think we should face this squarely, if only because the US also remains the world's biggest sponsor of Christian outreach. Also, I am emboldened to write in this way because I am British, only too aware of the fact that the last great proponent of Christian imperialism was Britain. I have been reading a recent biography of Rudyard Kipling (Gilmour 2003) an account which concentrates particularly on his imperialist politics. What it evoked, as far as I was concerned, were the parallels between British imperialism at the beginning of the twentieth century and American imperialism at the beginning of this. Appropriately one of Kipling's most famous 'imperial' poems, 'Take Up The White Man's Burden' was addressed to the American nation (and in particular to his friend Teddy Roosevelt) exhorting it to proceed with determination to its appointed task, the colonisation of the Philippines! Kipling sincerely believed that the 'white' European nations (he was probably talking here more about what he conceived to be moral qualities than racial differences) had an imperial *responsibility*. Empire was their appointed task, and though they received little thanks for discharging it, discharge it they must. The emphasis was very strongly on sacrifice. (Kipling had very little idea that it might be a matter of material advantage for *Britain* that India, for example, be kept under British rule. He never really looked at the economics of the matter.)

What would Kipling say today about the imperialism of the United States? Firstly he might have a good deal of time for the idea that the US could set new standards of 'democracy and freedom' in Iraq, indeed in the Middle East as a whole. He would also have felt that a good quick war might be a necessary way to achieve this. This rings a bell. The best argument for 'imperial' intervention that can be made even today is that the powerful have a duty to intervene where they perceive injustice. So the Iraq war was good and right because of Saddam Hussein's tyranny. Forget 'Weapons of Mass Destruction', forget links with Al Qaeda: Saddam needed to be ousted and we had the power to do it, so we did it. Kipling resorted to this line of argument at the outset of the Second Boer War in South Africa. The best reason for going to war with the Boers was that freedom loving Englishmen living under Boer rule in the Transvaal did not have elementary democratic rights (Gilmour 2003, 144). Or so he said. It was all nonsense of course. The Boer Wars were straightforward conflicts to determine who would rule South Africa in the future – the Dutch (and their supposed German sponsors) or the British. Economics (diamonds and gold) came into the picture, too, as did rival Boer and British cultures. It was easy enough however to describe the battle, as Kipling did, as an intervention by freedom loving British against the reactionary Transvaal government. Regime change was necessary!

It is not perhaps that intervention against tyranny and the like is always wrong, but we must beware the fact that potential winners in any dispute will always find the necessary arguments. The British were brilliant at it – not least Rudyard Kipling. If the United States is determined to go down the pathway of imperialism, I suggest its apologists take a good look at the hundred years or so of British pro-imperial propaganda (circa 1820 to 1920). All the arguments are there: 'it is our destiny', 'God is on our side', 'we are a freedom loving people', 'we are champions of democracy', 'as friends of the downtrodden we must act', 'the Western nations are purveyors of order and reason', 'as champions of science and technology we stand for progress', and so on. Does this sound like the claims of the US State Department at the beginning of the twenty first century? It does, though I am in fact listing what the British said about themselves a hundred years previously. Here is another less flattering catalogue (more what people said *about* the British): experts in 'gunboat diplomacy', exporters of high tech weapons, destroyers of small nations, subverters of 'foreign' cultures, economic imperialists by means of 'free trade', friends of tyrants (when it satisfied their purpose), builders of huge armies and navies, despisers of other races and religions, bombers of civilians and so on.

How fair and accurate are these parallels? Well, times have changed. The worrying aspect of this is that on the whole, if a comparison is made between British and US imperialism, the US version comes off worst.

- US imperialism is more dangerous than British because there is little to challenge it militarily. The British were never an unrivalled imperial power even in their heyday. The present economic situation may only make matters worse, particularly if the US decides to use military means to help to shore up its economic frailties. This is a much more dangerous situation than United States isolationism, often considered to be the more 'typical' strand in US foreign policy. It is in fact fast approaching the profile of the typical Empire, which assumes that it can impose its will on its neighbours with impunity.
- The British, as I have already suggested, were more responsible. They felt that they were in 'for the long haul' and that they were called to make significant sacrifices. The US enters a country like Iraq, overthrows its government and destroys its infrastructure, but will finally leave it to its own devices. Some have suggested that this in itself disqualifies the US as imperialists ('Manifest Destiny Warmed Up?' *Economist*, August 14, 2003) but this is an argument about words. Of course the American empire is different from the British one, but we certainly cannot ignore the use of American power to exercise world-wide control simply because it does not exactly fit an older paradigm.
- US economic imperialism, through its control of the IMF and the World Bank and its influence on the WTO, is much more pervasive and destructive. Britain tended to exploit its own colonies (India, in particular) but for the US the whole world is its economic playground.
- The US is more culturally insensitive. It has always had an isolationist streak (unlike the British who have not been able to afford that luxury) and its ignorance of other parts of the world is often profound. The British set to work to *study* their Empire; the US is not that bothered.
- The US government tends to be controlled by special interests e.g. the oil and coal lobby which trashed the Kyoto agreements. This means that the strong tendency to economic imperialism associated with economic globalisation and 'big business' has no sufficiently powerful countervailing criticism. It is a big question whether the present Obama administration can change this. By contrast the British government, even when imperialism was at its height, had to endure a constant barrage of criticism. (Consider, for example, the furious opposition to the Second Boer War mounted by the Liberal Party.)

US imperialism has its logic. It is the same logic that has bolstered empires throughout history. It runs like this.

> Our pre-eminent position of power is itself the evidence that we are 'destined' to be world leaders. Given that this is our destiny, we have the right to make it happen in all circumstances. Those who threaten our interests in the long run threaten their own. Attack is the best form of defence. 'God who made us mighty, make us mightier yet.'

The trouble is that we have heard it all before. As I have already said, the British perfected this sort of rhetoric a hundred years ago.

The imperial inheritance

It would be foolish to claim that the US is the sole source of imperialism or that imperialism does not have a global support system. There are, for example, many people in the once colonised countries (some of them vocal critics of imperialism) who benefit from the new imperial arrangements. They are those who manage to make the system work *for them*. In many cases they were the local beneficiaries at the time of the colonial regimes and they also became the inheritors. Today, most of the protest about the current economic arrangements, the WTO, the IMF and the like, comes from the West rather than the Global South. Why is this? Because in many instances developing nations are run by a small group of people who are ready to 'play ball' with the WTO and IMF; it is in their interests to do so, even if it is not in the interest of their own poor. Indeed the interests of governments in the developing world are very often largely *antagonistic* to those of their fellow countrymen (Goldsmith 2001, 24).

Take the matter of debt, for example. Third World countries have occasionally entered the debate, but on the whole they have been surprisingly quiet. This may be partly because the debt debate raises awkward issues about the way the borrowed money was spent in the first place. It may also be because a radical measure like debt cancellation may destroy the culture of borrow and spend on which some Third World governments have depended for so long, and may place them *outside* the international business culture, with the particular danger that no more loans are available, except on very stringent terms. Currently debt which needs repaying ties them into the system. At the very least, Western governments need them in order to get their money back.

This is not a popular thing to say. The West has a bad conscience about imperialism because, among other things, it is associated with racism. That is quite correct. It *was* associated with racism, particularly from the early nineteenth century onward. But racism was not the only factor, nor even the most important one. Much more important was the economic factor, and the status that went with it. During the British Raj, for example, Indian princes were, so to speak, admitted to 'the club', because they were wealthy aristocrats, and as long as they played by the rules of the game – they supported the existing imperial arrangements – they were forgiven the fact that they were not actually British or white.

Robert Mugabe is an example of a latter day imperialist. When his popularity began to wane he naturally played the race card for all it was worth as a means of getting himself re-elected in Zimbabwe. Why, however, did he not play it before, given that he has been in power for twenty years, and all that time his 'liberation army' has been without the land which, it now appears, they deserve? The reason is that up to recent times the arrangements put in place during the 'age of imperialism', where whites owned most of the land, actually suited him. Money donated by the British government to 'settle' the issue of land ownership went into the pockets of Mugabe and his friends. Commercial white farmers were keeping the economy afloat and attracting inward investment. Every government wants a thriving economy and inward investment. That is not surprising. But my point is that Mugabe had good reasons, for twenty years or so, to keep the *status quo* in place, and they were reasons which came out of *imperialism*.

World capital has always had imperialistic tendencies even within its country of origin. Britain, the great exporter of capital in the nineteenth century, was a country in which the majority of the British themselves were colonial subjects (Young 2001, 9-10). The global economic culture is the inheritor of these tendencies. In the ghettos of Western cities there are those who are in fact the colonial subjects of this new Empire and its rulers. These new *Herrenvolk* – partakers of the new imperial arrangements – link up with the others of their own kind word-wide, where in the same way, to a greater or lesser extent, they treat *their* compatriots as colonial subjects, only these are to be found in the slums of Manila or Mumbai.

Some intellectual tools

Radical Christianity is the only effective response that we have to the Domination System and we have made little enough attempt to raise this banner. Even the way that we teach in our Christian seminaries betrays our collusion with the thinking of imperialism. We need a new radical anti-imperialist curriculum. Without suggesting that this exhausts the matter, here are some possible ingredients.

- We need a more 'political' take on the gospels. It is becoming a commonplace in New Testament scholarship that we have read back into Scripture the sacred/secular divide that is a product of Enlightenment thought. Yet this approach is still frequently reflected in many of our commentaries and sermons today. Jesus is treated as a purely religious figure, when there was no such person in contemporary society. His open attack on the Domination System of his day is ignored in a hundred subtle ways.
- We need a more political take on the Bible as a whole – the Old Testament prophets, for example, were deeply concerned about the right ordering of society. The oracles they delivered had to do with false religion, economics, politics, and culture. Richard Horsley makes a familiar point:

> [B]iblical studies, along with religious studies generally, has remained in its private apolitical, self-marginalisation. Indeed, throughout the post-Holocaust debates, McCarthyism, the civil rights struggles, Vietnam war protests, the women's movement, anti-colonial struggles, and Third World cries for relief, biblical studies offered precious little response. That is surely largely because individualistic and depoliticised biblical and religious studies are unequipped to discern and address political-economic issues such as the globalisation of inequality. (Horsley 2000, 13)

One comment: Horsley's perspective may be familiar but look at the list of world events he offers. Imagine *not* responding to all that! What a scandal!

- The book of Revelation needs to be re-constituted as a political tract for Christians under attack in the Roman Empire. That is what it was written for and that is the way we should read it. It is a scandal of Biblical exegesis that we have turned it into a guessing game about 'times and dates' (Acts 1:7). Nobody understood apocalyptic literature in that way when it was first written and nobody should read it like that now. I have attempted to do some anti-imperialist commentary from Revelation in this book. I hope the exegetical approach commends itself to my readers.

- Radical Christianity has a history and this history needs to be resurrected. In line with the usual problem that 'history is written by the victors' much of our Church History concentrates on the people of power rather than the 'little people'. We need a 'Subaltern Studies' history of Christianity.[5] Years ago a worthy from the Plymouth Brethren, E.H. Broadbent, wrote a book called *The Pilgrim Church* which attempted to do just that. The scholarship may have sometimes been deficient by modern standards but he was on the right track. More recently the resurgence of Anabaptist studies suggests that there are more than one way of writing the history of the Reformation and the Protestant movement that came out of it. The Anabaptists were consistently anti-imperialist in their attitudes.It is also time for another look at Barth and the 'confessing church' in Germany, including the theology of the Barmen Declaration, Barth's statement on behalf of the German Confessing Church protesting in theological language against the betrayal of the German Christians who had allied themselves with Nazi ideology. This seems to me important because Barth represents, like the Anabaptists, the voice of the persecuted church, but there is no sense of withdrawal. Bonhöffer comes into this category too.
- What is the theology behind market capitalism? Capital accumulation as against 'sharing' is central to any philosophy of market fundamentalism. Francis of Assisi's father understood perfectly well that his son's radical Christianity would do his business interests no good whatsoever. In Barbara Kingsolver's *The Poisonwood Bible* the difference between a 'hoarding' community and a sharing community is neatly revealed in this conversation between the African schoolteacher, Anatole, and the American missionary youngster.

> 'When one of the fishermen, let's say Tata Boanda, has good luck on the river and comes home with his boat loaded with fish, what does he do?'
>
> 'He sings at the top of his lungs and everybody comes and he gives it all away.'
>
> 'Even to his enemies?'

---

[5] 'Subaltern' is a term commonly used in postcolonial discourse to mean someone of inferior rank. 'Subaltern studies' refers to a series of historical studies which attempt to 'read' history from a subaltern perspective.

'I guess. Yeah. I know Tata Boanda doesn't like Tata Zinsana very much, and he gives Tata Zinsana's wives the most.'

'All right. To me that makes sense. When someone has more than he can use, it's very reasonable to expect he will not keep it all himself.'

'But Tata Boanda *has* to give it away, because fish won't keep. If you don't get rid of it, it's just going to rot and stink to high heaven.'

Anatole smiled and pointed his finger at my nose. 'That is just how a Congolese person thinks about money'. (Kingsolver 1999, 318)

This is a clash between Western (modern) values and African (traditional) values. In the encounter between the West and the developing world, Christians should always have been on the side of traditional economics.

- Is there a link between the Christian imperialists of a by-gone generation and Christians who support dollar imperialism today? We have already seen that the language of imperialism transfers very easily from British imperialism in the nineteenth century to current US imperialism. Britain then saw itself as essentially the bearer of Christian civilisation; the US believes that it has the same role now. The danger is that 'spreading American values' can become confused with the spread of the gospel. Anything then which promotes American interests must be good for the faith. This link must be exposed and renounced.
- The decline of the church in the West and its link with the West's imperialism needs investigating further. A good deal has been written about the supposition that the Enlightenment, imperialism and the modern missionary movement (from 1800 onwards) were partners (Stanley 1990). More needs to be added, however, about the *damage* that imperialism did to the Christian cause.

Despite the propaganda, despite the dazzle of the system, despite the promised (more imagined than real) benefits, the proper Christian response to Babylon is resistance. 'Do not love the world' says John, 'the love of the Father is not in those who love the world' (1 John 2:15). A little later he defines this more closely: 'How does God's love abide in anyone who has the world's goods and sees a brother or sister in need and yet refuses help?' he asks (1 John 3:17). So we have to go on resisting 'the evil Empire' where the rich and the powerful monopolise the world's goods and a billion people go hungry every day. We have to believe that this can change and that it is through God's Kingdom that this change will come about. 'This is the victory which overcomes the world, our faith' (1 John 5:4).

Postcolonialism and the politics of dispossession

Colonial issues are essentially to do with land. Obviously, colonialism itself was a great land grab. Think what happened to the native populations of America and Australasia for a start. And not just them. The now famous story of the missionaries, the Bible and the land, I first heard told by Archbishop Desmond Tutu himself in an African context. For the few who are not familiar with it, the story goes like this: 'When the missionaries came to Africa, *they* had the Bible and *we* [Africans] had the land. Then the missionaries said "Let us pray." We all closed our eyes and prayed and when we opened our eyes, *we* had the Bible and *they* had the land!'. Interestingly, Archbishop Tutu went on to suggest that the Bible was such a revolutionary text that in the long run the Africans got the best of the deal![6] If colonialism has to do with the land, however, so has postcolonialism, though in a less direct way. The loss of rural livings and the consequent urban drift; the huge number of international migrants and refugees with their inevitable pathologies (dispossessed and dispossessing others); the continuing unfair distribution of existing land resources in decolonised nations; even the soaring house prices which make it so difficult for people to access decent living space in our cities are all postcolonial issues connected with the use of land.

If land use as an issue unites colonialism and postcolonialism, nevertheless postcolonialism has more positive aspects. In part at least, it is about re-establishing people in their own countries after the interlude of colonialism, and land being restored to its original owners. Also, it is not just a question of land. I am thinking here of a much wider rediscovery of 'lost treasures' which have been buried by colonialism and which need to be dug up again. With its inherent cultural imperialism and its rage for order, modernity as introduced by colonialism 'covered up' all sorts of 'possessions'. The question now is: what were they, and can they be recovered? Here are some examples:

---

[6] These comments were part of a sermon preached in St Aldate's Church in Oxford.

- Customary forms of government such as those celebrated by Mohandas Gandhi, and before him by writers such as John Ruskin and William Morris.
- Forgotten music and forgotten musical artists such as those discovered by Ry Cooder in Cuba, notably the now famous music of the *Buena Vista Social Club*.
- 'Fulfilment theology' which allows local Christians to draw upon their own cultural resources to construct a 'self-theologising' account of the gospel.
- Rediscovery of the geographical matrices that have formed peoples and cultures. See, for example, the idea of 'reclamation' described by Ched Myers (1994, chapter 11).
- Tribal groups, such as the Machiguengas celebrated by Mario Vargas Llosa, who keep alive and are kept alive by the narratives of 'the Storyteller' (1991).
- Wendell Berry's farming communities (in the United States) that, he suggests, are critical to the health of the nation – a contention which is a consistent theme in Berry's writings (2002).

All this may sound rather nostalgic, even obscurantist, a harking back to the 'good old days'. There are several things that can be said about this.

1. Can we always assume that 'what comes next' is better than 'what comes before'? Clearly not. In terms of political systems, for example, we would have to say that in Europe the dictatorships of the 1920s and 1930s were a retrograde step compared with the experiments in democracy that they replaced.
2. Can we necessarily assume that good things always survive the passage of time? Again, clearly not. Johann Sebastian Bach had almost been forgotten in the nineteenth century and it took a considerable effort on the part of musicians such as Mendelssohn to restore him to the repertoire. Similarly, radical changes often destroy as many good things as they introduce.
3. The power equation usually comes in somewhere. History, as we all know, tends to be written by the victors. Valuable cultural practices, such as language knowledge and skills, can be overlaid and even completely destroyed, simply because they belong to the vanquished – ask the Welsh or the native Americans. In the commercial world a number of technological innovations have failed and then been replaced by inferior ones, simply because they have been launched on the wrong market.
4. A possible theory is that Ricardo's 'comparative advantage' applies across

time as well as across space. An example would be the craft industries. No doubt, a certain sort of excellence is possible in our day when we have the advantage of sophisticated technology. (It is easier to produce multiple copies to a standard design, for example.) Could it be that another sort of excellence was more easily attainable when craftsmanship was more personal as in the apprentice system, more in tune with natural materials, and when the craftsman or woman was less likely to be distracted? When I worked in India I came across a three volume work *Flora of the Nilgiris* which consisted of a painstaking description of the herbs and flowers of the Nilgiri Hills. It had been produced by a member of the Indian Civil Service who clearly has plenty of spare time on his hands. The range of plants included was comprehensive, the descriptions were amazingly detailed and the illustrations exquisite. I very much doubt whether anything similar is being produced today or perhaps could be, considering the circumstances of contemporary life and the demands of modern publishers. In brief, certain epochs may have the advantage over the present in producing certain sorts of goods.
5. People who search the past for good models are not really that much different from those who search the present. Being alert to good possibilities in other cultures – as are, for example, the supermarkets in terms of food and drink – simply means searching *other people's* past. Every innovation of this sort is a traditional form elsewhere. I suspect that ninety per cent of our innovation is a borrowing.
6. If searching the past has its dangers so too does searching the future. Science fiction tries to, but then has to remind us constantly that it is, after all, fictional, in order to prevent us from becoming too afraid. The unknown future is too uncertain for us to appeal to it with confidence. We *think* it may be possible to invent a form of energy that will provide our needs and save the planet at the same time; but we are not *sure*. We have seen things like this go wrong too often. In the 1950s scientists were promising power – generated by nuclear means – that was so abundant and cheap that we would not even bother to charge for it. Now we see nuclear energy as, at best, a last resort, something we might have to go with because we cannot think of any alternative.

Of course there must be a sense in which we assert 'progress', though, I suggest, more after the fashion of journeying than from an evolutionary point of view. It is true that on life's journey we must not always be 'looking over our shoulders'; that we are often tempted to turn back and to quit, and part of the art of life is to keep going. (Requiring what the old translations of the New Testament call 'patience'.) Also, it helps very much if we have a goal, a *telos*, a future. In the matter of postcolonialism and the politics of dispossession, one of the ingredients of the postcolonial discourse is hope. 'The old order changes', empires are falling, 'a new day is dawning'. We catch the authentic sound of this in Jawaharlal Nehru's famous 'Freedom at Midnight' speech.

> At the stroke of the midnight hour, when the world sleeps, India will awake to life and freedom. A moment comes, which comes but rarely in history, when we step out from the old to the new, when an age ends, and when the soul of a nation, long suppressed, finds utterance.

A huge number of good myths centre round the idea of the dispossessed coming into their own – Ulysses coming home after the Trojan war; 'the once and future king' (who turns up in a number of national mythologies); Richard the Lionheart coming back from the Crusades, Aragorn returning to Gondor in *The Lord of the Rings* and so on.

I want to make a number of comments about this:

- Our heroes when they come home are starting again, but not starting from scratch. We cannot entirely escape the past. Despite Nehru's optimism he had to struggle with 'same old India'.
- New situations bring new dilemmas.
- 'Repossession' means that there are often a new set of losers. (Think of the state of Israel and the Palestinians.)
- 'Going back' must be combined with 'going on' (hybridity).

All of these comments make essentially the same point. *Repossession does not mean going back to the same situation that obtained before dispossession. It demands an effort to go on to something new.* Almost certainly that includes coming to terms in an inventive and imaginative way with the very forces – political, cultural, economic – which caused the dispossession in the first place. Politically the 'repossession' (the inverted comments are intended to show that I am not making a value judgement!) of their land, as they see it, by the Israelis will only work if they take into account the Palestinian presence and try to create something new. Edward Said saw this when he suggested that Israelis and Palestinians might come together over the mutual experience of dispossession and diaspora (2003b, 55). Postcolonialism can help us here. The point about the 'post' in 'postcolonialism' is surely that we are *both* living in a world in which colonialism still has to be taken into account (it would be fatal to pretend that it never happened) *and* that we are going on to something new, a sort of dialectic. If the thesis is colonial dispossession and the independence movements are the anti-thesis, then postcolonialism is the synthesis. However, I do not see anything inevitable or determined about this process. New hybrid solutions depend on a willingness to invent and experiment.

Postcolonial scholars, particularly more recently, have insisted that this dialectical process was going on in the colonial period, long before the success of the independence movements. We can think of Homi Bhabha's idea of 'mimicry' and Ashcroft's concept of 'interpolation' (see below in the chapter on Postcolonial Resistance) and the whole idea of 'the colonial transaction'[7] (Ingleby 2000, 333). This to some extent undermines Edward Said's thesis in *Orientalism* which over-represents the passivity of the colonised. Be that as it may, there is no doubt that a fearful struggle has been going on since the success of the independence movements to find a way forward into a new synthesis. Anti-thesis, so to speak, is the easy part, and some would like to remain in this phase. But what form will the new postcolonial arrangements take? That is the really difficult question. Mohandas Gandhi warned about the need to address this issue very early in the Indian independence movement. It was one thing to remove the British, he warned, but to come up with something that did not simply reproduce the faults of the colonialists would need some careful thought (Gandhi 1997, 28).

This is the big question for mission also. Some (particularly those in the Global South) would say that we must not hurry past the oppositional stage. They insist that dispossession must give place fully to repossession, and that that process should not be allowed to drop off the agenda. It is too early to forget the way that Christian mission was essentially tied to Western colonialism, indeed was itself a process of dispossession. It is Westerners (like this author) who want to talk about postcolonialism and synthesis and hybridity, when they ought to be saying: 'It's your turn now, we'll take a back seat for a while.'

I have some sympathy with this, but it will not do for a long term strategy, particularly for mission. The trouble with the anti-thesis of any dialectical movement is that, left to itself, it is too reactive, too destructive. It is a well known fact that trauma begets trauma (Said 2003, 75-7). Even political leaders in the Global South are beginning to agree. While honouring the dispossessed and reinstating them if possible, the postcolonial discourse does not invite

---

[7] The idea that in the colonial situation there was an exchange of power rather than a one way exercise of power from the coloniser to the colonised.

them to be constantly living as a dispossessed people. Psychotherapists and counsellors (Homi Bhabha's postcolonialism owes a conscious debt to psychoanalysis) know very well that, though healing may depend on the client's ability to go back to the past and 'repossess' it on their own terms, they must also be encouraged to use that as a starting point to strike out in new directions. Anger is good, but it is not enough.

Of course people can be helped to 'go on' when the perpetrators of the dispossession own up to the past and are sorry about it. You often hear people who have been harmed by others say something to the effect that 'they only wanted somebody to say "sorry"'. On the surface this sounds rather pathetic. Why do they not simply get on with life instead of (apparently) tying their future to somebody else's behaviour which they cannot control? Why indeed? It is something of a mystery, but nevertheless I believe people when they express their inability to move on without the help of their 'enemies'. It is how things work.

In mission circles we Westerners simply have not done enough thinking about how the peoples in the Global South see us as 'enemies' and are still waiting for us to put things right, if only in our attitudes. What the dispossessed need to repossess more than anything else – this is true generally – is their sense of worth, a sense that was fatally impaired by mission that always saw itself as essentially having its origin in the West ('from the West to the rest'), as consisting of sending and receiving nations. 'Can any good thing come out of the Global South?' No, obviously not, or we would not be spending our lives and our treasure trying to 'reach' them.

Reversing the situation is largely a matter of economics. One of the great things we can do for mission in the twenty first century is to undo the economic imbalances that still mean that, all too often, the nations of the Global South (especially Africa, but parts of Asia as well) are beggars at the West's door. For example, I do not think that it is enough that we are planning to 'bring over' missionaries from Asia, Latin America and Africa to 'save' the West, at the West's expense. What we really need is mission movements in the Global South that are strong enough (economically and in other ways) to be planning and implementing global strategies of their own. It is beginning to happen of course. South Korean missionary agencies have this sort of strength, as do some from other parts of Asia. Latin America may be on the way. Sadly, you hear a good deal of criticism of these mission agencies, particularly that they are 're-inventing the wheel', not learning from two hundred years of the West's missionary experience, 'making the same old mistakes' and so on. No doubt, in some cases, they are. They are the 'teenagers' of world mission who want to do things their own way and do not want to be bound by their parents' world, and of course teenagers make mistakes – that is how they learn. The people who are virtually disqualified from giving them advice, however, are the former authority figures in their lives – usually their parents. I suspect that in terms of mission strategies it is time that we Westerners learnt to be quiet, certainly to speak more circumspectly. The new mission agencies do indeed need new models and new guidance, but they will probably not get it from the West.

If all this sound rather too 'us' and 'them', the really interesting experiments in mission structures, to my mind, are the hybrid mission teams, which on one view could be considered the new mission synthesis. If mission from 'the West to the rest' was thesis, and if the new missionary movements from the Global South are anti-thesis, then mission teams may be synthesis. It will be fascinating to see whether they can really work. I suspect that, to date, the jury is out, just as it is on the hybrid church. In both cases, as in society at large, successful hybridity will require a massive amount of imagination, inventiveness and flexibility (not to mention sacrifice and humility). Can you imagine the Palestinians and the Israelis getting it together in a new 'diasporic' Middle Eastern state? Are the new churches and new mission teams really going to be able to sort out issues of language and culture and the identity issues that go with them? It seems unlikely, but equally it may be the only way ahead.

Postcolonial Resistance

My impression is that we Christians are in need of new forms of resistance. We find it very difficult to oppose things that we feel are wrong and yet retain what the Apostle Paul calls 'a good conscience'. As soon as we enter the world of assertion, or confrontation, or organised opposition we feel guilty. Other people are 'political' on our behalf and we are not sure what our reaction should be. We settle uneasily for 'a quiet life', aware that this is probably not far from a culpable indifference.

This is depressing because there is so much that needs a forthright and forceful response – not accommodation, sympathy, or understanding, but *resistance*. Postcolonialism as a discourse is helpful here, because it has its *raison d'être* as a form of resistance to something – colonialism and its attendant attitudes –

which is clearly an evil and yet which is so pervasive that it cannot be avoided, it must be dealt with. Further it shows us that authoritarian regimes can be subverted by non-violent means. Interpolation, representation, mimicry, 'magic realism' are examples of postcolonial techniques which provide us with a vocabulary and praxis of dissent. However, before we look at these, I also want to take another look at the subject of 'violence'.

The anti-colonial movement was characterised by a whole range of tactics of civil and militant resistance, a spectrum which ran from armed struggle at one end to Gandhi's *satyagraha* at the other, though even Frantz Fanon, who is usually associated with the violent response, said that armed struggle was the tactic of last resort (Young 2004, 26). Theorists also tried to distinguish different sorts of violent response. Jean-Paul Sartre drew a distinction between violence initiated by exploited groups – a sort of organic expression rising from the community, and violence initiated by sectarian groups which had no community basis (Young 2004, 25). He accepted the Algerian war of resistance against metropolitan France, but not movements such as the Red Brigades in Italy and Bader-Meinhof in Germany. Clearly terms such as 'armed struggle' and 'violence', need refining, and once we have done so (and perhaps added some necessary warnings such as 'the one who takes the sword will perish by the sword') it is much more difficult to issue a blanket condemnation. In practice we are often inconsistent. We approve of, let us say, the resistance to the Nazis from 1939 onwards, but not of the violent reactions to colonialism. Again, how do we distinguish 'independence movements' from 'self defence' or 'protecting my own home and family'? It is worth all critics of violence as a liberationist tactic taking a look at the history of such movements as Nelson Mandela's ANC in South Africa, which began with a non-violent approach and which changed (after the Sharpeville Massacre in 1960) to an armed struggle.

All the same, I imagine that Christians are much happier with Gandhi or Martin Luther King than Frantz Fanon and Che Guevara , and I think rightly so. Walter Wink in his classic (and essential) work *Engaging the Powers* (1992, 171-275) makes a powerful case for resistance by means of what he calls 'Jesus' Third Way', a non-violent, confrontational approach. This is all immensely attractive , and I certainly could not improve on the general idea. We clearly need to find 'a place to stand' somewhere between 'fight' and 'flight'. What this chapter might add to is Wink's 'tactics' (186-7). Let me explain.

Interpolation

Here I am leaning heavily on Bill Ashcroft's book *Post-colonial Transformation* (2001). Ashcroft's idea is itself a response to Edward Said's concept of 'Orientalism'. Said, extending the thought of Antonio Gramsci and Michel Foucault, contended that colonialism depended as much on an imposed way of thinking as on physical factors such as conquest and occupation. Western colonialism in particular constituted 'the Orient' as a (naturally) inferior Other, thereby establishing the West's identity and that of the colonised at the same time, in a way that would make their unequal roles permanent. Also, the inferiority would be accepted by the colonised as 'the natural order of things' leading to a passive role and an absence of resistance.

The main criticism of Said's thesis has been that he posits too passive a role for the colonised. There was, after all, a good deal of resistance, and worldwide the anti-colonial movements have succeeded in expelling the foreign imperialists by means of the independence movements. However, doubts continue to be expressed both about the actual nature of this success and the manner by which it was achieved. . What about neo-colonialism? Has not the West simply continued colonialism by other means since the independence movements? Again was it possible that the manner in which colonialism was challenged only showed how well Western Orientalist hegemony had been established? Nationalism itself – the engine of the anti-colonialist movement – was a 'derivated discourse'. That is to say, even this trump card of the independence movements was drawn from the Western pack. Similarly, Gayatri Spivak asks in a famous essay 'Can the subaltern speak?'. Is it really possible for the voice of the marginalised, either in history or today, to be heard? By and large, her answer is 'no'. It is only possible to be heard by using the 'language' of the oppressor and the result of this is that the original voice of protest is hopelessly distorted, or worse 'taken over' by the oppressors and invested with *their* meanings.

Ashcroft does not accept such a gloomy picture. He points out that dominant groups have always been resisted, often successfully, and adds that this is not necessarily by violence. For one thing, those in charge, including colonialists, usually learn that they cannot rule without some sort of co-operation with their subjects. The basic principle of 'interpolation' is that the colonised does indeed use the cultural capital of the imperial system, but not in some hopeless gesture, rather to dismantle it (Ashcroft 2001, 58). The subaltern *can* be heard precisely by appropriating colonial speech. An obvious example, given by Ashcroft, is the 'voyage in' by intellectuals from the Global South who confront the metropolitan culture and do so by using its own techniques (48). Another example is the multiform varieties of the English language which have developed in the world. While English has spread worldwide in an imperialistic way, it has not been able to establish itself as a standard code, rather it is regularly dismantled and re-assembled to follow different codes by users in different contexts (65). Actually, Lamin Sanneh's well-known thesis in *Translating the Message* (1989) is a commentary on interpolation. In translation work, even if the translator is, say, a Westerner, he or she almost always has to rely upon local wisdom, and this transfers power away from the centre. Again, while Bible translators certainly bring with them the tools of learning developed at the centre, they use them to produce versions that allow languages at the periphery to express in their own way their insights into the gospel and to develop an indigenous theology which may challenge the Western theological hegemony.

Clearly, interpolation of whatever sort, is a form of resistance. It is the opposite of a passive acceptance that 'the leader's way is always best'. It does not totally reject authority, of course, particularly the 'authority' of new and useful knowledge, but it appropriates this knowledge and uses it in ways that benefit the subaltern. There can be something 'tricky' (I am not using the word as a pejorative) and non-confrontational about this. 'I will play your game' says the subaltern, 'but by my rules'. Or, 'I will accept your rules, but show that they may have different possibilities and consequences than you expect'. I am reminded here of Walter Wink's exegesis of Jesus' stories about confrontation in the Sermon on the Mount. The Roman soldier insists that I carry his pack for a mile, but does not know how to cope when a second mile is offered. The judge has awarded my oppressor my outer garment; let him take my underwear as well. How embarrassing for him as well as for me! My superior has given me a derisive backhander; let him treat me as an equal and give me a punch instead. (1992,175-84). This is all at the personal level, but the principle is wider than that. Colonialists can teach people that their system of government – empowerment of the people through democratic means – is superior, but what happens when the 'inferiors' actually take up their right to vote and as a result ask you to leave.

In the church the same principle applies. In the struggle to establish an appropriate role for women, patriarchalism was combated, it seems to me, not so much by mustering the theological arguments, but by women acquiring and displaying the skills which were supposedly masculine, and showing that they could deploy them as well as, if not better than, men. (Contrast Samuel Johnson's male chauvinist remark about women preaching being 'like a dog walking on its hind legs; it is not done well but one is surprised that it is done at all'.) This is analogous to Jesus' response to those who criticised him for forgiving sins. 'You are not allowed to do that' say the religious leaders. 'Well, let me do something even harder', says Jesus, 'and then we can argue about it' (Matthew 9:2-7).

Ashcroft's most vivid illustration of interpolation is the petrol station at Mbarara (2001, 157). Set up from outside the village by a multi-national oil company for its own purposes – to provide a re-fuelling point for cars on the national highway – at first glance the station is an instrument of exploitation. It uses up more electrical power than the rest of the village put together, while serving none of the village's obvious needs. However, that is not the whole picture. The villagers begin to see that the station could fulfil their purposes as well. As the best lit meeting place in the village it becomes in effect the village centre at night time. The bicycle taxis use the facilities to inflate their cycle tyres; women come to top up on paraffin for their family cooking (using second-hand Coca Cola bottles!); people sit around talking all night.

Though the analogy is far from complete, we might compare this situation to the function of some village churches. The church is introduced to the village by a well-known multi-national agency (the Church with a capital 'C') and initially appears to serve purposes which do not immediately connect with the village. It may also be, however, the most impressive building in the village and may serve as a more than ordinarily useful meeting-place. People may find that some of their needs – for friendship, intellectual stimulation, financial support in times of crisis, and so on – are met. What once appeared an alien institution is 'taken over' by local people as theirs. Of course, Christians would say that the church also introduces them to the gospel and that this is its most important function. I agree with this, and I am not simply trying to give sociological reasons for the church's 'success', rather I am saying that a church which is accepted by the community has a better opportunity to spread the gospel than one that is not.

Mimicry

A similar resistance process is the idea of mimicry. Originally the 'mimic men' (as in V. S. Naipaul's novel of that title) were the colonial subjects who tried to copy the colonialist, usually because the colonialist appeared to be part of a more successful culture. But Homi Bhabha (1994), in particular, extends the idea to include those who are mimics in a much more complex way. First of all, 'mimic men' were something that was required; the colonial authorities needed them as intermediaries. One is reminded here of the famous quotation from Lord Macaulay in his Minute on Education in India .

> We must at present do our best to form a class who may be interpreters between us and the millions we govern, a class of persons, Indian in blood and colour, but English in taste, in opinions, in morals, and in intellect.[8]

However, a policy of this sort has consequences. Mimicry confronted the colonialist with a version of himself or herself that was 'almost the same, but not quite'. This then raised the question as to whether other versions might not be as valid as the original. If the colonised returns the gaze of the coloniser, this reminds him or her that the colonised can be subject as well as object. Thus the observer becomes the observed and this 'partial' representation ('like but not like') questions the original observer's identity. 'If you have created this simulacrum who is like you, but not you, then who are you?'

From a Christian point of view all this seems rather harsh, even wicked. Surely we are to learn to respect and imitate our leaders, and not 'mimic' them. In the light of Bhabha's definition, however, we do not need to look at mimicry in this way. Mimicry, as described above, is not necessarily a deliberate strategy on anybody's part and even if it were, it would primarily be a reminder to those who have authority that if they intend to use people, this has consequences. If, to succeed in their plans, they need people who are like them, then the empowerment of others that this implies may mean a diminution of their own power. The mimic is 'like but also unlike'. In the end he or she will want to do it their way, and this will be, if only ever so slightly, a different way. Of course this will be a threat to an authoritarian leader, but if so, it is a good threat and will ultimately be for the right working of the organisation. Both sides must live with a certain ambiguity. On one hand those in authority must learn that, unlike God, they cannot fully create in their own image. On the other side, the object of that authority must balance between 'following the master' and 'being true to oneself'.

It would be good if this relationship were informed by love and not fear. Authoritarianism is a great producer of fear. People imitate other people for

---

[8] Macaulay delivered this Minute to the Committee of Public Instruction in India on 23 February 1835. The full Minute can be found in Bureau of Education. Selections from Educational Records, Part I (1781-1839). Edited by H. Sharp. Calcutta: Superintendent, Government Printing, 1920

fear of the consequences if they are seen to be different. Perhaps also authority figures try to create clones of themselves out of fear – how else can they control people? But we can also imitate people because we love them and admire them and want to be like them and follow their example – a good 'mimicry' in fact. Even so, the ambiguity remains. I can never be fully like the person I am imitating and I am suggesting that this form of 'resistance' is good for everyone concerned.

Archaeology and Magic Realism

As we know, postcolonialism assumes that the world is shaped by the colonial experience, particularly Western colonialism, which introduced modernity and Enlightenment values into traditional societies – at least that is the theory. Postcolonialism examines what that shape is, especially how former colonies are now progressing, and also what traces colonialism has left on the former colonising powers. Postcolonial studies, however, have recently taken on a wider remit. One idea is a sort of archaeology. Where indigenous forms of culture have been buried by the colonial experience, work is being done to 'unearth' them. Restored to their former use, they are put to work to critique, and perhaps subvert, the prevailing modernist orthodoxy. This can be a form of resistance.

The idea of 'archaeology' reminds me of what is going on in Wim Wenders' film *The Buena Vista Social Club*. The musician Ry Cooder goes to Cuba and manages to unearth a group of talented performers who had once played together at the Buena Vista Social Club, but have now largely been forgotten. Their music was traditional Cuban music (and the tradition went right back behind and before Cuba as a nation: one man speaks of the guitar which he plays as the *laud* which had been brought to Cuba by the Spaniards, who had themselves received it from the Arabian civilisation that contributed so largely to Spanish culture) but it erupts on the modern world of Cuba, Amsterdam and New York, with all the force of a volcano once thought extinct but now brought back to life. For the old men (and one woman) it is little short of resurrection. Of course you could say that their music had not so much been repressed as forgotten. But are these such different processes? Memory and salvation go very closely together. Amnesia is a great weapon of Empire, used to cut us off from the roots which nourish our existence.

Another example of this would be the technique called 'magic realism', used in the writing of novels. This term was originally coined to describe a particular literary *genre*. More recently, however, it has been used to refer to any use by contemporary authors of myth or 'traditional' material derived from local sources, written or oral. The material then calls into question the assumptions of Western, rational, linear narrative, and re-calls the pre-modern cultural worldview in a way that shakes the reader into a more pluralist mind-set. At a literary level we might say that the conventions of novelistic social realism are being challenged. On a much broader front, however, what is happening is that the very canons of Western, rational, Enlightenment discourse are being challenged. The world is not quite the way we Westerners see it. It is more 'uncanny' than we think. The 'uncanny' as defined by Freud is when the experiences of childhood which have been repressed, break through to disrupt our everyday adult experience. Similarly the repressions of the beginning of Western modern history (what the Enlightenment suppressed so as to introduce order and reason) break through the veneer of 'civilisation'. As David Huddart puts it (commenting on the thought of Homi Bhabha):

> This is an extremely striking thought: post-colonial criticism is psychoanalysing Western modernity. This analysis finds that modernity has repressed its colonial origins, origins that install a foreignness within its identity from the very beginning. What is uncannily revealed…is that foreignness within the self (Huddart 2006, 93).

Just to take one example - typically the postcolonial novel has a role in 'writing the nation'. The 'imagined community' as Benedict Anderson calls it, is invented and bound together by these narratives. However, the introduction of 'magic realism' into the account suggests that the nation, to be properly described, must be seen to include more than the rational structures bequeathed by the colonists, but also 'magical' elements derived from the traditional past. In brief, postcolonial reading practice 'looks to the colonial past as part of a process of thought, producing new answers to the problems of how we live now' (Huddart 2006, 33).

As the world church wakes up to the realisation that it, too, lives in a postcolonial era, I would expect some of this archaeology to be going on. Along with a gospel expressed in largely rationalistic terms, with its emphasis on text and preaching, and its opposition to enthusiasm and mysticism, we may see the resuscitation of forgotten indigenous forms. Indeed, in one area of our church life I think this is already happening, especially in Pentecostal and evangelical circles, namely in our worship music, the way in which the black African music and worship styles have become dominant in many of our churches? We may also see it increasingly in such areas as dance, healing, ecstasy, respect for ancestors and the like. In 'writing the church', so to speak, every congregation will want to bring to light the depth and riches of the cultural experience actually represented by the membership, and where some of this is not simply hidden but buried, then there will be work to be done, just as there is in building a nation. Of course we shall need to be selective. The big mistake that is often made about culture is to call it either all good or all bad (usually mine being good and theirs bad!). We really must get away, however, from the idea of cultures as 'separate, pure, defensible entities'. Every culture has elements of the divine and the demonic and perhaps much in between that is merely human. Not everything that is 'dug up' from the past will be good. But then not everything in our present cultural practice is good either. We Enlightenment people, for example, have an impressive record of rigorous textual study and exposition of the Bible. There is no reason why we should not hold on to it. However, we also have a fear of almost anything that moves us in our worship (literally and metaphorically) which is certainly not healthy.

Finally, though I am taking it wildly out of context, I like the idea of appropriating the phrase 'magic realism'. In the church our realism needs a touch of magic and our magic needs to be anchored in reality.

Palimpsest

How can the gospel be introduced to a culture without, on the one hand, destroying it, or on the other, surrendering to it? Postcolonial thought can help us here with the idea of a *palimpsest*. Originally, a palimpsest was simply a piece of manuscript on which the previous entry had been rubbed out and replaced by another. Here the idea is applied to a particular place imagined as a manuscript which has been written on by its culture. The point is that no inscription (no way of 'writing' the culture) is indelible. It can be overwritten by the consequences of habitation, by the way that people subsequently live in that place. As I mentioned, this idea has been used in postcolonialism. Colonialism may have 'written itself' on a place, through maps and boundaries, through choice of names and ways of seeing and representation, but 'no inscription is indelible'. A place may be re-appropriated and given new meanings by the people who continue to inhabit it.

In the same way missionaries originally wrote their version of the gospel story on a particular culture and we have to accept that there may have been an element of cultural imperialism about this. Whatever the case, subsequently (i.e. subsequent to the arrival of the gospel) the people who inhabit the place need to re-write their cultural story on the place in question, but now with the gospel included. This is a process and will therefore take time. Place, and the people who inhabit the place, are much more important than we often imagine. That is one reason why we cannot read the Biblical text in a one to one way. To take one simple, but contentious example, the fact that Paul says to Timothy that in the church (in Ephesus probably) 'he does not permit the women to teach' (1 Timothy 2:12) is a perfectly reasonable injunction in the circumstances where women had no education, theological or otherwise. Today, where men and women are often equally educated, and where there may be as many women as men in our congregations who have theological expertise and ability to instruct others, he would say something different.

What was originally written on the document, even if it was not indelible, was important. For one thing it may have been part of the instruction of those who subsequently erased it. The creation of a palimpsest was a practice that came from a time when manuscripts were so scarce and so valuable that you had to re-use them. But before you did so, you took notice of what had been written there already. Similarly 'writing' a culture in a particular place, necessarily entails erasing, at least to some measure, what has already been written in that place. But places are unique, too valuable to throw away. So in this writing process, choices have to be made. In the place that is my church, in my locality, women can teach or they cannot. In Ephesus they could not. We need not forget this. Not forgetting it does not mean never changing the rule, but prompts us that teaching in the church is a skilled task and that we need to give time and attention to raising up a skilled teaching ministry if we have not got one. 'Let the women learn' is the main thrust of the passage in 1 Timothy 2.

Representation

Postcolonialism is constantly circling round the idea of *representation* – how we see things and describe them, how we appropriate history and tell its story, how we create essentialisms and dualisms where neither exist, and so on. As we have seen, in some ways the whole discourse of postcolonialism was kicked off by Edward Said's take on the Western representation of the Orient in his book *Orientalism* (2003a).

However, postcolonialism did not invent the idea that history is a process of (mis)representation; it only shows, by highlighting one aspect of this process, how imperialism has a cultural aspect and that this process goes on, even though formal colonialism is over. Postcolonialism is an on-going protest against 'history written by the victors', the victors being the colonialists who not only commanded the cultural high ground when they were the rulers of colonial territories, but have gone on doing so since. There is an example of this in Sardar and Davies's book *Why Do People Hate America?* (2002, 163-9). The authors show how historians who have suggested that the Iroquois people in North America may have had a significant influence on the American constitution have been subjected to fierce criticism by the white establishment. Why is this? Because if it was allowed that indigenous Americans had shaped the Constitution this would challenge a number of received opinions, including: the conventional understanding of Native Americans and their role in American history, the authority of Western scholarship, the 'mythic vision of where America comes from' and 'the exclusivity and hierarchical pre-eminence of Western civilisation' – all of these. It thus becomes a powerful identity issue. It also has political implications. If Native Americans have contributed little of value to the formation of the nation, then the nation owes them little. However, if the reverse is true...

The importance of all this to issues of identity, politics and obligation means that the struggle over representation will certainly continue and have practical consequences. A familiar example of representation is 'Remembrance Day' as observed in many countries. Typically it has to do with remembering servicemen who 'gave their lives for their county'. In Britain it tends to concentrate on the two World Wars (when Britain was on the winning side) and phrases such as 'those who gave their lives so that we might enjoy freedom' are common. These expressions tend to 'remember' the Second World War as against the First; because in the Great War it is difficult to know what anyone was fighting for. They also tend to 'forget' the colonial wars (such as the Suez War) where the British were using their military superiority to subjugate others. Also, typically, left out is the remembrance of all the brave soldiers who fought against us. So Remembrance Day is also 'Forgetting Day'.

In postcolonialism representation is specifically a site of resistance. This is where a stand must be made. Much postcolonial discourse therefore has to do with 'writing'. The work is actually done through 'writing', in the wide sense of the word, meaning the way that we describe or represent matters. As Derrida reminds us metaphoricity *constructs* the social, as we play out its implications. For example when we describe the church as 'the body of

Christ' we are using a metaphor but one which is not simply descriptive but which powerfully shapes our understanding and therefore, at least potentially, our behaviour. We are in the process of constructing a new community.

Walter Benjamin can help us here. He thought very deeply about the meaning of history, concerned as he was about the disasters of his own day (he died in 1940) and the way that European fascism was 'junking history'. In fighting this enemy he gave the historian, at least a certain sort of historian, a key role. 'Only that historian will have the gift of fanning the spark of hope in the past who is firmly convinced that *even the dead* will not be safe from the enemy if he wins. And this enemy has not ceased to be victorious'. And again, 'Every image of the past that is not recognised by the present as one of its concerns threatens to disappear irretrievably' (Benjamin 1999, 247). Thus, as we have already seen, a crucial part of the work of historians and social scientists is *retrieval*. Already contemporary thought has buried, or attempted to bury, so much along the way, that history must very often take up the role of archaeologist, or in more sinister mode, gravedigger and exhumer. Benjamin sets all this under the sign of *redemption* and so should we. 'Only a *redeemed* mankind receives the fullness of its past' he says (246).

The important aspect of this historical project from a missiological point of view is its completeness. 'Nothing that has ever happened should be regarded as lost for history' – Benjamin again (246). The theological equivalent is Jesus' words: 'whosoever will may come'. Thus we are not permitted to write history that represents only the truth of the victors. From the standpoint of the gospel we hear Jesus announce 'good news to the poor' and 'the year of the Lord's acceptance' to every person, culture, nation or tradition that has been thrust beyond the margins. Benjamin makes the same point only he puts it negatively.

> Whoever has emerged victorious participates to this day in the triumphal procession in which the present rulers step over those who are lying prostrate. According to traditional practice, the spoils are carried along in the procession. They are called cultural treasures, and a historical materialist views them with cautious detachment. For without exception the cultural treasures he surveys have an origin which he cannot contemplate without horror. They owe their existence not only to the efforts of the great minds and talents who have created them, but also to the anonymous toil of their

contemporaries. There is no document of civilisation which is not at the same time a document of barbarism (248).

So even our mission history may be a 'document of barbarism' when it describes the 'triumphs' of Western missionaries and ignores 'the anonymous toil of their contemporaries'. It is for this reason, says Benjamin, that we must 'brush history against the grain' (248).

Benjamin's appeal to history is also a reminder that we cannot approach the future as if the past had never happened, as if the future of mankind was a 'progression through homogeneous, empty time' (255). Here again we see a road marked out for us Christians. Too often history has been written in an imperialistic or triumphalistic way! Or we think that we can forget the sorrowful past and start the future from scratch. We would like to put things right, perhaps, but we do not have the time to take the past seriously. Progress demands that we push on. In his polemic against Progress (with a capital 'p') Benjamin conjures up a picture of 'the angel of history' who is as helpless as we are to go back and 'awaken the dead' and for the same reason. The famous passage needs to be quoted in full.

> A Klee painting named 'Angelus Novus' shows an angel looking as though he is about to move away from something he is fixedly contemplating. His eyes are staring, his mouth open, his wings are spread. This is how one pictures the angel of history. His face is turned toward the past. Where we perceive a chain of events, he sees one single catastrophe which keeps piling wreckage upon wreckage and hurls it in front of our feet. The angel would like to stay, awaken the dead, and make whole what has been smashed. But a storm is blowing from paradise; it has got caught in his wings with such violence that the angel can no longer close them. This storm irresistibly propels him into the future to which his back is turned, while the pile of debris before him grows skyward. This storm is what we call progress (249).

How much of our Christian history needs re-presenting, and in what way? Firstly, we must be careful that re-presenting is not just a nostalgic journey back into 'the good old days'. It is seldom if ever true that there was a 'golden age'. Reading some works of Christian history you might get the impression that all godly behaviour and all good doctrine reached a climax in the Reformation; alternately it was during the Victorian era exemplified by a 'Christian Britain' and a vibrant missionary movement. Christian history certainly should include an identity-forming re-assertion of 'roots' ('remember the rock from which you were quarried' – to change the metaphor) but this must be balanced by reminders that there are lessons to learn from the sorrows and failures of the very people who are our admired spiritual 'ancestors'. All of this needs to be wrapped up in the general justice principle of honouring those who deserve to be honoured. A 'feminist' history of the modern missionary movement rightly recalls what has often been forgotten, that women played an essential role in the spread of the gospel worldwide.

Most of us are in 'the firing line' here. One could easily collect a lengthy catalogue of historical events which make uncomfortable reading for almost any theological and ecclesiastical tradition (starting with the David and Bathsheba incident). Let me suggest a few:

- Martin Luther was an anti-semite.
- The first Western (Protestant) missionary to China was employed in the drug (opium) trade.
- Evangelicals in the first half of the nineteenth century believed in the social gospel.
- C.H. Spurgeon was a keen user of tobacco. So was C. S. Lewis.
- The Edinburgh Conference (1910) was a direct ancestor of the ecumenical movement.
- Benjamin Warfield believed in evolution.
- Martin Lloyd Jones experienced 'the second blessing'.

It is of the essence of the postcolonial historical project that it honours the 'subaltern', as we have seen. This has huge consequences. Because, as we now know, subaltern history has never really been written? Also have our historians promoted the subalterns of the past to the approval of the contemporary establishment in order to ignore the uncomfortable message of *their* subalterns? Jesus had something to say about this. He accused the people of his day of honouring the memory of the prophets while belonging to the same 'family' (their 'ancestors') – and by implication approving of the same behaviour – as those who killed the prophets in the first place (Matthew 13:29-36). A modern example might be the tributes paid by the political establishment in the United States to people such as Martin Luther King. The inescapable conclusion is that it is the controversialists, particularly those from among the subalterns, who were the prophetic voice of their day. The 'postcolonial voice' with its desire to represent 'the other', to speak for suppressed minorities, for the still-colonised and migrants, in general for 'the wretched of the earth' is today, and every day, the voice we need to discern. It is very difficult to do so.

What about the church?

What project do we have to listen to those who are powerless? Even in the church their voice is very faint, almost inaudible. In order to hear it we shall need to change our systems of power, to be much more quiet, more patient, more humble. Without wanting to idealise it, the early church seems to have envisaged some sort of open fellowship where everyone had a say, and power flowed inward from the periphery. Gift could be bestowed by the Holy Spirit on anyone and while exercising that gift the gifted one had (temporary) leadership conferred on him or her (1 Corinthians 12:29-31). This whole breathtaking arrangement did not last very long, however.

Today's church is still hopelessly 'colonial' in its attitudes, and is ruled by the equivalent of colonial powers. So here, in conclusion, are some practical suggestions based on a postcolonial philosophy, which we might measure against the practice of our own (local) church.

- Obviously, first of all the church should be autonomous in the sense that it should not be controlled by any 'foreign' power. Nowadays, this is not usually a problem, though some denominational structures (the Roman Catholics perhaps) are still rather hierarchical, and in some charismatic circles there is an unhealthy tendency towards centralised 'apostles' interfering in the running of local fellowships.
- Much more common are hierarchical and authoritarian structures within individual local churches and, of course, they are equally unwelcome and need to be resisted.
- Also within the church the rights and roles of the marginalised, the poor (in every sense) and the disadvantaged need to be constantly championed, and this will mean a wholehearted tolerance of diversity. Obviously this will also mean different things in different churches, but the role of women, of ethnic groups with different cultural practices, of the young, of the elderly, must be recognised.
- If, for any reason any group is being exploited to the advantage of another this needs to be recognised and dealt with. We have an example of this sort of thing, and how it was dealt with, in Acts chapter 6. All should participate freely and fairly in the life of the church.
- Equally no one group should be allowed to use their 'identity', particularly

if it is grounded in tradition, to get their own way.
- Finally, the church will encourage free and constructive dialogue which will encourage every church member to be involved in the running of the church and also in determining its direction.

The strategies described in this chapter – interpolation, mimicry, archaeology and magic realism, palimpsest, new modes of representation – are meant to provide practical methodologies for the building of healthy communities. I have not just borrowed some political philosophy (postcolonialism) and, without much reference to Bible, theology, or Christian tradition, tried to transplant it in an 'unspiritual' way into the life of the church and the nation. Rather my method is part of a wholesale attempt to develop a Christian political philosophy. I am unhappy about the way that many people – Christians, but not just Christians – use the word 'political'. Politics refers to the way that we run our public lives (as against our family or private lives). The public sphere, while more difficult to control, deserves to be run quite as much in a godly way as our families. Churches are public institutions in that they bring together people from different families (private situations) and ask them to behave in a corporate way. They need good rules and ways of behaving together, just as much as any other corporate activity. Every corporation, every church, has rules (usually a mixture of written and unwritten); the question is: what are they and do they work? I contend that the 'rules' mentioned above are biblical (and can find biblical passages to support all of them), but would be happy to debate the matter with anybody, because I admit that biblical interpretation is not at all an exact science, and that Christians have disagreed about 'church government' down the centuries. However, I also contend that the onus of proof lies with those who wish to say that we do not want to live by the rules above, because they are, I think, rules which we would all want to be applied to ourselves, or in other words they are all examples or outworkings of 'the golden rule' – do as you would be done by. We have all suffered from authoritarian personalities and a hierarchical use of power; we all need to be respected and honoured even when we are 'different'; we all feel the need to participate 'freely and fairly' in the life of the church and this includes having a say in the way things are run and in planning the future; we may all have been browbeaten by those who are using church tradition as a weapon to get their own way. There is nothing extraordinary about this; we just hope that it is not going to happen to us.

Also, finally, truth is one. Rules for the good life of the church apply equally to society at large. Read the book of Proverbs. The 'good life', personified by Wisdom, is not just for the household or the Temple but is to be proclaimed 'in the open air', 'in public places', 'at the top of the bustling streets' and at 'the approaches to the city gates' (Proverbs 1:21,2 REB).

Postcolonialism and the global culture

It is clear that we live in a globalised world and that globalisation entails very significant cultural change for us all. Such simple everyday events as watching the television or going shopping connect us with a huge variety of new experiences and products from all over the world, and this can change our lives. But there is a further question based on that fact. Changes happen in people's culture because of globalisation but is there a global culture as such? Are we perhaps moving towards a time when there is just one culture for us all, and what is that culture like? If there is such a movement, what threat, if any, does this pose, and has the postcolonial discourse anything to say to this situation? I want to begin by trying to describe this global culture, but, of course, if I am unable to give a coherent account, it may be that it simply does not exist. and that too would be an answer to our question.

A global culture?

First of all, the global culture is inhabited by people who belong to many different national and ethnic groups. It is not conditioned by place; you do not have to live in any particular country or city in order to qualify for membership. However it is not global in the sense that it is universal It does not touch upon the whole of life and not everybody is able to join in. It has its own language (in the sense of technical terms, jargon, in-jokes and so on), appropriate dress, events, heroes, but you do not have to belong to a particular national or regional group to belong, in the sense that you might say of someone 'once a German always a German'.

The culture that it is nearest to, and to which it has the most obvious links, is Western modernity (with occasional nods in the direction of postmodernity with regard to life-style) and we might even specifically nominate that of the United States, at least in its 'export' variety. Its modernity consists of a continued metanarrative of progress, democracy and capitalism, including such virtues as efficiency and scientific measurement. It is an agent of the democracies, but not necessarily democratic in itself. The global culture is oligarchic and bureaucratic rather than democratic. In economic terms it is a product of the 'New World Order' and is a near neighbour to the Bretton Woods institutions, particularly in their most recent incarnation as apostles of 'free trade', deregulation and the like. It is frequently guilty of 'economism', the belief that economics is at the base of everything, and justifies everything. There is a widespread belief, not confined to the economists, that at some profound level 'you can't buck the market'. Thus economism invades every part of our lives. As Jonathan Sachs has said:

> [P]olitics in the West has become ever more procedural and managerial, concerned with delivering maximum public services at minimum cost while bypassing substantive moral questions about what kind of world we seek collectively to make. John Rawls calls this, one of the credos of contemporary liberalism, 'the priority of the right over the good'. (Sachs 2002, 34)

The global culture is very closely linked with 'big business' and finance, indeed without this connection it would hardly exist at all. There are exceptions – the world of academia (especially science) is one, and the world of entertainment (including sport) and the arts is another, but as these have often been commodified to a large extent, the exceptions are not as important as they first appear.

As it depends on relatively sophisticated communication systems, with rare exceptions, the global culture is only available to those who have access to them. It is characterised by intense mobility, aided by these same systems. Globalisation favours people who are 'on the move' or 'in touch'. Paris yesterday, New York today, Tokyo tomorrow, is not the exception, but the rule. (There is an alternative which goes 'I spoke to Paris yesterday…etc.) Rootedness in a locality is positively a hindrance.

The global culture is in practice only open to those who are wealthy or who are on their way to being wealthy or who aspire to be wealthy. Manuel Castells puts it this way:

> Under the new, dominant logic of the space of flows… areas that are non-valuable from the perspective of informational capitalism, and that do not have significant political interest for the powers that be, are bypassed by flows of wealth and information, and ultimately deprived of the basic technological infrastructure that allows us to communicate,

innovate, produce, consume, and even live, in today's world. (Held & McGrew 2000, 350)

The technology (air tickets, international communication devices, access to the media, a subscription to the *Economist*) is not an optional extra in the global culture. Are not the poor, certainly the ultra-poor, automatically excluded? As soon as the poor connect with the global culture – one thinks of the ubiquity of satellite television – they come into the third category, those who aspire to be wealthy. They are no longer content with 'village life', even if this offers them a supportive community, a healthy environment, a satisfying occupation and a reasonable standard of living.

You may be asking at this point whether I am distinguishing sufficiently between global business and global culture? For example, globalisation might also include the numerous poor migrant workers who cross international boundaries to look for work. However, it is probably true to say that these people are not so much part of the global culture as its victims. Were slaves part of the Roman Empire? Yes and no. They were certainly not those who shared in its ethos and style, nor in many of its benefits. Today's biggest and most powerful club is the global business culture. This may not look like an exclusive club. More and more people are getting onto the inter-net, which is largely unregulated. Quite ordinary citizens can wield extraordinary net-power by creating a computer virus, which may have world-wide effects. True, but it is one thing to attempt to pull the system down, quite another to share in the benefits. Again it might be argued that plenty of 'ordinary' people are making money (not so much recently!) on the internet and at another level that it is encouraging to see an Indian city like Hyderabad beginning to gain a share in the wealth generated by the IT revolution. True again, but forcing your way into an exclusive club, and even changing the rules a little, does not mean that there is no club and that others are not excluded. The English sahibs and the Indian rajahs have mostly departed from the clubs set up by the British Raj, but the clubs have not ceased to exist. One set of wealthy and privileged people has replaced another. The poor are still sweeping the floors and serving the drinks. The big question is not whether there are fortunes to be made but whether there is a systematic equalisation of wealth.

Within the global culture there are a number of global sub-cultures, such as the international sporting culture, the youth culture, the internet, International Non Government Organisations (INGOs) and many others. Some of these sub-cultures may be integral to global culture. The obvious example is the business culture, as already mentioned. The youth culture is probably another example. The world has 800 million teenagers – the most ever. Teenagers and young adults like to travel, they are very fashion conscious and they have reasonably good purchasing power. Many analysts have suggested that young people are the motor behind globalisation – not perhaps in the sense that they are the initiators or even the controllers, but that they are the essential consumers. This may have more than cultural relevance. It was largely young people who forced the issue of the fall of the Soviet bloc.

The global culture has a low-level relationship to tradition and 'culture' in the sense of previously agreed aesthetic norms. The global warrior must be able to cope with and enjoy a wide variety of cultural experiences ('I enjoy, Japanese, Chinese, Indian, Italian cuisine and live by the 'when in Rome eat like the Romans' rule!) but this is not the same thing as becoming rooted in a particular culture. Because of the need to move, *not* to be rooted, to 'do business' wherever the opportunity arises, the global culture has developed its own shorthand culture. Its language is mostly English, its aesthetic is 'hotel décor', its relationships are ephemeral (by design), its cuisine is 'international bland', its dress is the business suit, its drink is Coca Cola or some alcoholic equivalent, its currency is Mastercard.

Not surprisingly, it is an impersonal and depersonalising culture. Take the massive money transactions that are carried out by means of the television screen, without any reference to what this might mean to actual people. (Rather like some aspects of modern warfare, when the real damage done to real lives is hidden behind the images which seem to represent little more than a sophisticated computer game.) Businesses are no longer attached to communities (ask the miners, the steel workers, even the car workers) or if they are, they are communities who know that at any minute the business might be transferred somewhere else where the work can be done more cheaply.

It is a culture where change is the order of the day. Traditional patterns seem to be dissolving. Just think of the way that the whole area of gender relations has become a confused and contested domain, or the way that accepted family values such as 'the sanctity of marriage' have come under attack. Even more disturbing is the fact that people do not know how to respond to change. They are deeply concerned about the environment, perhaps, but, despite their concern, do not know what to do about it. Political systems in this, and in other areas as well, seem unable to deal with the problems we face. There are plenty of movements for protest and action, but because they are also by-passing traditional political structures we are not sure whether they are part of the problem or the solution. Manuel Castells says: 'we live in a historical period characterised by widespread destructuring of organisations, delegitimation of institutions, fading away of major social movements' (Castells 2000, 3). Furthermore, the sheer speed of these changes is destabilising. David Harvey speaks about the acceleration of turnover time, in production, exchange and consumption. Examples he gives are the increasing use of shift systems in the work place, 'just in time' delivery, credit cards, and the increasing 'consumption' of services, the lifetime of which – think about something like a rock concert or attending a health club – is generally shorter than those of commodities (Harvey 1989, 285). Yet much that we value, or ought to value, takes time and care to establish, relationships being the obvious example, but many other things as well. Great institutions, traditions of excellence, flourishing neighbourhoods are not, any more than Rome, built in a day.

The effects of globalisation on traditional culture: three possibilities

If a new global culture is emerging what effect is it having on traditional cultures? The process of global cultural change leads, it seems to me, to at least three theoretical outcomes. Firstly there is the possibility of newness. Why should we stay with the 'old ways' that are tied to local and particular cultures, when brand new forms of global culture are emerging, which often seem preferable? Viewed in these terms it is only reactionaries who see the erosion of local cultures as a loss.

Secondly, there is 'glocalisation' or hybridity, where newness is created, not by sweeping revolutionary innovation, but by a mixing of the old and the new. Ulrich Beck quotes Salman Rushdie to the effect that 'A bit of this and a bit of that is how newness enters the world', (Held & McGrew 2000, 102) a saying which might be thought typical of someone who has moved so effortlessly into Western culture and yet has not forgotten where he comes from. This leads to all sorts of invention and innovation, from Bollywood to curry becoming the English national dish. In India, McDonald's serve mutton and a vegetarian menu. *Sesame Street* in China has the same characters but the content contains Chinese not American values. 'We borrowed an American box and put Chinese content into it' they claim (*National Geographic* August 1999 p.16).

Thirdly there is the resistance to the global culture. Here we move smartly into postcolonial territory. The conflict between Islam and the modern world would be an example. Unlike 'glocalisation' which tends to be a smooth and even pleasant process, this resistance tends to promote conflict and confusion. Many young British Muslims, for example, are torn between the desire of their parents and close associates that they should make a stand for their Islamic culture and the natural attractions of a 'modern' culture. The film *East is East* deals precisely with this issue. While the film is very funny, it is also very sad. Also, according to one account, it was not very popular with Asians living in Britain. Perhaps they felt that it made too much humorous capital out of something which for them is a deeply felt personal struggle, or, simply they felt that they were being misrepresented. In any case the clash of an immigrant, in this case Islamic, culture with the home culture is familiar territory (though an area that needs constant attention). All the key conflictual words and phrases – 'insecurity', 'lack of identity', 'cultural confusion' – come to mind. This process – where globalisation is seen as a threat – is the more serious because it tends to produce communities that are toxic. Religious fundamentalisms are all too often rampant ethnicities, cults and gangs and clubs, with values determined by what they are defined *against*. We have plenty of these and they are usually a reaction to the rootlessness of the globalised world. Anthony Giddens describes this as a world of 'pure relationship' in which the strength of the relationship depends not on social ties, such as are provided by the family or community, but on the emotional rewards inherent in the relationship itself (Giddens 1999,61). Whatever the case, we continue to be in a world which is producing fierce opposition to the perceived values of globalisation.

Responding to cultural change: some examples

The three outcomes just mentioned need further exploration. Judging the actual impact of cultural 'invasions' is a tricky business. Difficult as it is, it remains something Christians should try to do. Here I want to look briefly at some case studies in cultural globalisation, beginning with the film and TV business.

Held and McGrew et al. have pointed out that there is huge dominance of the world film and TV markets by the Western media, particularly that of the US. As early as the 1970s the US was exporting something in the region of 150,000 hours of programmes a year with very little reverse flow (Held & McGrew 1999, 359). In terms of this particular aspect of culture therefore, globalisation means Westernisation, particularly in view of the extraordinary penetrative power of satellite television. The usual questions arise. Is this a good thing? Is it 'inevitable'? Does it mean a completely new way of life for our (meaning the world's) young people? Do we want our values set by organisations that are largely profit driven and over which we seem to have so little control? Of course some distinction must be made between the way Western nations dominate the media and the actual process whereby films and TV programmes bring about Westernisation and globalisation. In theory it should be possible for non-Westerners to watch any amount of films and TV and not to be affected by the values portrayed in them. Also, as we have suggested, 'glocalisation', whereby local values are *combined* with those of the 'invaders' must certainly be taken into account.

A second case study is provided by the global music industry. One way to become a household name world-wide is to become a music star. The biggest names are in popular music, but Western classical music is also now enjoyed almost everywhere. Music has been carried by people as they moved about the globe - think of the way that the rhythms of Africa have arrived in music stores in Europe via America, a process which has involved such widely spread historical events as the Atlantic slave trade and the arrival of American troops in Europe during the second world war – and has altered cultures along the way. The American youth culture has been exported partly by means of its music culture. This change has dominated the music scene in Europe and elsewhere. Have a look in any big music store, and you will find that the biggest section is devoted to this sort of music. Traditional music cultures have found it hard to compete. It is not that there are no music traditions outside the West. It is just that unless you are connected to the world wide music industry you are unlikely to get much of a hearing.

The fate and role of a traditional music culture are exemplified by the story of *rai*. Modern *rai* emerged during the 1920s when rural migrants brought their own music with them to the city of Oran in Algiers. The resulting musical style was a mixture of influences – Spanish flamenco, Sufi music from Morocco, French music hall, Berber music, and so on. The lyrics were always considered rather *risqué*, indeed subversive of good morals and religion. It rapidly became the music of choice of Algerian young people, particularly the disaffected and unemployed. There were massive cassette sales and the new stars *chebs* (male) and *chebas* (female) gained celebrity status. As Algerians emigrated to France they took their music with them and *rai* became popular among French young people whether of North African origin or not. However the immigrants saw it particularly as *their* music, as an expression of solidarity among those who were confronting European opposition and racism. Since approximately 1988, when *rai* 'arrived' in the US, it has been part of the World Music scene. There has been an attempt to de-radicalise it, however, with *rai* seen as a vehicle of teenage rebellion (like rap) rather than an expression of ethnic solidarity. As Gross, McMurray and Swedenburg have put it (Inda 2002, 203):

> A more subversive reading would see *rai* as part of a wider endeavour to bring about "the gradual dissolution of 'white' culture by all the peoples who, having been forcibly subjected to it, have assimilated the tricks, the techniques necessary to contaminate it" (Juan Goytisolo).

More recently *rai*'s core audience has been somewhat diminished in France and the young people have abandoned it for rap. Rap, unlike *rai*, tends to be multi-racial and apolitical and there is an underlying tension between music such as *rai* that expresses the sentiments and aspirations of a particular culture and music which is, perhaps deliberately, a mixture of many cultures and so not representative of any one of them. Consider the comment made by one musician (Rabha Attaf); 'I will continue preaching for the mixture of cultures…The more hybridisation we have, the less we'll hear about claims to [a pure] culture' (Inda 2002, 218). Others felt that a loss of culture was a loss of identity, and it was their Maghrebi identity which gave them the only 'place to stand' in a hostile French environment.

> *Rai* performance and consumption re-create a relatively free and protected cultural zone…in which Algerians in France can feel 'at home'. *Rai* performances are also ritual occasions for the expression of pride and protest, where, as in music performances among African Americans and Black British, a 'moral, even a political community is defined'. (Inda 2002, 220)

At the same time *rai* fans continued to be pleased that it had made it onto the world stage. The fact that many enjoyed it world-wide created the sensation that *rai* was both 'ethnic' and multi-cultural. Though in some ways *rai* had been commodified and homogenised by its adoption into world music; it remained a valuable cultural source for those on the move (also as a result of globalisation).

A third example is tourism. Held & McGrew write: 'What other activity exposes so many people, (an estimated 561 million spending $380 billion in 1995) from so many social strata, to such a wide, immediate and tangible experience of other cultures, locations and frames of reference?' Yet the matter is even more complicated than this. They continue: 'The very presence of tourists, especially in any large numbers and carrying significant economic consequences, transforms the cultural and economic character of the locales they visit' (Held & McGrew 1999, 361). So there are two cultural revolutions going on simultaneously. Tourists are learning about new cultures, something which changes them and their habits in all sorts of ways. In the process, however, they are affecting those who receive them. Whole neighbourhoods are being revolutionised to cater for 'the tourist trade' and locals are beginning to learn new ways in order to provide visitors with 'a home from home', while, at the same time trying to maintain their own distinctive cultures.

Three examples, then, of cultural change agents – television and film, the music industry and tourism, all of them apparently innocent enough, indeed in many cases pleasurable and profitable – which remind us that the our worlds are deeply affected by cultural globalisation on a day to day basis, and that these changes affect not just the periphery of our lives, how we spend our leisure time for example, but our value systems and even our fundamental sense of identity.

So we are confronted by at least three interconnected but different scenarios. We began with a global culture that is modern, based on sophisticated technology, patronised by wealthy businessmen and apparently bringing the world together in a new way. We followed this up with talk of toxic communities and lack of identity leading to insecurity and outrage. Our last image was of a culture that is largely welcome wherever it is encountered but is changing the way we think and behave in a quiet and pervasive way. So which is the true picture? The answer is all three. Peter Heslam speaks of interconnectedness and fragmentation, of inclusion and exclusion (Heslam 2002, 6). The picture is complex and change is taking place in many ways.

Leaving the local

Embracing a global culture means, almost by definition, 'leaving the local' and this introduces us to the whole vexed question of 'community'. There is much anxious talk about community in Christian conversation today, but little that ties down the concept to specifics. It is an indication of the individualism of our Christianity that even when we consult the Bible, that profoundly community centred text, we come up with individualistic answers. Happily, one scholar at least, Ched Myers, provides a welcome exception. Myers sees 'the Kingdom of God' as expressed *in a fundamental way* in rootedness in a particular locality and suggests appropriate economic, political and ecological strategies as a result (Myers 1994, 364-7). Community is 'the efforts of unlike people to live well in specific places' (he is quoting Daniel Kemmis: see the citation in Myers 1994, 346) and, by definition this is not possible unless we can identify specific geographical locations. Myers' argument is that where mobility is more important than roots, spirituality can die. Raymond Williams makes the same point about socialism.

> A new theory of socialism must now centrally involve *place*. Remember the argument was that the proletariat had no country, the factor which differentiated it from the property owning classes. But place has been shown to be a crucial element in the bonding process – more so for the working class than for the capital-owning classes – by the explosion of the international economy and the destructive effects of deindustrialisation upon old communities. When capital has moved on, the importance of place is more clearly revealed (Harvey 1996, 29)

Appealing to the history of the United States Myers suggests that the 'original trauma' of European displacement led inexorably to the dispossession of other peoples from their land. Later people were displaced from rural to urban lives and later again from settled neighbourhoods in towns to 'suburbia'. This has divorced people from a relation to culture, land or community (Myers 1994, 342). In the same way, Simone Weil thinks that immigrants are a problem because they do not have, by definition 'roots'. She notes that the US is a nation of immigrants (Weil 2002, 50). Myers develops this theme much further and proposes various antidotes to this rootlessness. For our purposes we should note that this displacement is an underpinning reality of globalisation. As David Smith has put it:

> Peoples whose lives have been shaped by non-western religious world views are pressurised into abandoning socio-economic systems that have proved capable of ensuring their survival for centuries, in favour of an alien economic structure that offers short term benefits for the privileged part of the population while endangering the very survival of the people in the long run. (Smith D. 2003, 93)

Of course, this detachment from the locality is what many people want, indeed it is the tension between local and global which remains one of the great conflicts of modernity. Every young man or woman who has to decide to leave the village and go out into 'the big world' is caught up in this. There is a wonderful description of the multiple tensions that arise out of this sort of situation in Raymond Williams' novel *Border Country* (the title itself is significant). The young university teacher, Will, having used his education to 'get on in life', returns home to his dying father, Harry. His father as a younger man had also had opportunities to widen his work experience but had chosen to stay rooted in village life. His contemporary, Morgan Rosser, by contrast, had always had an eye on the wider world. Disillusioned by the failure of the General Strike, he had decided to go into business on his own – another break away from the life of the village. In a pivotal scene Morgan tries to persuade Harry to join him in his business. He is contemptuous of those who just go on in the same way.

> They're strong enough, Harry, in their own little patch, their own fields. But what they don't realise is there's far stronger things, not like people at all, breaking in from outside. If a man digs hard enough he'll eat: that's all they see of it. But a miner digs, just as hard, and it isn't the same. The coal has to go out and come back as meat, and a lot can go wrong with that. Even here it's the same. It isn't just what they grow, but what happens out there, places they've never seen and know nothing about.' (Williams 1988, 180)

We can see here Morgan's continued resentment that the miners had not been able to control their own fate and also his feeling that he wants to get his hands on the controlling forces himself. However, as Harry realises (he turns down Morgan's offer) there is a price to be paid.

We are still paying that price today. The loss of 'tradition' ensures that we have no way to carry on when 'experience' fails us. When circumstances turn against us, as we say, and our usual stock of happiness and contentment is 'past its sell-by date', what else have we got in the fridge? When tongues cease, what language shall we speak? Further, without a language of our own, who will protect us from the idolatrous images of the advertisers and the sound-bites of the spin-doctors? We are given over to the inexorable spread of a global culture, with its consumerist values, its relentless hedonism, its heartless carelessness – 'eat drink and be merry for tomorrow we die'. Living without tradition, without significant roots, means that I have no way of resisting adverse weather. Tradition is like a well-built house. It is a place to live, and within which I can flourish without always fighting the elemental battles to do with shelter, warmth, food and hygiene. I *can* live out in the open, but it is often more difficult to do anything much but survive. I am naturally preoccupied with the weather, and I get on much better when it is good. Severe weather is a real problem. Thus it is that 'rootless' people are fine until a (metaphorical) storm blows up. (Jesus said something about this in his parable of the two builders.) Our modern worship songs are adequate when we wish to rejoice; not so useful when the time has come to weep. A similar illustration is that our tradition is like a language. Without it (e.g. in a foreign county) we are reduced to the status, very often, of simpletons. Everybody else seems to know better than us what is going on. We can survive without a knowledge of the past, but we are severely disadvantaged even in the performance of the simplest tasks.

Destroying local communities

'The idea of a national or global community is meaningless apart from the realisation of local communities' (Berry 1993, 120) asserts Wendell Berry, while at the same time lamenting their destruction.

> The social and cultural pluralism that some now see as a goal is a public of destroyed communities. Wherever it exists, it is the result of centuries of imperialism. The modern industrial urban centres are 'pluralistic' because they are full of refugees from destroyed communities, destroyed community economies, disintegrated local cultures, and ruined local ecosystems. [Berry 1993, 169]

Human communities, and they come in a thousand shapes and sizes, are so often invaluable repositories of human wisdom, experience and experimentation in successful living, and we destroy them at our peril. As a general principle human dignity needs the support of appropriate economic arrangements. No doubt big business and big government are a threat to our independence even now, and where this is the case it works through the undermining of community. As Tom Sine has put it:

> We are rapidly moving into a future in which the family farm, the small retailer and the corner shop are becoming artefacts of a bygone past. (Sine 1999, 79)

I live in an English city, Gloucester, and try to be aware of the dynamics of my own neighbourhood. I see that community threatened in a number of obvious ways. Commercially the small shopkeepers cannot, on the whole, compete with the supermarkets. This is bad for them, but also for those residents who cannot afford to run cars and who have lost the services of the corner shop. The food in the supermarkets is probably less healthy than the locally produced and sold food, but there is little that I can do about that. I have choice inside the supermarket but not really choice to buy elsewhere (except at another supermarket). The supermarkets are friendly enough, but impersonal compared to the local shopkeepers who you can, if you want to, have a real relationship with. So community breaks down at another level. Local transport arrangements worry me increasingly. The roads are very busy and not at all safe for pedestrians, cyclists, old people and children. They are also very frustrating for motorists, with long queues at a number of points to do with the railway crossing and a cluster of public services (hospital, schools). There are two big through roads which cut through the heart of the area and which make it very difficult for there to be any sense of unity. There are too few public spaces (though we live near a very pleasant park) and people have got out of the habit of congregating together. There are too many single purpose spaces – car parks and the like – which are underused and also rather threatening spaces at night. Again this discourages congregation. Property prices have shot up recently and it is difficult for people to move into the area and for there to be the spectrum of people that we need to build community. In the city as a whole there are cheaper parts of town and also much more expensive areas and the ever growing differential in prices means that the town is divided into income ghettos. People have to commute some distance for their jobs and that too means that they come home in the evening late and tired and without any desire, understandably, to meet their neighbours or to take part in communal activities. From a Christian point of view, churches do not represent neighbourhoods, but rely on people travelling to church, often from some distance. Home entertainment makes it quite difficult to organise locally based public entertainments and activities and the local rugby club has been globalised, with a nationwide following and an international team, not to mention exorbitant ticket prices. Nothing about all this is very new or surprising. I dare say it could be replicated all over the country. It is so unexceptionable that it seems hardly worth commenting on, yet perhaps that is the point.

How many features of globalisation can we see here? The nearest supermarket to our neighbourhood is owned by an American firm, notorious for grinding down its small competitors. Transport arrangements reflect a government which understandably does not want to make itself unpopular with the powerful car lobby, and which, like governments before it, has simply not been able to control the growth of private transport. It may be unfair to blame the government in that we all love our cars, but the world wide interests of automobile manufacturers and oil extractors are not being sufficiently challenged in the light of what we are doing to our communities by means of the motor car.

TV of course brings the world into our front room – that is a cliché. But we underestimate no doubt what that does to our ability to nurture local culture. Professional sport, part of the TV package, is now very much presented to us as both a global enterprise and part of everyday life. Local sporting loyalties, once very much part of community life, have been replaced by Manchester United and 'Engerland'. The World Cup (2006) was a huge global event. It awoke more excitement in the College where I teach than anything that happened locally by a long shot. September 11, 2001 in turn overshadowed any local political issues. I stood recently in the municipal elections. On one occasion I telephoned one of our local radio stations to suggest that they might like to interview me, or something of the sort, particularly as I was standing for a new party which had not previously contested elections in the city. I was politely told that the station did not 'do' local elections because they were not sufficiently newsworthy. My response from other sections of the media was almost equally lukewarm.

All this may sound rather trivial. In truth shopping and transport arrangements, the distribution of public spaces, property prices and the media may not threaten my life in a fundamental way. These sorts of issues, however, have a much more powerful effect in parts of the world where there is more poverty. Jeremy Seabrook's book *In the Cities of the South* is just one which describes the devastation that is being wrought among poor city communities by the day to day effects of current economic policy. Here he writes about part of Bangkok.

> Klong Toey is cut off from the rest of the city, bordered on one side by the port and on the other by a raised expressway which soars some 20 metres above the rail track leading to the port. Along the railway line, squatters and vendors have built rough shelters and stalls. On the other side of the railway a dusty highway crowded with trucks also leads to the port. The expressway – a somewhat exaggerated term for a highway that is frequently at a standstill – was to have been the answer to the chronic and immitigable congestion of this overgrown city. (Seabrook 1996, 184-5)

Already the victim of economic 'development' you would have thought that this beleaguered community would have been left in peace to try and build a place fit for human habitation. Not a bit of it.

> The social and physical isolation of Klong Toey has not preserved it from the rise in land and property values. The Port Authority itself requires more land for containers, while the Bangkok Metropolitan Authority wants to sell some land it owns in the slum to a developer for another shopping mall (to add to the sixty or so already constructed). The BMA has proposed the sweeping away of large parts of the existing community, with the removal of the people either to the peripheral areas of the city or to new high-rise apartments on part of the Klong Toey site. (Seabrook 1996, 185)

This sounds a reasonable idea (even if destructive of a community now more than fifty years old) but many of the dwellers do not have any title to their land and therefore to new housing elsewhere. Also the new flats are quite unsuitable for families. And so on and so on. The problems of Gloucester pale into insignificance compared to the everyday struggle to survive in Klong Toey. Yet the causes are much the same. The life of communities is being destroyed by 'development', 'progress' and globalisation.

How do you destroy a community? Well, economic means will do very well. As Simone Weil notes, 'Even without a military conquest, money-power and economic domination can so impose a foreign influence as actually to provoke this disease of uprootedness…Money destroys human roots wherever it is able to penetrate, by turning desire for gain into the sole motive.' (Weil 2002, 44) This process seems to go on without any conscious direction - another of our so-called 'inevitables' – but there may even be a reason why a rootless mass is preferred. For example, employers are 'secretly inclined to prefer to have in their factories a drove of unfortunate, rootless individuals', as Simone Weil has noted (Weil 2002, 63). We might say the same for many administrators, bureaucrats, politicians and the people they control. Whatever the case, the argument is always on the side of modernity, in favour of what is always thought of as 'progress' and what is sometimes unhelpfully called pluralism. Those who oppose are always 'against progress' or seen as obscurantists or traditionalists. As Wendell Berry has it: 'They [the definers of 'pluralism'] affirm the pluralism of a society formed by the uprooting of cultures at the same time that they regard the fierce self-defence of still-rooted cultures as 'fundamentalism', for which they have no tolerance at all' (Berry 1993, 169).

The global youth culture

In the context of the destructiveness of the global culture it is worth thinking about the global youth culture. Is the youth culture that has spread world wide a destructive force which we need to resist or is it just one more culture with both good and bad and much in between? At a conference I attended recently there was a major disagreement as to whether the global spread of a youth culture was a bad thing or not. A speaker had made some adverse remarks about young black Africans watching MTV. A younger man wanted to defend the youth culture – what's wrong with MTV anyway? – and an African representative was uncomfortable about Europeans telling Africans what they should or should not watch. Others felt that we have long bemoaned the spread of 'Westernisation' and an uncontextualised western gospel, why not stand out against the same secular influences as they affected our young people. Later the question of choice came up. In Francophone Africa, or so the argument went, young people were rejecting the life style of their African origins (too traditional) also of their French heritage (too elitist and colonialist) and choosing a global (American) culture as their own.

Whatever the outcome of this argument, I am sure that we have underestimated the way that traditional community life is being undermined by the cultural impact of globalisation on young people, particularly through the already mentioned television, film and music industries and their ability to advertise themselves. As Dewi Hughes has put it:

> What is most significant about the impact of these industries is the way they create an image of the Western, primarily North American, way of life that seems so attractive to people in the homes of the poor, where any artefact from the West is treasured and displayed – as if an empty perfume bottle or a page of a magazine somehow gives the homeowner a stake in the much coveted Western life-style. (Hughes 2002)

A friend of mine visiting Thailand was hoping to spend as much time as possible in a remote village in order to assimilate the local Thai culture. On arrival at the village he was dismayed when the children gathered round him and asked the question which was most urgent in their minds, 'How you ever been to see Manchester United?'

The destruction of 'life-worlds'

Joel Kovel adds to our theme of traditional society under attack by speaking of 'life-worlds' (Kovel 2002, 52ff). This gives an economic dimension to the picture. Typically, he suggests, in the case of the life-world of an indigenous people there is a disruption of their relationship with the land.

> With the productive foundation of society interrupted, a complex and disintegrative chain of events is set in motion. As the 'old ways' no longer make sense, a kind of desire is set loose, and as this is now relatively shapeless and boundless, the virus of capital, with its promise of limitless wealth, is able to take hold. This is always accompanied by the mass-cultural invasion that encodes capital's logos in the form of commodities. Once 'Coca-Cola the real thing' replaces traditional reality, the internal colonisation that perfects the take-over of peripheral societies is well under way. (Kovel 2002, 54)

Or to put the same point in another way:

Perhaps the most difficult aspect of this fight [against the destruction of life worlds] is the need to deprogramme developing world peoples away from the modern culture that has penetrated our societies, so that lifestyles, personal motivations and status structures can be delinked from the system of industrialism and its corresponding creation of culture. (Goldsmith 2001, 155)

This penetration is often quite subtle. Encroaching capitalism tends to meet the colonised life-worlds half way. (In mission circles this is called contextualisation!). This 'glocalisation' is quite pleasing to post-modernists. It is also pleasing to capitalism, which commodifies everything that it touches, while breaking up existing life-worlds and creating new desires and needs (Kovel 2002, 54). (For further discussion on 'glocalisation' see 'The local fights back' below.)

Western secularism

At a more fundamental level, there have long been concerns about the effect of Western secularism and rationalism on traditional worldviews and the way that this might influence the reception of the gospel. Well before globalisation was a commonly accepted term, we have been aware of the impact of the Enlightenment and modernity as part of western cultural imperialism. Here, for example, is a classic statement of concern from Dan Beeby.

> The Gospel flourished and still flourishes in many parts of the world for the same reasons that it once flourished in Europe, and that is because the cultural opposition was only on the surface and not at the deepest level. Deep down the door was open.
>
> In accepting Western culture, will flourishing churches in many countries find their future situation exactly the opposite? On the surface they are free to choose in the religious supermarket, but what about deep down? Is the door going to be ajar? Our European schools and universities, our factories and farms, our banks and politics – almost everything public – function without reference to revelation, deity, heaven, creation, redemption, miracle, prayer, worship, judgement, confessed absolutes, and eternal life. (Beeby 1994, 7)

Have we answered Beeby's concerns? Somehow we in the Western church cannot bring ourselves to believe that *we* are the problem. Yet the truth is that we still do not know how to cope with the rationalistic foundations of our society. In many cases we have not even asked the key questions. 'How does the old knowledge class, the pastor scholar, relate to the new knowledge class, the technical experts?' asks Hutchinson (Hutchinson 1999). Also, has contemporary society made up its mind whether the new age of globalisation is a material age – politics, economics, sociology – or a spiritual age? Has the church? Can we 'cross over' from one to another? Another question is about the extent that traditional *methods* can be dispensed with. Too readily, we opt for a 'scientistic' world view, substituting bureaucratic efficiency, with its dependence on statistics and measurement, for spiritual power. Mission organisations, for example, have not been slow to realise the importance of film and TV as having a global reach. Consider for example the work of

SAT7[9], or the world-wide distribution of the Jesus Film. Against this some might argue that the world of 'virtual reality' is precisely what we do not want. Consider the mission statement of Rupert Murdoch's News Corporation:

> Just as our assets span the world, our vision spans art and humour, audacity and compassion, information and innovation. Every day hundreds of millions of people are entertained and enlightened by the authors, the actors, printers and producers, reporters and directors who fulfill [sic] our mission. (Cited by Timothy Garton Ash in his article 'Fight the Matrix' in *The Guardian* June 5 2003.)

I think we have had enough of this sort of thing.

The local fights back

As we have seen – the second of our three outcomes above – we need to bear in mind that globalisation often encounters communities that, so to speak, are ready and able to 'take it on'. These communities do not accept the ideology of globalism: for example that it is inevitable that there should be a cultural homogenisation, but rather construct new possibilities which are neither part of the so-called global culture nor part of the receiving culture, but a mixture of the two. This is akin to the 'hybridity' discussed below at the beginning of the Section on New Formations. Another possible name is 'globfrag' (Kelly, 1999, 160ff) chosen to indicate that globalisation creates fragmentation as well as uniformity. There are reasons for this, of course. Postmodernity is not all that friendly to homogenisation, nor is environmentalism. We have seen elsewhere that some modern technology makes 'small people agendas' a possibility. Good old-fashioned nationalism is by no means dead and where nations can see trading advantages in getting together, then regionalism (the European Union is the obvious example) can theoretically act as a counterbalance to cultural homogenisation. Better development theory has moved away from modernisation as in the recent work done by Robert Chambers (Chambers 2005).

When I send my students out to track down global influences here in Gloucester, I ask them to do *two* things: find out what is new and find out also what has happened to the new things as they have been assimilated by the good folk of

---

[9] Sat7 is a Christian broadcasting organisation based in Cyprus. It uses satellite television as its primary media method.

this part of the world. Sometimes it is the latter which is the more impressive. Gloucester City docks, once a workplace for the thousands of traders who used Gloucester as an entrepôt as they transferred their merchandise from the Atlantic to the Midlands, is now a tourist and business centre replete with museums, pubs, cafes, shops and offices. The tourist trade is one of the world's biggest global businesses, and Gloucester is not inclined to miss out. It has adapted its traditional working centre to a new reality. To my mind this says more about Gloucester than it does about globalisation. As David Lyon has pointed out 'globalism often seems to be a sort of economic triumphalism which rejoices every time a 'world product' becomes on offer in some remote locality' (Lyon 2000, 101). But his point is that this triumphalism may be misplaced. Certainly the spread of a global culture is by no means the only thing worth commenting on. Local adaptability to changing circumstances may be equally remarkable.

As an aside, the language of evangelism and church planting can be equally dismissive of the local. As if the real innovators, the real movers and shakers are the strategic *global* planners (schools of world mission and the like). However we should remember that in any significant advance of the gospel, local people are involved too, and, it may be, at a deeper level. When Jun Venceer announced at a WEF meeting in Canada, 'We've come to celebrate the globalisation of the church' what was actually celebrated was politically and culturally sensitive local initiatives from all over the world ([Lyon 2000, 101).

Dewi Hughes has suggested (Hughes 2002) that there are three ways in which Christian thinkers have taken on what he calls 'uniformitarian globalisation'. Encouragingly, in the light of a possible critique of Bible translators as thoughtless modernisers, he cites protestant/evangelical Bible translation as empowering local cultures. Hughes's point is that Bible translators have a vested interest in language and culture. Sometimes they have even had a crucial role in preserving local languages which have been under threat. William Carey's role in the development of Bengali as a language is not forgotten. The valuable role played by missionaries such as Caldwell and Pope in promoting the Tamil language, still remembered and celebrated today in Tamil Nadu, is another example.[10] Similarly, Hughes suggests that Christian development theory is an antidote to uniformitarianism because it is learning to adopt methods such as Chambers' Participatory Rural Appraisal which is based on 'humility towards and respect for the knowledge and abilities of the poor'.

---

[10] The classic text on this whole process is Laminh Sanneh's *Translating the Message* (Sanneh 1989).

Hughes knows much more about development theory and practice than I do, and I hope he is right. I suspect we have a long way to go yet, however, before we can claim that we have thoroughly disengaged our development theory from modernist ideologies of progress, indeed in the thinking of many, including many Christians, I suspect that this has hardly begun. Hughes's third point, contextualisation, does I think indicate a place where Christians can stand to resist homogenisation and to promote a welcome diversity. For many years now there has been an increasingly sophisticated understanding of the theory and practice of contextualisation (led by missionary anthropologists such as Paul Hiebert and Charles Kraft) which has led to much worthwhile empowering of local communities and cultures. Of course more needs to be done, but I think the theory is in place. Hughes, himself, distinguishes between contextualisation as inculturation, of which he approves, and contextualised theology which he thinks is not the genuine article. The latter he illustrates by citing 'certain types of Liberation Theology'. This theology he suspects 'is a means of modernisation that can be applied universally to the poor' and therefore not to a particular culture. I would argue however that in practice poverty takes many different forms and these forms are determined by local circumstances. (The Korean idea of *minjung* theology is an expression of this.) If you go, for example, into an Indian village, the unhelpful generalisation would be to say that the villagers belong to 'Indian culture' or 'Hindu culture'. Appropriate inculturation depends rather on sociological and political analysis, the very tools that Liberation Theology wants us to use. Certain members of the village (those that are poor) need to identified, in order to determine how the 'good news for the poor' can be applied to their 'culture'. This is not applying a universal means of modernisation but rather taking the context of powerlessness seriously.

Once more, not all of the products of the clash between globalisation and the local are healthy. Some of the newly created communities, because they are a reaction to the rootlessness that is experienced in a globalised world, may be dangerously reactionary. The vicious nationalism that is a feature of the Balkans, for example, seems to me both a product of the fear of loss of identity (something which began under the Communists, but which continues today with the advent of globalisation) and also a desperate harking back to the past. Despite the appeal to the past it is something new which is being produced, a far less secure and settled community, much more dependent on ephemeral factors such as charismatic leadership, nationalist slogans, the creation of rivals, and 'heritage' rather than history.

Thus, to repeat and summarise, the debate about the effects of cultural globalisation on communities is a complex one. Some notice the way that communities are being swept away. Others see 'Westernisation' or secularisation as the villains in chief. Yet others point out that globalisation does not have it all its own way. The 'local' receives and adapts new trends and produces something new, or turns back to the older ways. Certainly, while we need to remain aware of the powerful effects, past and present, of cultural imperialism we must also be careful not to overlook either the world wide resistance to it or the occasional happy outcomes. We must beware the idea that the recipients of cultural imperialism were, or are, merely passive victims. It is possible to demonstrate that a more accurate picture of classic imperialism would be that the 'victims' were very often able to pick and choose from what was being offered to them by the imperialists. (See the chapter above on Postcolonial Resistance.) This applied to missionary imperialists as well as to other cultural agencies. Here is Andrew Porter's account, for example:

> The history of the missionary enterprise offers many examples of indigenous societies taking advantage of missionary resources, not in any abject or desperate surrender to an imposed set of values and conditions, but positively as their chosen and most effective strategy for ethnic and community survival (Porter 1997, 375).

No doubt the same mechanisms are at work today as locals respond to globalisation. However, the matter is complex. There is a fierce debate going on at the moment between those who want to, understandably, get away from the centre/periphery model so central to colonialism. They question the whole idea that non-western societies can do little else but *react* to globalisation. On the other hand there are those who are keen to point out that colonialism is still alive and well and that colonial attitudes and practices cannot be simply ignored in an attempt to widen the source of action.

Christians or missionaries may play a number of roles in this clash of cultures. As we have seen, the advent of Christianity may reinforce local cultures, for example by affirming them through translation work. Alternatively, Christianity may provide a bridge between traditional and modern society ('mediating modernity'). This would make them the apostles of hybridity, so to speak. While the missionaries will often be representatives of the modern in a pre-modern world, they can try to make sure that the influence of modernity on the locality is benign. Presumably this would entail acting as 'gatekeepers' to some extent, though whether it is possible to act as a gatekeeper to globalisation is questionable. A more positive way of describing this process would be to say that somebody needs to equip people who are facing the onrush of modernity with the necessary skills to cope with the inevitable changes that modernity brings. I take it that this was the strategy of the *Iniciativa Cristiana* as described by Maurice Sinclair in his book *Green Finger of God* (Sinclair 1980) – I give an account of the work of the *Iniciativa* in the section on 'The Great Economy' below. The missionaries saw that the indigenous tribes people of the Chako in Argentina were deeply threatened by the arrival of the modern state and its commercial enterprises. It was not possible to isolate them from these developments, but they could be helped to survive. A third possibility is that Christianity can be seen as itself a threat to the local culture. This is certainly the accusation of many anthropologists. The advent of Christianity may become a force that undermines many traditional practices, even if not whole cultures. A straightforward example would be the marginalising of indigenous medical wisdom by the missionary doctor and his hospital.

Global and local: an ecclesiological perspective

It is not often that the church receives compliments from Marxists but here is one from David Harvey.

> The churches' ability to work at different spatial scales provides a number of models for political organisation from which the socialist movement could well draw some important lessons. (Harvey 2000, 51)

Harvey is right about the church's potential for working 'at different spatial scales'. For example, the theme of combining global and local is echoed by the familiar juxtaposition of universal and local when we think about the church. The importance of both these concepts has been insisted upon by Christians, in fact we may feel that the church itself was set up originally on a model – you might call it 'decentred interconnectedness' – which reflects this. While at the very beginning of the Christian era there is a 'mother church' as described in the Acts of the Apostles, Paul's missionary methods envisaged autonomous local churches (though not independent ones). Later centralising trends (Rome as the geographical and administrative centre, a Papacy at the head of an ecclesiastical hierarchy, uniform creeds etc.) were, in my opinion, contrary to the original apostolic pattern and contained their own nemesis. Certainly, the idea of a universal church is authoritatively stated in the Christian creeds but also the idea of the importance of belonging to a local Christian community has New Testament warrant and is, besides, a near universal practice. In the church with which I worshipped in Ootacamund in South India there were three congregations, different in language and culture. As an appropriate acknowledgement of 'the local' they were encouraged to express themselves through those languages and cultures in worship, teaching, and evangelism. However we did not forget the global. The congregations were *united* in a common leadership and the common use of finance and buildings as well as occasional joint celebration, in order to demonstrate to a town bitterly divided along ethnic, caste and class lines, the way that Christ had made peace by his cross.

Like many tensions of this sort it is not easy to keep a healthy balance. 'All one in Christ Jesus' is a motto to which we can subscribe, no doubt. But what does it mean in practice? What about cultural differences? Where do they come into the picture? Do our calls for unity all too often mask our desire to have things our own way? On the other hand does an insistence on cultural difference amount to little more than a narrow defence of my own upbringing, even my own preferences? Consider the situation in the College where I used to teach which is a multi-cultural community. The students certainly needed to be wary of an apparent global unity which tended only to mean that non-western students were expected to do things the Western way. On the other hand neither did we want students to use their cultural diversity to emphasise their differences – the Africans sitting all together at one table and the Koreans at another.

As I say, we have to keep two things in tension here. It is partly a matter of 'here there is neither Jew nor Greek' and partly 'every tribe and kindred and nation' before the throne. Similarly, was the Babel event in the Old Testament a blessing or a curse? The people were scattered and their languages confused, and that was some sort of curse, and yet at the same time this 'scattering' may have saved them from a greater evil. Pentecost was not altogether a reversal of Babel. People heard the divine message 'in their own languages'. Diversity remained, but the confusion was removed. Paul certainly celebrates a common citizenship for those in Christ. The 'powers' are divisive, the gospel unites (Ephesians 2). Even so, Ephesians 3:10 speaks of the church demonstrating 'the wisdom of God in its infinite variety' (REB translation).

This idea that there are good aspects to both local and global can be translated to world structures. Take economics for example. Global trade in itself seems a good thing. It is not an end in itself of course, and where something is available locally then it would be best to buy it there, but there is something to be said for David Ricardo's 'comparative advantage'. This is often quoted by economists, but what is less often quoted is that Ricardo believed that trade should be carefully balanced so that one country should not become hugely indebted to another and also that investment capital should be anchored locally and not allowed to flow from a high wage country to a low wage one (Ellwood 2001, 16). Similarly free trade is often a good idea, but does it have to be over vast distances? Is *regional* free trade one possibility? Each region decides whether and when they want to enter into bilateral trade agreements with other regions (Sine 1999, 78). Regions and localities often need to be protected. 'We must not simply open our markets to any and every product regardless of whether it benefits our economy, destroys our employment, or destabilises our society.' Adam Smith believed in 'the market' but what he had in mind was small manager-owned enterprises located in the communities where the managers lived. The managers would naturally have an interest in the future welfare of the community in which they were situated (Ellwood 2001, 17).

On this last point we need to remember that there is often great hostility towards those who defend local communities. Wendell Berry's eloquent defence of the Luddites makes precisely this point.

> To this day, if you say you would be willing to forbid, restrict, or reduce the use of technological devices in order to protect the community – or to protect the good health of nature on which the community depends – you will be called a Luddite, and it will not be a compliment. To say that the community is more important than machines is certainly Christian and certainly democratic, but it is also Luddism and therefore not to be tolerated. (1993, 131)

How to hang on to the local

A number of writers recently have emphasised the importance of 'the land' as a Biblical motif. This is usually linked with the provision made for the people of Israel, not simply to have a land of their own, but to maintain a just way of living once the land was theirs. So the now famous Jubilee legislation was not so much about the forgiveness of debt – that was a means to an end – but an attempt to make sure that families received back the land which had been given to them in perpetuity, but from which they had been alienated.

The Old Testament ideal was 'every man (family) under his own vine and his own fig tree' (Micah 4:4). Having your own land was not only a guarantee that you had food on the table but also gave you independence, literally a place to stand. When big government (the king and his courtiers) or big business (there were capitalist landowners in Israel too – see Isaiah 5:8) tried to take you over, then you had, at least in theory, the means by which to resist them. Thus ownership of land was translated into political and commercial power. This was considered to be a vital aspect of covenant legislation and the breakdown of these arrangements in Jesus' day occasioned some of his fiercest criticisms of the ruling elites.

Another aspect of Biblical concern for community was the importance of the tribe. 'Tribal', as a description often has an ugly ring about it, but this is not so in the Bible. The importance that Jesus gave to 'the twelve tribes of Israel' (see e.g. Matthew 19:28) suggests that he was interested in a project which might even be called 'retribalisation' (Myers 1994, 355-8). Obviously this goes back to the arrangements before the monarchy in Israel, and reminds us of the strand in the Old Testament that incorporates the idea that the monarchy was something of a mistake. We might even say that the monarchy was a manifestation of 'Empire'. What the monarchy tended to do, was precisely what Yahweh warned should not happen. It centralised government, created a standing army, opened the way for destructive foreign alliances (the trouble with foreign royalty was not that they were foreign but that they did not understand the covenant – the story of Naboth, Ahab and Jezebel (1 Kings 21) is a classic in this respect) amassed too much wealth at the centre, and ultimately produced the inequalities that in turn produce tyrants and slaves. (See Deuteronomy 17:14-20.) What was destroyed along the way was the sort of good community that you can read about in the book of Ruth.

It would clearly be wrong to idealise all small community life, particularly the traditional village. An ex-student of mine writing from a development project in Moldova commented:

> There is a lot of truth in the prejudice people have about country life: there is a lot of hatred and jealousy, gossiping, and everyone knows everything about all the others. There is also the alcohol problem. There is a lot of drinking going on. I can often hear my neighbour shouting at his wife when he is drunk. She is the woman that I rent the house from, and she came to me once afterwards to cry. It was just after Easter, nobody was working and lots of people had been

drinking for a couple of days. There were many problems when everyone had to go back to work: many suffered from hangovers and were all very easily irritated. My landlady had taken a beating. There was a lot of tension between all the people.

Yet we need not despair either. Jesus' response was to offer the rule of God and to build a community which reflected the values of this rule, indeed which made the rule visible 'on earth as it was in heaven'. Building good communities is what the Kingdom of God is all about.

Postcolonialism and Development

Despite heroic attempts by a number of organisations – TEAR Fund, World Vision through their MARC publications, the Micah Network, Integral, just to mention a few – to pull the whole Development discourse into Christian praxis and to give it an adequate rationale within mission, or vice versa, the truth remains that the Development discourse as such remains in deep trouble, and it might be better if we Christians – theologians, missiologists and Christian Development practitioners in particular – took notice of the fact. It is not at all that I want to go back on the idea that mission is holistic. What I am saying is that we have allied ourselves with an ideology and praxis of Development which has been insufficiently interrogated by the Christian encounter (Collier & Esteban 1998).

Did we start at the wrong place?

When I first became involved in Development work I was hugely influenced by Maurice Sinclair's book *Green Finger of God* (1980). I very much liked the idea that 'development' and 'revelation' were virtually interchangeable terms. I followed this up with Paolo Freire's 'big idea' that humans fail to 'develop' because they are part of an unjust order characterised by violence and oppression. What is offered as an alternative to 'being more' (development) is 'possessing more', the drive towards which is precisely the mechanism which hinders a truly creative existence (Freire 1996, *passim*).

What I might have heeded was the warning in Tom Sine's essay (1981), which I read at much the same time, suggesting that 'development' had a secularist origin and a doubtful future. Since then I have been teaching Development Studies (not to mention Globalisation) and the doubts have only increased. My reading of the Development discourse is that it is indeed flawed in its ideological basis, that is to say, in its origins, and it is this, along with my increasing appreciation of the postcolonial perspective, that provokes my questions.

If we begin with the post Second World War era – a reasonable starting point as the Bretton Woods institutions, the World Bank, the International Monetary Fund and the World Trade Organisation (though not necessarily by those names) came into being at that time, as did the widespread use of the term 'development' – then it is worth remembering that the Bretton Woods conference was not intended to 'make the world safe for democracy' but rather 'safe for capitalism'. The idea was that the victorious powers of World War Two (especially the United States, but excluding the Soviet Union) were attempting to create a global commercial system – one not possible in a period of world war – which was open to the free flow of capital and the free exchange of goods. They made out, as is natural, that this was something which would be of universal value. (Of course it was convenient for the US and her allies that they could commend to the world an ideology and praxis that confirmed their already existing commercial ascendancy.) In political terms this was a substitution of neo-colonialism for colonialism proper. The US was happy to see empires as such disintegrate – for one thing they tended to represent trading blocks from which she had been excluded – but that did not mean that she was abandoning the advantages of being the premier Western trading nation, with the strongest currency and the most powerful corporations (not to mention the military muscle to back up the commercial advantages). Quite the reverse: Bretton Woods and other similar arrangements were meant precisely to drive home the American advantage. Neo-colonialism was the name of the game.

These tendencies were not left uncontested, and in a number of ways. From the first there were other possibilities. Some countries opted for a more managed capitalism, often with an element of state socialism, the pattern more or less advocated by John Maynard Keynes.[11] Obviously, communism and a redistributive socialism was on offer until the end of the Cold War, and many countries in the Global South were attracted by the anti-imperialist 'spin' that Lenin had given to world communism. 'Tricontinentalism' or the 'non-aligned movement', an attempt to form an association of newly independent,

---

[11] Keynes was the British representative at Bretton Woods, but lost out to his American counterparts on the major issues.

postcolonial states which owed allegiance to neither of the two Cold War superpowers, was another feature of the post war period. Then there were the 'liberation' movements: feminism and other gender issues, anti-racism, peace and disarmament movements and more recently, environmentalism.

All of these – various forms of socialism, Tricontinentalism, 'liberation' movements – were seen as 'the enemy' by market-driven, neoliberal capitalism of the sort espoused by the Truman Doctrine, President Truman's declared intention in 1947 to pursue an anti-communist world strategy, and brought to maturity by Reagan and Thatcher in the 1980s.

Now if we place neoliberalism, capitalism, the Washington Consensus (i.e. using the Bretton Woods institutions to implement a neoliberal economic policy) etc. on one side, and all those movements I have mentioned on the other, then it is out of the former that the Development discourse comes, and it is perfectly fair to ask what might have been the consequences if it had come from a different place. Obviously, in one sense, there is no going back as if we could start again. (We are all familiar with the story of the Irishman who, when asked for directions to a certain destination, suggested to the enquirer that he should start from somewhere else!) Nevertheless, though history cannot be changed it can be interrogated. I add a few of these interrogations.

(a) Had we been Keynesians we might have invested more in the state and more in the idea that the state can be used as a vehicle of justice, a mechanism like the Jubilee legislation in the Old Testament, for wealth distribution. Here is a quote from Keynes to illustrate what I mean.

> For nothing can preserve the integrity of contract between individuals, except a discretionary authority in the State to revise what has become intolerable. The powers of uninterrupted usury are too great. If the accretions of vested interest were to grow without mitigation for many generations, half the population would be no better than slaves to the other half (Skidelsky 1992).

(b) Socialists, in theory at least, believe in the famous dictum, 'from each according to his/her ability, to each according to his/her need.' How might this have worked out in our churches/communities/nations under committed Christian leadership?

(c) Tricontinentalism believed that a certain amount of legitimate power should and could belong to nations that were *not* themselves the victors of World War Two but *were* the victims of colonialism and might now expect a place in world leadership. Suppose *these* people were now running our development agencies.

(d) Liberation movements, responding explicitly to the cry of the victims of racism and discriminatory gender politics, to the protests of those who want to 'give peace a chance' and to the warnings of the environmentalists, might all along have been the best focus of our development enterprises.

These are hints and guesses, but what I am sure about is that, as I say, we must interrogate our current assumptions. Have we inherited the wrong model? Is it possible that development, as we have it today, is simply not transformative?

Are we part of the problem rather than part of the solution?

A friend of mine is a highly qualified and experienced environmentalist specialising in waste management. He was recently in Sri Lanka working for a relief agency advising on waste disposal in the aftermath of the 2004 *tsunami*. Apparently the work went well and he enjoyed the opportunity to use his skills in the Global South. He was well looked after, staying in a well appointed hotel and was picked up every morning to be driven to his work which mostly took place in an air-conditioned office. His colleagues were friendly and helpful and so were the (rather few) people he met on the street. In the evenings he was able to relax, have a good meal and swim in the hotel pool. He was extremely well paid, indeed he believes that he will be able to fund other (voluntary) trips to Sri Lanka on the back of this assignment.

There was a snag, however. He was a Christian.

Why was this a problem? There are a number of reasons.

He felt isolated from the 'real' people of Sri Lanka and in some respects isolated, full stop. He describes himself as in a bubble, and, in truth, it was a bubble that at one level helped him to perform better, although it also made him feel guilty. It was a bubble that his employers were keen to keep in place. They did not want him 'wandering off' on his own adventures. He was an expensive investment that they needed to protect.

Of course it was a 'Western' bubble or a 'globalisation' bubble. It conveyed a certain message about the good life, the superiority of Western knowledge and technology, and the rewards that go with them; also the need that the Global South has for help from outside. So this was the second reason or problem: the work he was doing conveyed a message of superiority, of elitism. This had nothing to do with his own attitudes. It was the system to which he belonged that conveyed the message whatever he did.

This little story illustrates, I think, some fundamental difficulties that we have inherited in development work and in mission more generally. To put it rather crudely, we can never win the battle if we are part of 'the enemy'. This comment will immediately draw the response that this is an unfair way of describing matters. Development workers and mission agencies are trying to *help* people who are in need. The people they minister to *want* the gifts 'the enemy' is offering them. That may be so, but it is more complicated than that. Consider:

(1) People want help, but within a framework of respect and friendship. Think of Bishop Azariah at the Edinburgh Conference of 1910 who thanked the missionaries assembled for their sacrifice and generosity over the years, but startled everybody by adding that what Indians wanted most from the missionaries was friendship!
(2) People want things that are bad for them. I am not being paternalist here. All too often modernity is like a virus or an addiction. My friend told me several times, with real concern, that one of the things that worried him most was that the few Sri Lankans he met who were 'outside the bubble' were desperate to get into it. Or if they saw no realistic chance of being truly on the inside, at least they wanted some of the accruing benefits. They had a wonderful civilisation of their own, of course, often with much better values that the West's – their lifestyle was less stressful, less greedy, more sustainable, more family-centred, more healthy, more environmentally friendly – but someone, somehow, had convinced them that their values were worthless and that the civilisation which had served them to good purpose for centuries, was now to be abandoned as quickly as possible.
(3) People want Western technology and so on, because we have effectively destroyed their way of life and so 'there is no alternative'. Urbanisation is an example of this. Who wants to live in the slums and informal settlements of the Global South? Not many of us. But it is better than starving on a non-productive farm.

In brief, the whole development business is an off-shoot of the Enlightenment project with its dedication to 'progress', its scorn of the pre-modern and traditional societies, its secularist and materialist assumptions, its commercial values and finally its underwriting of Empire. People are attracted by it and also destroyed by it. My friend suggested that the only counterculture that was providing any sort of refuge in this storm was the culture of traditional (or even sometimes fundamentalist) Islam. It was offering religious values that, in the minds of its adherents, had transcendent worth, which trumped the worldly values offered by the Western development agencies. When we talked about this, the best we could say was that very often Islam offered countercultural ways that were typical of 'fearful religion'. But the question is: can we Christians offer something better? Are the choices solely between anarchy and fear? And this brings us back to my friend in Sri Lanka? If he feels uncomfortable about being part of the Enlightenment project on one hand, but is equally disturbed by the high priests of traditional religion on the other, what else is there on offer? How, in brief, can love rule? This, it seems to me, is the key development question.

Can you contextualise into the Empire or do you need to fight it?

The question follows immediately: can a Christian development praxis find a place within the discourse of the Enlightenment project? Is it in conflict with it or can it be effectively contextualised within it in a healthy way – borrowing the best insights and avoiding the worst excesses – or is it sufficiently distinct as a praxis so that it offers a prophetic critique of secular development. Alternatively is it so deficient in theory and practice that it has *nothing* to say. Somebody I know who works for the World Bank is dismissive of missionary sponsored development in his area of expertise, largely on the grounds that most missionaries simply do not know enough economics!

I am not sure that I know the answers to these questions, but they are the same questions that scholars have been asking for some time about the relationship between gospel (Christ) and culture (Niebuhr 1951). Or we could use Walter Wink's idea of the 'powers' (1992) in which case the question is: 'are the powers redeemable?' Wink thinks that they are, others disagree (Howard-Brook & Gwyther 1999, 265).

Missiologists will see the issue, perhaps, as one of contextualisation. Are we involved in a little thoughtful contextualisation as far as the culture of the secular Enlightenment is concerned, or a life and death struggle against an implacable foe? If it is the latter, and we are trying to do our good works from 'the belly of the whale', if (using the imagery of the book of Revelation) great Babylon has swallowed us up and it is simply not possible to build the New Jerusalem from there (Revelation 18:4) then it is time we took notice.

In my case I have found teaching Development Studies very difficult while at the same time teaching a course on Globalisation. Globalisation, in the sense that it stands for an increasing commitment to 'the culture of economism' is quite easily identifiable as one version of the secularist dream. But 'development' appears to me to be more of the same. Theological reflection on both comes to the same conclusion. It concerns me that development as currently practised seems to have little other purpose than connecting with modernity. Though we have learnt to say that we are respectful of the wisdom of others, and that they have to 'own' the projects that have been initiated, in fact we are only there in the first place because of the *newness* of the enterprise. Also, we behave, too often, as if the essential part of any productive enterprise is that it will be connected to the market. But is this connection with modernity what people really need?

What about power?

Through it all the central issue remains one of power. Is not development in its truly transformative sense a power encounter which we developers should be determined to *lose*. ('I am among you as one who *serves*.') Our customary approach is rather that I will teach you to play my power game, as powerfully as you can, though of course you will have to play it by my rules. The 'rules' are the usual ones: foreign 'capital' (money, expertise, good connections) can be used in order to 'exploit' the situation so that local resources (labour, raw materials, time) can be made more productive. Power resides with the 'capitalists'. More productivity is certainly a possibility (though by no means a certainty) but it will almost always benefit the few (foreign capitalists and those within the locality promoted to join them) and not the many. Local skills will be neglected if they do not connect with the 'new productivity'.

Here are a couple of illustrations, one from my own experience and one from the Bible.

(1) While I was working in India I was able to observe a fishing project, run by a particularly benign European nation, which was intended to improve the lot of fisherman who earned their living on a day to day basis by fishing in small boats in coastal waters. The project introduced

more highly mechanised fishing using large power driven trawlers, and there was a particular emphasis on prawns which were to be sold to the wealthy Middle Eastern countries. A number of ice factories and prawn processing facilities were also established. The trade with the Middle East flourished and a good deal of money was made, particularly by the trawler and factory owners (often the same people). The 'ordinary' fishermen did not do so well, however. Their small boats certainly could not compete with the trawlers and most of them were forced to sell their boats and take up employment as deckhands on the trawlers or as factory workers. Wages there were reasonable, or they were as long as trade prospered, but when there was a downturn in the prawn market, many of them were laid off. Unfortunately they now no longer had any boats to which to return and the usual outcome was destitution.

(2) The Israelite tribes wanted to establish a monarchy because they needed more political 'productivity'. The new harsh world of Philistine political power was a threat to their local tribal system. So they opted for a power system that played by 'international' rules (1 Samuel 8:5), and to some extent, at least for a while, it worked. The Philistines were defeated and David and Solomon raised Israel to an unprecedented pinnacle of power. The trouble was what they lost along the way. All the distinctive features of covenant monarchy – no foreigners unacquainted with covenant behaviour, no standing army or arms trade, no harem, no excessive wealth, familiarity with the law and so on (Deuteronomy 17:14-20) – were forgotten. Community itself was eroded by this and the final result was civil war, division of the nation, conquest by foreigners and exile. In other words, in the long run they were not better off; they had destroyed the covenant community which was the ultimate guarantee of their safety and prosperity (see Deuteronomy 11:22-5, 20:1).

What about community?

All this leads to a simple thesis. You cannot do transformative development work without good community. Building community comes first . Harking back for a moment to our discussion on 'origins' it seems to me that this is one theme that runs through all the alternative discourses, 'the might have beens'. 'There is no such thing as society' said Mrs Thatcher, but with one voice Keynesians, socialists, tricontinentalists and the whole crew of liberationists reply 'oh, yes there is, and until we understand how it works and how we can make it work better, we shall never learn the true secrets of development.' Surely Christians want to say the same thing.

Good community is built on 'covenant' values. Power alone will not do, in fact despite likely initial successes, the end result may well be destructive. (By 'power' I mean, of course, greater wealth, knowledge and connection.) Entering a community on the basis of power, even if it is a simple 'I can do this better than you' may have a number of power-full consequences, such as attracting people to the project who see it as an opportunity to 'get on', (that is, to get beyond the service of the community to a place where they can serve themselves instead) or connecting the community to those outside who have no stake in it, no fear that it might be destroyed, indeed may have reasons to wish its destruction. Covenant kings, supposedly for the safety of the nation, made foreign alliances only to find that they were caught up in a tangle of power relations where they were dealing with ruthless Empires whose only aim was aggrandisement at the expense of their neighbours. Isaiah of Jerusalem knew all about that and issued the appropriate warnings (see e.g. Isaiah 31:1). If I were advising a community which was being approached by a big development agency, my first advice would be extreme caution, some sort of commentary on 'Beware Greeks bearing gifts'!

So is it not possible to access new power without some sort of disaster ensuing? Not without love, and power and love are seldom found in each other's company. It is certainly necessary to secure the community first – which is what love means.

This emphasis on the viability of the community means a number of things. Development workers have to understand the community, they have to know it and learn to love it. Flying visits simply will not work. Anything destructive of community will have to be avoided like the plague. I would go further and say that if development is going to work it will have to *build* community. That may be the newness it can bring. Christians should begin, perhaps, by planting a church which will serve as a 'sign of the Kingdom', as a picture of the true community. In this sense you cannot do good development without playing politics, and this does not contradict what I have said about power. It means that unless we adjust the power equations – by promoting just relationships in a supportive community (think 'covenant' again), then development will only accentuate disparities of wealth to the detriment of the majority. In brief, we have to 'break the funnels' and that is political work. But this is just another way of saying 'community comes first'. So the key question is the one that Jesus asked his disciples: 'How shall we describe the Kingdom of God?' Jesus' community was one where the greatest gift to be offered was service, the first were to be last and the last first, the shepherd(leader) laid down his life for the sheep, and so on. We know these things, but do we realise that they are vital to development work?

Here we can mention the Book of Revelation again. When we read this book we need to understand that we are dealing with a tract addressed to churches under severe pressure from the values (religion, politics, economics) of the Roman Empire. The author presses on his readers the unlikely thesis that the way ahead (salvation, 'overcoming', victory) lies in being faithful disciples of 'a slaughtered lamb' with all that that speaks of vulnerability and sacrifice. Conversely the Roman Empire, with its immense wealth and patronage, is, in some senses, already an expended force, a fallen power (Revelation 18:2). There is no future there. The destroyers of the earth will be destroyed. The boat is leaking and will shortly sink. You will soon see desperate attempts to jettison the cargo, but it will be too late.

Have we got the right perspective?

The sobering question is: where are *we* now? What about the Christian development discourse – the question we started with?

On one view this is a matter of scale, or perhaps, which is the same thing, a matter of timing. The author of Revelation is fighting very hard to put his situation in perspective. His readers, because the Roman Empire 'filled the universe', hardly needed to be reminded that they were in danger of being overawed by the size and power of their opponent (Revelation 13:4). (Elsewhere the same author, or one like him, simply says 'the whole world lies in the evil one'.) What John expects to help his readers is his 'revelation' of the bigger picture. It is the Lamb who opens the seals of the book of history - not the Roman Emperor. Something else, some other powerful reality, must be taken into account. Close up, the Beast seems invincible, but this is not how it looks to someone like John who 'has seen heaven open'. Notice that this is the 'upstairs, downstairs' of apocalyptic. It is not the argument that says, 'In the end things will come straight'. Rather it suggests that if you only had the right perspective, you could see things as they *really* are *now*. (John speaks as a prophet. Compare the ministry given to Jeremiah as described in Jeremiah 1:10.)

There is a perspective of time also. To go back to the Old Testament, when the Israelites asked for a king, what was pressing in on them was the immediate threat of the Philistine presence. This sense of urgency, a sort of survival mentality, betrayed them; not only on that occasion, of course, but on a number of others in their history. Remember Ahaz (we read about it in Isaiah 7 and 8) who rashly called in the Assyrians to help when he was threatened by an alliance of two of his northern neighbours against him. He should have trusted God and kept quiet! I worked many years ago in a Christian organisation where the leader was willing to throw away already agreed principles of action in the name of survival. 'What's the use of our principles', he implied, 'if we end up on the scrap heap?' Of course, there was a simple answer to that. If you betray your key operating principles, you are on the scrap heap already!

Have we a prophetic word for today?

So the 'prophetic words' which need to be addressed to today's development discourse must now be determined! Somebody needs to do the job who is 'standing in the council of the Lord' (Jeremiah 23:18) like the authentic Old Testament prophets. (See the story of Micaiah in I Kings 22, especially verses 19-23.) Based on what we have been saying at the very least we need:

- A severe examination of existing institutions, even good ones, which are failing in the bigger purpose of maintaining or creating the good community
- A presentation of more adequate models of community
- A renewed emphasis on a strong 'justice' element in our work
- A forthright criticism of power
- A distrust of inappropriate alliances.

All this must be done in the face of a proper understanding of today's Domination System. In outline this will include the following characteristics:

- Intolerance of diversity (cultural homogeneity)
- Centralisation
- Military/commercial/religious domination
- Uneven development
- War on the saints
- An increasing attempt at global control

Resulting in:

- Constant crisis

- Ecological stress
- An exploited underclass
- 'Civilian' casualties
- The diseases and sorrows of Empire

Too many questions, you might think, and not enough answers. Agreed. All the more reason for a little reflection.

Chapter Three

New Formations

Hybridity or The Third Space

If it is true that the colonial syndrome is still with us, that decolonisation has given way to neo-colonialism, then it must also be true that some sort of response to colonialism is still a necessary feature of our world. This situation applies to mission, too. What is an appropriate response? We cannot afford to live as if our colonial history never happened and equally we cannot afford simply to accept the transference of our colonial values from West to South and perhaps back again.

The biggest difficulty may be that we continue to see things in terms of the old 'us and them' division, something which is more a way of thinking now than a matter of geography. The South, according to this psychology, is only knowable through an almost inevitably false representation. The West defines its virtues by contrasting them to the South's lack of virtue, and the South responds by reproducing the behaviour of which it is accused. For a while it seemed that the idea of multiculturalism might be an antidote to this pervasive stereotyping. But I suspect it has the same divisive effect. Different groups stake out their identities in ways that tend to emphasise their differences. (There will be more on identity politics below.)

In view of this *impasse*, here is a proposal. We need to develop ways of cultural interaction, of forming community, that both destroy existing oppositions and create newness, resulting in what I am going to call, using the terminology of some postcolonial thinkers, 'hybridity' or 'a Third Space'.

Strangers

What intellectual resources do we have to fund the construction of this community? The answer is 'not many', and the 'modern' situation is uniquely difficult. I am drawing here on the analysis of the sociologist, Zygmunt Bauman, who on the whole is rather gloomy about the possibility of contemporary community building. *Life in Fragments* is the title of one of his better known books! According to Bauman, for a large part of human history other people were either neighbours or aliens. Aliens could enter your social space only as an enemy to be repelled or as a guest – by definition a temporary nearness and confined within certain rules, or as a neighbour-to-be, in which case the newcomer had to learn to behave like the neighbours do. The unattached person in the Middle Ages, for example, was one either condemned to exile or doomed to death. If alive, he immediately sought to attach himself, at least to a band of robbers.

A totally new situation emerges in the modern city. However much we work to avoid this, aliens appear within the confines of the life-world, and they refuse to go away. They are neighbourly aliens (actually neither neighbours nor aliens), socially distant, yet physically close. We could call them *strangers* and they create a good deal of uncomfortable confusion.

Not surprisingly, what we try to do is to select the objects of our proteophobic sentiments[12] and then try to expose them to eliminating strategies. There is the *anthropophagic* strategy: we eat up, devour, and digest strangers, if they are useful to us, absorb them, make them our own. By contrast there is the *anthropoemic* strategy. We throw the carriers of danger up, expel them, either into permanent exile or into guarded enclaves where they can be safely incarcerated without hope of escaping. These *phagic* and *emic* strategies are operated in parallel. They are, however, only very partially successful. The company of strangers is now a part of normal life. The strangeness of

---

[12] *Proteophobia* is the dislike of situations in which one feels confused. True community, I would contend, thrives more often on confusion rather than certainty.

strangers, socially distant but physically close, is not now a curable disease (Bauman 1993 chapter 6).

The good news is that this may provide us with a new starting point. It may now be possible to start with the acceptance that we are all strangers, all different. I am not really referring here to the well known idea of 'cultural diversity'. This tends to put everybody else in a museum as an exhibit, something Westerners are particularly prone to, because we have inherited 'modernity's monolithic discourse'. So, Westerners are 'normal' everybody else is exotic. We need to realise that Western culture does not enclose everybody else in this sense; it, too, can be marginalised; also that dominant and subordinate cultures cannot really learn about each other while leaving the structures of power intact (Hesse 2000, 8). Until we treat Christians from the South as equals, we shall not know ourselves or them. It is very difficult to learn the truth from one's subordinates. We have to change the relations of power or fear, to relations of love.

As I have said, we can accommodate these differences by creating what Homi Bhabha calls a Third Space, by embracing *hybridity*. This allows neither a cosmopolitan universalism nor a particularised multiculturalism. The former lacks an ethnic enunciation, the latter has nothing else (Hesse 2000, 27). We can illustrate this with the following incident:

> When Nelson Mandela visited the US in 1990, one of the T-shirt slogans was: 'IT'S A BLACK THING YOU WOULDN'T UNDERSTAND'. Some reactions were understandably critical. The message should have been, 'It's a *human* thing, you better understand'.

Here again we are resorting to the binary mind set. We can do better than this. The Third Space allows not so much a new identity as an identification. Identity is about me, about who I am. Identification is about me and another, indeed not just another but an 'other', someone who is different from me . Of course, we carry with us the traces of feelings and practices we bring as a subject, but identification enables us to add traces of other meanings and discourses. This gives rise to something new and unrecognisable. The process demands 'a non-sovereign notion of self and my own culture'. It refuses to 'totalise'. Our culture is not 'the only show in town'. It also refuses to judge everything by a pre-given model or paradigm. This is difficult of course (for all of us, but for fundamentalists in particular) because they (we) find it difficult to cope with uncertainty. But we have to abandon our certainties and enter an area of *negotiation*. As someone has said, rather cynically, about marriage, 'even though there is a war on, in the end you have to *negotiate*' (Bhabha 1990, 211-6).

Culture itself, and certainly the Christian community, needs to be seen as an in-between space – a place of translation and negotiation, something available to us in quite new ways. My son, an Englishman, decided to marry a woman who came from Mizoram in North East India. Of course a wedding needed to be planned, but the question immediately arose as to what sort of wedding, in terms of cultural 'colouring', was it going to be. They are both Christians, so that would seem to solve some of the problems, but in other ways it complicated matters. I asked the bride whether she was going to wear red (the traditional colour for brides in India) but she said that her community, staunchly Christian for many decades, would only be happy with white. In the event, the bride's family, all Indian nationals, mostly wore European outfits. The groom and the groom's family however almost all wore Indian clothes. This was just one area where some invention was required! The combined effect of the many discussions and negotiations which took place was that the wedding did not really look like any other wedding. We had invented a unique ceremony with a unique culture!

From the point of view of mission, perhaps it is through this sort of translation and negotiation that we are going to create the multi-cultural mission teams we are all so anxious about. Each would have a brand new culture, negotiated among the members. Paul wrote to the church in Galatia that 'here there is neither Jew nor Greek'(3:28). Like him, we need to be more aware than ever of *mixed* situations, characterised by hybridity and confusion of identities. If I am neither Jew nor Greek, what am I? Too many of our mission strategies today are based on the 'people group' pattern. This clearly had its value, particularly in freeing us from our Eurocentric models, but it is an inadequate model for today's world just as it was for the Roman Empire. It owes too much to the idea of cultural purity and pays too little attention to the phenomenon I have just described.

This can also be applied to the nation state. For many nations in our world today, the trouble is that much of their history happened somewhere else, so they do not know what it means (Bhabha 1994, 239). The immigrant has come to tell them, uncomfortably, what that meaning is (241). So Homi Bhabha speaks, hopefully, of 'the emergence of a hybrid national narrative' which makes it possible for us to receive 'other histories' (240). Notice that, in terms of the nation state, this new postcolonial space never quite adds up, it is always less than one nation and double (241). Diaspora formations challenge the nation state (and globalisation) in that they are situated both inside and outside the nation.

Identity

The 'hybridity' project raises the issue of identity, and we could do worse than begin with the testimony of Raphael Mokades. After recounting a number of incidents from his past and circumstances about his background he writes:

> So there you have it. I'm black and I'm brown and I'm a brother and I'm Indian and I'm Jewish and I'm Muslim. White people have told me I'm white, too: after all I went to Oxford and I talk properly, don't I? Wherever I go I can fit in. So I'm everything. But I'm nothing. I fit in, but I'm never at home. I'm not part of a 'community'. I'm Jewish, but I don't practice, and I'm about as unlike your average north London Jew as it's possible to be. So talk of 'people from ethnic minority communities' makes me feel a bit left out. I don't spring from a community. I'm not alone, either. Among my friends I count a woman who is half-Zimbabwean, half-English; another half-Filipino, half German Brit; a guy who is half Dutch, half Nigerian and so on. All of us have complex identities (*Guardian* Dec. 29, 2005).

You will have noticed already that the postcolonialist discourse moves away very sharply from any idea of 'essentialism'. It believes that cultural identity is a human construct. This is a great help in two ways. If you are living between two cultures and it is difficult to identify fully with either, then a *constructed* or negotiated Third Space comes in useful. Similarly, the fact that we have a *human* construct also allows us to admit that culture is not perfect, that all systems of knowledge are flawed, muddled and scrappy. Out of these 'scraps' we find a new way – a sort of 'scrapheap challenge' – which overcomes of necessity a purist or essentialist way of looking at things. Here it might be appropriate to quote Salman Rushdie's tag again: 'A little bit of this and a little bit of that, that's how the newness comes'. There are no thoroughbred cultures, only mongrels. Paul Gilroy makes a distinction between 'roots' and 'routes'. 'Third Space people' have decided to create new *routes* for themselves as an alternative to finding their *roots* in a particular community identity (See below under Migration and Diaspora, Identity Issues).

The difficulty is that we are talking about the considerable intellectual and emotional effort needed to construct a *new* culture. Stuart Hall encourages people to be positive – so many people are dispersed, perhaps dispersal and fragmentation become *the* representative modern experience. Dispersal becomes central (Jeater 1992, 115). Instead of accepting that cultural identities define essential differences, people can *celebrate* the complexities and interdependencies of their cultural heritages (118) Conversely, on this basis the enemy is identity politics, particularly where identity is discovered in opposition to others, as in male/female, Jewish/Palestinian, black/white etc. (116).

Is it really possible to build identities beyond cultural and national boundaries? Does this mean that we have to give away, at least to some extent, our cultural identity? Though we should not underestimate the difficulty of this task, I believe it is certainly something to aim at as Christians. Consider the New Testament call to be 'pilgrims and strangers'. Consider also that there is nothing even vaguely like nationalism in the teaching of Jesus. Chris Sugden has put it this way:

> The universality of the gospel, which relativises all other definitions of identity and claims to loyalty, does not replace or suppress people's identity; neither is it a recipe for uniformity. It is meant to create a community marked by mutuality of relationship where people have to find their identity in partnership with others who are different from them. (Kirk 1999, 80)

Do we actually see this in the church today? Multi-community churches are quite common now, but I am not sure that this is the same thing as creating a third (hybrid) space. In Ootacamund in India where I lived for many years we tried very hard to create a multi-community church and had some success, but we did not get much beyond the idea of separate communities happy to work together. We had three different congregations – English speaking, Tamil and Badaga[13] – with shared finance and joint leadership. Creating a new culture was something else, however. More challenging is Paul Hiebert's 'Critical Contextualisation' (Hiebert 1987), something he developed in a church planting context. He hoped that new churches would create a new Christian identity by drawing on a mixture of their new found faith, their

---

[13] The Badagas are a tribal group who migrated to the Nilgiri Hills round about the seventeenth century. They are the largest single indigenous group in the Hills and have reatained their own language

traditional cultural practices and the invention of brand new practices where appropriate.

> Those *within* the culture should evaluate practices in the light of Scripture and their new understanding of the gospel. They also decide what they are going to do about it. The missionary/pastor is consultant but not director. There are all sorts of possibilities:
>
> - many beliefs and practices will be kept
>
> - some will be rejected
>
> - modification: giving old practices Christian meanings
>
> - adoption of practices drawn from their own new Christian heritage e.g. baptism
>
> - creation of completely new, culturally appropriate, symbols and rituals.

We could think of this as what Manuel Castells calls a *project* identity. Castells suggests that we all begin with a *legitimising* identity (what we grew up with) and where we feel that this is threatened it may produce a *resistance* identity. But the healthy response is to go on to a *project* identity, where we construct a new identity in response to our overriding life goals (Castells 2004, 8). Tempelman calls this a *civic* identity, whereby identity is not a given substance, but something which is determined in a pragmatic way in an ongoing dialogue between my own tendencies, impulses and needs and those of the community and even with those outside the community (*Political Studies* March 1999, 23). So the Apostle Paul is prepared to become 'all things to all people' so that by all possible means he might save some. He adds 'I do all this for the sake of the gospel' (1 Corinthians 9: 23). The project determines the culture, rather than *vice versa*.

Confusion

It may help us here to be a little more confused. Thomas More was reported to have said when his enemies were trying to pin him down with exact definitions: 'I trust I make myself obscure'. Similarly, Ann Morrisy talks about 'obliquity' as a mission strategy (Morrisy 2004). It is not always the best tactic to come head on at something, the oblique approach may be better.

The philosopher Gillian Rose was fond of talking about 'the broken middle'. For her the middle was the space that is given us between the beginning where there is still potential, a cluster of possibilities, and the end where those possibilities are foreclosed. She thought of it as the *broken* middle because it is often a place of loneliness, fear and anxiety – and moral choice. You never do reach the End. The Middle is a place of never-ending beginnings (Bauman1995, 72-5). In Laurie Anderson's song, *Big Science*, there are only imaginary traces of the future, a future which, as yet, has no representation or substance (Rutherford 1990, 13).

> Hey Pal! How do I get to town from here? And he said: Well just take a right where they're going to build the new shopping mall, go straight past where they're going to put in a freeway, take a left at what's going to be the new sports centre, and keep going till you hit the place where they're thinking of building that drive in bank. You can't miss it. And I said: This must be the place.

The Kingdom is like this. We don't have a blueprint, only hints and guesses. The Third Space is a margin which resists the centre, and yet in this process of decentring it is itself transformed into something new. For example, Israel's resistance to the Egyptian 'centre' (as described in the Old Testament) led to the creation of a new nation, an appropriate illustration because the Third Space is often thought of as a desert, 'an uncanny space', a place where the certainties are undone and people lose their original identities. As Saul Bellow has put it 'The old forms of existence have worn out, so to speak, and the new ones have not yet appeared and people are prospecting as it were in the desert for new forms.' (Rutherford 1990, 9). Think of the testimonies of Hosea and Jeremiah (Jeremiah 2:2-3, Hosea 2:14), where Israel in the desert was still waiting to be a nation and yet in some ways all the better for that.

> I remember the devotion of your youth, your love as a bride, how you followed me in the wilderness, in a land not sown. Israel was holy to the Lord, the first fruits of his harvest. (Jeremiah 2:2-3)
>
> Therefore I will allure her, and bring her into the wilderness and speak to her words of love. (Hosea 2:14)

Can we find a community where we can begin to turn our potentialities into our actualities without losing our freedom? I doubt it. Can we eat of the tree of the knowledge of good and evil without precipitating another fall? I think not. In the Garden everything is still potential. The attempt to realise that potential leads to disaster. When did I lose my freedom? Well, it was just at that point when I began to ask what my freedom was for?

Somehow we have to accept that the rule of God is a place where we do not know as clearly as we would like to. We see through a glass darkly. Rowan Williams in a tribute to the late Gillian Rose in December 2005 called it 'joyful erring'. 'We do not know what our interests are', he said, 'I must fictionalise a version of my interests because I do not recognise myself.' He argued that Rose's commitment to the 'mutual recognition of misrecognition' is a fruitful flight away from foundationalism. It is the hybridity that is so confused and confusing that every statement is a mis-statement, every sighting a mis-recognition (Rochenko 2005). We can no longer work out, for example, what it means to be British. That is a good thing. All the forms of foundationalism — based on denomination, kinship, locality, ethnicity, credal orthodoxy, gender, easily identifiable allies — are becoming confusingly muddled. Rejoice! The Kingdom of God is near.

Just to pursue this a little further. Rose makes a sharp contrast between what she calls *dialectic* which implies objective and absolute truth ('We see…') and what she calls *repetition* which implies perspectivism or contextualism ('…through a glass darkly') (Rose 1992, xiv). She wants us to linger in the space between these two and not to try to mend the gap. The broken middle should remain broken. In terms of what I am calling postcolonial mission, this might be a *third space* somewhere between the perspectivism of the post-Christendom West and the 'objective and absolute truths' of the Global South. Rose's preferred term is 'aporetic'. An *aporia* can mean simply a 'difficulty', something which cannot be resolved, there is 'not a ford' which unites two banks of the river: you cannot get across. It also means something which does not fit, which has a crack in it ('that's how the light gets in' to quote Leonard Cohen) which allows for movement or further discussion, it is not monolithic (167).

Let me give you Rose's illustration. It is from the Abraham and Isaac story in the Bible, which she sees as a struggle between the 'law' and the 'personal appropriation of right and wrong'. How do we see Abraham's situation? In making his decision about Isaac, does the law outweigh any human perspective or do we accept this as a never-before-heard-of confrontation between the single one and his God (13). Rose suggests that both imply loss of the divine voice? Is there a middle way that recovers the divine voice? Abraham exemplifies this middle way. He is an exile and pilgrim, and his position outside a settled community makes it possible for him to hear God's voice authentically, but he is not a solitary. As Miroslav Volf puts it, 'Abraham is not "a lonely modern self". He remains bound within relationality. In effect he is surrounded by a wandering community. Contrast Odysseus who wanders on his own' (Volf 1996, 42). What we need is some sort of travelling community such as the New Testament seems to envisage and which might provide a pattern for modern day missionary teams. The settled community has no need for divine intervention (it feels), or indeed for any principled intervention, because it has the law. The solitary has nothing against which to measure the message it believes to be divine. One has too much context, the other too little. Wendell Berry puts it this way:

> To choose community over principle is to accept in consequence a diminishment of the community's moral inheritance; it is to accept the great dangers and damages of life without principle. To choose principle over community is even worse, it seems to me, for that is to accept as the condition of being 'right' a loneliness in which the right is ultimately meaningless; it is to destroy the only ground upon which principle can be enacted, and renewed; it is to raise an ephemeral hope upon the ground of final despair. (Berry 1981, 208)

The hope is that diaspora people who have created their own hybrid community and who are in the 'broken middle' have the opportunity to experience one way out of this dilemma.

There are themes here that need to be followed up. One theme might be reconstructing the history of the last two hundred years, especially its mission history, accepting neither the certainties of the Enlightenment nor the tyranny of context, but looking for the new hybrid communities, and the religious experience and theologies that went with them, which emerged in each new culture. Another might be to enquire how we can sustain that 'middle' place where the actuality and the potentiality meet, living according to the 'now...but not yet' principle, so beloved of theologians? A third theme could be looking harder at the characters and situations in Scripture and history that are clearly on the margins – exiled people and desert places. Might not

Abraham be the paradigmatic missionary? Is it not true that Israel only truly becomes a missionary people when in exile?

Let us return to the more practical matters of constructing a community. The church struggles with the whole issue of creating new community and in doing so mirrors society at large. We rejoice in the apparent display of unity seen in something like a large multicultural festival (the Notting Hill Carnival in London would be an example) only to be dismayed at the way that people go back to their own, somewhat segregated communities, after the carnival is over. Similarly Christians go to their conventions (in the UK something like Spring Harvest or Keswick) happy to proclaim that they are 'All one in Christ Jesus' but then go back to their local churches and find it difficult to work with other Christians, especially where those Christians have different styles of worship or theological emphases, perhaps based on different cultures and ethnicities.

Are there ways in which people can *create* common cultural experiences which can bring them together? That is my question. There are plenty of superficial answers about – a shared music or support for the same football team. In this respect globalisation's business culture is interesting and so are Castells' 'resistance identities' and the cultures or sub-cultures that go with them such as the anti-globalisation movement, and, of course, various fundamentalisms. Our faith, however, demands something deeper. Paul is very radical in this area. He speaks about the 'one new person'. Jesus is even more radical. Kinship (at the end of Matthew 12) is replaced by 'whoever does the will of my Father'.

> And pointing to his disciples, he said, 'Here are my mother and brothers! For whoever does the will of my Father in heaven is my brother and sister and mother. (Matthew 12:49, 50)

Here community is formed by building the Kingdom. One description of the Kingdom is 'all my relations', a native American expression. We cannot build the Kingdom without accepting and acting on the new relationships that Christ brings. So, are there any *Biblical* resources for a description of a missional community?

How Shall We Describe the Kingdom of God?

'How shall we describe the Kingdom of God?' is always the question.

R.T. France points out in his commentary on Mark that after the initial announcement of the Kingdom by Jesus the idea seems to disappear until some chapters later we have the calling of the disciples (France 1990, 26). In other words Jesus begins to build the Kingdom by creating a community of disciples, and by teaching them its principles. Obviously this is a complex subject and we shall return to it, but I want to suggest here three controlling metaphors that Jesus uses (in teaching about the Kingdom) which may help us. Firstly, a picture of a house that is falling. Secondly, the idea of neighbourliness. Thirdly the idea of fruitfulness.

At the end of the Sermon on the Mount Jesus warns that his teaching is the only secure foundation for the nation (Matthew 7:26,27).

> And everyone who hears these words of mine and does not act on them will be like a foolish man who built his house on sand. The rain came and the floods came, and the winds blew and beat against the house, and it fell – and great was its fall! (Matt. 7:26,27)

Later (Matthew 24) Jesus foresees the destruction of the Temple State; the vineyard is taken away from the original proprietors and given to others; those for whom the great banquet was prepared never make it to the feast. We have reached a moment of crisis in which Jesus offers a new community, a new Kingdom, but he knows that the nation is about to refuse that offer. The rich young man, who belonged to the ruling class, was offered the Kingdom but refused the terms of entry. Other rich people were making the same choice for the same reasons. As N. T. Wright says: 'This was the challenge that Jesus gave to his contemporaries: give up the interpretation of the tradition that has so gripped you, which is driving you towards the cliff-edge of ruin' (Wright 1996,383). I dare say that Jesus says the same thing to our generation. We, too, are on the edge of the precipice. (To quote a twentieth century prophet: 'It's not dark yet, but it's getting there.'[14]) For the purpose of this book we could call the tradition that is driving us 'neo-colonialism', or 'globalisation'. It refers to our unjust wealth, our superior attitudes, our determination to be rulers, to be in control. But *this house is falling*. Beware that we are not caught up in the crash.

---

[14] The words are from a song by Bob Dylan.

The second 'big idea' is a re-definition of *neighbourliness*. We could obviously use different words or phrases: equality, a community of sharing, affirmation of the other, the promotion of diversity, and these are indeed some of the issues that postcolonialism naturally throws up. In any case this defines the Kingdom, it is its fundamental law. Jesus does not simply teach a spirituality which helps us to know ourselves better, or even a spirituality which helps us to 'to know ourselves and to know the true God' (Augustine) but rather he teaches us to discover and know ourselves by knowing and loving God *through* the experience of *loving the neighbour* who images God.

But who is my neighbour? Well in Jesus' parable of the Good Samaritan it is the one who comes from the 'other' community and who is in need. It is not all that difficult to discern my neighbour (he is usually lying there by the roadside needing help) only it will be a different person in different contexts. I suspect that in the Third Reich it was quite specifically the Jewish family that I happened to encounter who were in trouble with the authorities. Today it might be a Muslim neighbour or even someone from a group that society has taught us to despise, such as a partner-beating or child abusing neighbour – and you can insert at this point the name of any person or group or community which you find threatening and yet which also makes a claim on you. However, let us take our Muslim neighbours as a test case. In the parable what we might call 'the duty of care' rested on the Samaritan (and the priest and the Levite, of course) because the person by the wayside *needed his help*. Muslims in the West are, by and large, a beleaguered minority. They suffer the usual disadvantages of minorities and at the moment are particularly threatened by an association with terrorism. It is our responsibility as Christians to see to it that they are respected and given space to follow their own religion and culture; treated in fact in the same way that we would wish to be treated if we were living in an alien culture, where we were suspected of criminal activities despite having nothing to do with them. But, you might say, is it not true that Christians living in Muslim majority societies are routinely treated unfairly? True (in some cases), but all the more reason that we Christians set an example of neighbourliness. In the parable we do not read that the Samaritan was let off helping because Samaritans were customarily treated as second class citizens by Jews. In fact, it was partly this returning of good for evil which demonstrated what it truly meant to be a neighbour.

The third controlling image is *fruitfulness* – all those pictures of seeds yielding a hundred fold, of a harvest growing secretly, of mustard seeds turning into big trees, of nets full of fish, of unexpected treasure, of widespread healing, of fair wages for everyone, of poverty banished, so that in the very first effective manifestation of the Kingdom community in Acts 4, there were no poor people among them at all.

In the Bible fruitfulness and justice go together. In their fascinating commentary *Colossians Remixed* Brian Walsh and Sylvia Keesmaat claim that Colossians is contesting the contemporary political orthodoxy that 'Rome and the emperor are the beneficent providers and guarantors of all fruitfulness.' Set against this is a counter claim that the gospel is bearing fruit in the whole world (2004, 74-5). When Paul makes this counter claim he is doing so in the context of the parables of Jesus, the teaching of the Old Testament prophets (e.g. Isaiah 5), and the OT connection of prosperity (fruitfulness) with justice as in Psalm 67 or Psalm 72. He is invoking a completely different 'way of political and economic being in community' to that of the Roman empire (75). In Colossians, to quote our authors, the church is the embodiment of Christ which meets 'as a body politic, around a common meal, in alternative economic practices, in radical service to the most vulnerable, in refusal of empire, in love of this creation'; the church 'reimagines the world in the image of the invisible God' (87).

As the authors also say, how difficult it is to *imagine* what a life that is an alternative to the dominant culture is like (82). It is, of course, a tactic of Empire to try and make us *forget*. (This is especially true for exiles. They are expected to forget their homeland. But, beware amnesia.) I would add that Jesus also warns us against forgetting. 'Do you not remember?' he says. So what have we forgotten, or what have we not been told? Or perhaps it is a matter of overload. To get back to Colossians again, apparently in Paul's day, Rome's image was everywhere. Walsh and Keesmaat remark 'Images of the Empire were as ubiquitous in the first century as corporate logos are in the twentieth century' (83). So I thought this quote from Barbara Ehrenreich was relevant.

> Wal-Mart when you're in it, is total – a closed system, a world unto itself. I get a chill when I'm watching TV in the break room one afternoon and see...*a commercial for Wal-Mart*. When a Wal-Mart shows up within a television within a Wal-Mart, you have to question the existence of an outer world. Sure you can drive for five minutes and get somewhere else – to Kmart, that is, or Home Depot, or Target, or Burger King, or Wendy's or KFC. Wherever you

look, there is no alternative to the megascale corporate order (Ehrenreich 2002, 179)

We are too numbed or satiated by the pervasive images, for the imagination to do its work (Walsh & Keesmaat 2004, p. 84).

It is significant that the American farmer philosopher, Wendell Berry, insists upon calling the Kingdom of God 'the Great Economy' (1987, 56). The word 'economy' as we know, does not just have to do with money. Literally it means 'the law of the household', how we run our daily affairs. When Jesus told his disciples to 'seek first the Kingdom of Heaven (God) and its justice' he was asking them to enter a community in which daily affairs (questions of food, clothing, shelter, work, leisure) were conducted in a just way. (One is reminded of Peter's 'social security' question in Matthew 19:29.) Elsewhere Jesus calls this 'the abundant life'. I think that this idea of 'the Great Economy' is at the heart of mission. There is no mission, or to state it more carefully, we cannot be part of God's mission, without just economic arrangements.

The community which Jesus forms, is also a healing community, another description of its fruitfulness perhaps. Matthew 10:1-4 identifies the Twelve and describes their ministry as exorcism and healing. For the new community healing is what happens when the king rules. 'Then shall the eyes of the blind be open, and the ears of the deaf unstopped: then the lame shall leap like a dear, and the tongue of the speechless sing for joy.' (Isaiah 35:5,6). When the New Jerusalem is manifested it will have a garden and a river and a tree, 'and the leaves of the tree will be for the healing of the nations'. Matthew makes a point (in chapter 4) of describing the various sorts of people who are healed, people with 'pains' probably wounds from torture or war, demoniacs, epileptics, paralytics. It is obvious that the Empire was a desperately diseased place. One of Rome's apologists, Aristides, praises Rome's accomplishment in bringing *salus*, health, to the nations (Carter 2000, 124-7). But the scenes described in the gospels show how false that impression is. And things are no different today. Why is there so much anxiety and depression, so much fear and rage? Why are our doctors' surgeries full, our counsellors and psychotherapists so much in demand? Why are there so many drugs, legal and illegal? Why so many failed marriages and lonely people? Why is 'stress' a word that everybody reaches for? All these are the diseases of our particular empire. And just as the Romans exported the diseases of Empire, so we in the West export our illnesses too. We have already thought about the 150 million street children world-wide. Why are they there? It is because of the breakdown of family life as a result of poverty. Where does poverty come from? It is a disease of Empire. We cannot pick off these problems by means of individual efforts and indeed that was never the intention. What Jesus offers is the healing community. A place where the pained, the demoniacs, the moonstruck, the paralysed of our society can come and find their illnesses begin to mend.

Does the idea of the Kingdom disappear to be replaced by mission, as some scholars claim? Not at all. There is no mission without the Kingdom. 'Lord, is this the time when you will restore the Kingdom to Israel' asked the disciples (Acts 1:6)? Answer. 'Yes, that is what is going to happen through your going to the ends of the earth'. The Kingdom is what mission in the book of Acts is all about. Jesus explained it (Acts 1:3), Philip preached it (Acts 8:12), Paul argued about it (Acts 19:8) and proclaimed it (Acts 20:25). Acts begins with restoring the Kingdom, along the way the believers will enter the Kingdom if only they will persevere (Acts 14:22); and right at the end when the gospel has reached Rome, Paul is still proclaiming the Kingdom (Acts 28:31).

In conclusion we can say that, at least for us Christians, the 'third space' is a Kingdom space. As we try to build these new communities we have to accept the failure of other models of community. Jesus was quite radical about this. 'This house – the one that in his day consisted of the Jewish Temple state – has fallen'; and the same is true of the national, ethnic, and religious houses that we are putting our trust in today. On offer instead is the neighbourliness of what I have called the 'hybrid' community, where we learn to identify and accept the 'other', where my enemy becomes my neighbour. Also on offer is the fruitfulness of a community marked by justice and healing, in which the diseases of Empire are replaced by the tree of life, the leaves of which are for the healing of the nations.

Migration and Diaspora

The massive movements of population that are a feature of today's world create all sorts of political, economic and social challenges and for Christians a variety of mission opportunities and dilemmas. Understanding the world of refugees, asylum seekers and economic migrants, not to mention the response of local people to them, demands sophisticated legal and sociological tools as well as a knowledge of history and global politics. No small task.

> Today the mobility of labour power and migratory movements is extraordinarily diffuse and difficult to

> grasp. Even the most significant population movements of modernity (including the black and white Atlantic migrations) constitute lilliputian events with respect to the enormous population transfers of our time. A spectre haunts the world and it is the spectre of migration. All the powers of the old world are allied in a merciless operation against it, but the movement is irresistible. (Hardt & Negri 2000, 213)

True, but what does this mean for Christians trying to make sense of the world, particularly those who are, as we say, 'working with refugees'? Also, have we done any theological analysis? Michael Schluter postulates the idea that the rise and fall of nations can generally be understood as a reflection of their conformity to God's law. For example, he suggests that the high rate of population mobility associated with the free market approach to economic development tends gradually to a breakdown in community relationships which runs contrary to biblical laws. Working with refugees and understanding the free market are joint enterprises (1994). My point here is that, whether Schluter is right or not, he is attempting to see contemporary events within a theological framework.In many instances, migration is closely linked with colonialism. It is a postcolonial phenomenon, which continues to link the colonising and colonised nations. The presence in Europe of people whose not-too-distant origins were in Africa or Asia or Latin America reflects the bonds created by the Spanish, French, Dutch, Portuguese and British empires. Difficult postcolonial issues such as multiculturalism (ethnic differences), language barriers, uneven development, inter-generational strife, identity crises and the like stem from this movement of peoples. In the same way Europe has become the testing ground for a number of new missiological issues such as monoethnic churches in a multiethnic society and witness to the gospel in a post Christian society (often by Christians who have no experience of a post Christian society!).

All this makes Europe today one of the most interesting continents as far as mission is concerned. We see a society which is 'mixed-up' in ways that are quite unique. It is not just a matter of immigration. The United States, Australia, and Canada – just to make a selection – have experienced huge waves of immigration, indeed are nations largely made up of immigrants. But they have, speaking generally, handled the situation by promoting a sense of new-found oneness among their people. They have been greatly aided in this by the way that immigrants have been able to forge a new life for themselves without the presence of a settled population. (Sometimes the land was genuinely unoccupied, sometimes the original inhabitants were pushed to the margins or eliminated.) Immigrants to Europe, however, have encountered centuries- old civilisations and even more importantly, they have remained the minority. On the whole, too, they have formed a *diaspora*, that is to say that have retained strong links with their place of origin. (To use the old test: you cannot imagine an Australian wanting to support England in an England versus Australia sporting contest. In a match between England and Pakistan, however, a 'British Pakistani' might well support Pakistan.) Another difference might be the relative isolation of the immigrants. The original settlers of countries like the US and Australia had little opportunity to return to their homeland, even if they had wanted to. Partly this had to do with the fact that they were often *escaping* from the old to the new, and partly because transport systems were comparatively slower and more expensive – return to the homeland and regular visits were not easy to manage for people who had 'sold up' to make the move in the first place. I suspect that the vast majority of immigrants nowadays can afford the (relatively cheap) air fares to visit friends and relatives at home, and asylum seekers are quite few as a proportion of the whole. People are 'on the move' more than ever before today and in all directions (see below). A third factor is, as we have seen, a typically postcolonial situation – the pattern of settlement in European countries is directly influenced by the former colonising-colonised relationship. Nigerians come to Britain, Moroccans to France, Angolans to Portugal, Indonesians to Holland and so on. But the former colonies were not, almost by definition, peopled by those who had close religious, ethnic and cultural affinities with Europeans. As a result postcolonial 'flows' have enriched the European mix dramatically.

People on the move

Postcolonialism is tied in with globalisation. For example, the movement of people from their homes in the Global South to the West is the result of both. Postcolonialism provides the links and the global culture demands and then favours those who are prepared to be mobile.

By one description most people in the affluent world are economic migrants. Very few people stay at home when it comes to finding a job. The difference is that globalisation has made it both easier and (often) more necessary to make that move. Not equally easy, however. Unequal development within globalisation means job mobility and open frontiers for some, it means forced migration and hostile frontiers for others. Postcolonial migrants are more often in this second category. 'Economic migrants' is a loaded term, nowadays, because they come in a number of varieties. They may be people who simply want to earn a better living, and have marketable skills for which they can get a better price away from home. (Oddly enough, considering the outrage commonly expressed in affluent countries about 'economic migrants', *some* of these people appear to be welcome outside their own countries. Britain, for example, is recruiting nurses for the National Health Service from all over the world at the moment. This just goes to show that our response to migrants is largely selfish. If we judge them necessary to meet our needs, we are happy to have them; if not, not.) Then there are those who need to make new arrangements for their families as a matter of survival. They simply cannot provide for their own by staying at home. Globalisation in its revolutionary communications mode has sometimes made these movements possible where they have not always been an option before.

Identity issues

The discarding of our rooted identity is sometimes painted in very attractive colours in our society. For example, many of the leading postcolonial writers and thinkers are keen to describe their 'rootlessness' as an advantage rather than a curse. Paul Gilroy, as we have seen, speaks about 'routes' rather than 'roots'. By this he means that the diaspora person 'does not have secure *roots* which fix him (sic) in place, in a nation or an ethnic group; rather he must continually plot for himself itinerant cultural *routes* which take him, imaginatively as well as physically, to many places and in contact with many peoples' (McLeod 2000, 215) . This situation is not lamented, it is celebrated. The postmodern desire to be freed from 'totalising narratives', that is to say to be freed from what is perceived to be the dead hand of tradition, or 'single' explanations of a 'given' society, gives the vote to those who have severed their roots, gone on into new experiences and then brought their new wisdom back to bear on the societies they once left. This may indeed be a service rendered. But beware! The young man or woman who goes away and comes back with new knowledge, may also have forgotten (or never known) the old knowledge, without which the community may not be able to survive. In fact there are two traditions here and we must not confuse them. Of course news from outside can be a necessary challenge to any community. But so can remembered wisdom. The *erzähler* or European village storyteller (celebrated by Walter Benjamin) (Benjamin 1999, 84) could either be itinerants, like soldiers or sailors, or rooted residents, like tillers of the land. It is the wisdom of the latter, I suggest, that is most often neglected today.

I am reminded here of Ched Myers' point about the way that the Puritans tried to forget what they had done to the native Americans. One of the many powerful moments in Myers' book *Who Will Roll Away the Stone?* is where he retells Nathaniel Hawthorne's story of Young Goodman Brown's walk in the forest with the devil. The devil reminds the alarmed Puritan that his forefathers had been deeply involved in the brutal pioneer days of the first settlements, including the persecution and even extermination of other groups. Goodman Brown marvels not just at the fact that these things happened, but that nobody ever told him about them: 'I marvel they never spoke of these matters' he says. Ignorance of the past makes it irredeemable (Myers 1994, 131-2). An example from another source might be the Polish folk and their strenuous attempts to forget what they had done to the Jews during the second world war, so brilliantly described in Charles Powers' novel, *In the Memory of the Forest*. As Simone Weil reminds us: 'Loss of the past, whether it be collectively or individually, is the supreme human tragedy' (Weil 2002, 119).

The global culture has a vested interest in destroying the past. The world of consumerism, fashion, tourism, fast food, one-night stands, advertising, photocopiers, marketed experiences, planned obsolescence and disposable everything is the sworn enemy of traditional cultures, except inasmuch as they can be appropriated and turned into hard cash. (People do not look at paintings, nowadays, they ask how much they might be valued at if they take them along to an auctioneer.) Yet the past is essential to identity. Imagine a world in which our memories had failed completely and we had no knowledge of the past. We would have lost our identities. In fact we sometimes need our identities to be rebuilt. People need to be given a past, as happened for the replicands in Scott Ridley's movie, *Blade Runner*. We also need an environment, something which is not overly uniform, like a snowfield or the sea. Think of the movie *Waterworld*, where the world has been inundated to such an extent that all the landmarks have disappeared, or John Dominic Crossan's famous quote about postmodernism 'There is no lighthouse keeper. There is no lighthouse. There is no dry land. There are only people living on rafts made from their own imagination. And there is the sea' (Crossan 1975). In any landscape, or seascape for that matter, unless there are recognisable features we cannot find the way. We are immobilised by a featureless life. What is up or down, left or right, backward or forward? If we set off in that direction (rather than this) are we likely to come back to the same point from which we started? If we are adrift on a featureless sea without compass or guiding star, what is the purpose of setting off, particularly if we have no clear idea what our destination might be? Dante's image is equally powerful. He spoke about being lost in a forest – the *selva oscura* – a place without paths or signposts. But what are the signposts that we customarily rely upon? They are not the new and unfamiliar things. That would only add to our confusion. They are those familiar things that link us to the past. For Christians they are probably the 'traditional' means: prayer, fellowship, worship, Bible study, Christian books, natural revelation, teaching, counsel, history, theology or just the wisdom and fellowship of other Christians who have not lost the path. But do these now form part of our Christian identity? Sadly, many today favour what some have called the world of 'pure relationship'. This, in turn, is connected only to the random 'highs' of the sort of Christian experience which does not require the continuum of a Christian tradition and which is defined in terms of immediate feelings and the warmth or otherwise of up-to-the minute relationships.

When people *do* have a past and a landscape, that is to say an identity, they can go ahead along the pathway. 'Stuck' people who cannot go on in life are in fact very common in our society. Some of them are stuck because they have not dealt with the past and it is still damaging them, like adopted children who feel the need to find out about their natural parents and cannot get on with life until they do. Many people today also suffer from a dangerous amnesia. They have willed themselves into forgetfulness or they have had vital memories withheld from them. The loss of the past is intimately connected with the destruction of community. (It is noticeable how many of our films today centre round issues of identity: *Blade Runner, the Truman Show, Toy Story, Sliding Doors, the Matrix*, and how many round the search for community (*Friends, Career Girls* – indeed all the Mike Leigh films – *the Sixth Day, American Beauty, Brassed Off*, etc). Memories, says John R. Gillis, are a vital part of our identity both as individuals and communities. Both memory and identity are being eroded by an increase of mobility typical of the globalised world. He speaks of 'men (sic) terrified that they had become rootless as a result of their own upward and onward mobility'. (Gillis 1994, 10) This process is on the increase, and applies now to everyone.

> As global markets work around the clock and the speed of communications shrinks our sense of distance, there is both more memory work to do and less time and space to do it in…Today time takes no prisoners. Pockets of pastness – ethnic neighbourhoods, rural backwaters, the intact family – are fast disappearing. Those who were once perceived as our connection to the past – old people, women, immigrants, minorities – are swimming in the same flood of change that

previously created such a profound sense of loss among elite males. (14)

This disconnection with the past 'opens up' the future. There is nothing anymore to 'hold us down'. This sounds attractive but it also has its dark side. As we have seen a lack of any sense that we are heading towards a conclusion also de-motivates and de-radicalises us. Radical people, of whatever stripe, need a future, and it is hope that radicalises them further. Of course this has its dangers, in that utopian politics have all too often sacrificed the present in brutal ways. Privileging my future over yours can simply be another description of tyranny. There came a stage when Marxism, for example, began to stumble on its inability to deliver. The promised utopia did not seem to be any nearer. It was hijacked by power hungry tyrants and ruthless bureaucrats. Yet, particularly in its early days, it spoke to millions, especially the oppressed of the earth, because it had hope. It may be that in the West Christianity is in danger of being abandoned for the same reason as Marxism. We have failed to deliver and our failure is both a cause and a consequence of our abandonment of hope.

Whatever our response to this, we should, I think, be sorry about the apparent death of utopian politics. For us, too, a world without hope, without a strong sense of 'building for the future' is a dangerous one. Hope is a vital part of the Christian prospectus. (Romans 8:20,1 with 24,5). It is the certainty of the end which helps us to assert its values in the present and to stick with them when they are opposed and rejected. This is the 'revolutionary patience' of Marxism and the faith of which the author of the book of Hebrews writes. It is important that we maintain this vital connection between present experience of the rule of God ('the Kingdom of God is at hand' – spatially) and future hope ('the Kingdom of God is at hand' – temporally). Letting go either end of the rope closes us into our own little world of experience.

Diaspora

The name 'diaspora' may have behind it the simple idea of dispersion, but it has now become something of a technical term, with a number of features. First of all, it involves a dispersion from one place or 'centre' from which all the dispersed take their identity, though there can be a variety of foreign destinations. All share in a common memory or myth of this 'homeland' (even if they are born somewhere else!), something which is so important that there is no likelihood that it will be forgotten. The fact that they remain 'strangers', a perpetual minority in their host nation, keeps the myth alive. If, by chance they are assimilated to such an extent that they disown or forget their place of origin, to that extent they are ceasing to be part of the diaspora. Many hope to return to their homeland, and even if this is not the long term plan, they are often keen to visit from time to time if they are able to do so. They are also often very willing to take part in enterprises that benefit their homeland, whether this is to their individual advantage or not. All this means that the ongoing connections with their homeland are an important aspect of their self-identity.

Postcolonialism is very comfortable with some aspects of the idea of multiple identities. This is useful when looking at diaspora people who typically have a confused identity. To a greater or lesser extent they are required to 'fit in' with the culture of their host country. At the same time they can never do this fully. Part of their identity is always shaped by 'home'. Or to put it the other way round, even if they are determined not to lose the identity that they brought with them, some of it 'wears off'. Diaspora people returning to their country of origin after a long stay away, often find that to an uncomfortable degree they are treated as outsiders by their own folk. Somehow they are different. Even though this idea of confused identities has been viewed as positive by some in the postcolonial literature, we should remember that it is also a source of much pain.

Postcolonialism may have a place for confused identities, but national discourses are far less accommodating. Diaspora formations challenge the nation state (and globalisation) in that they are situated both inside and outside the nation. The *Umma*, the community which unites Muslims and to which they have a loyalty which is stronger than that to any particular nation, is part of the logic of diaspora (Hesse 2000, 20-1). So is the Kingdom of God for Christians; it is always less than one nation and yet much more. I should point out that in nationalist terms this is a dreadful heresy, which often makes our rulers profoundly uncomfortable (Bhabha 1994, 322). But then in this sense God's Kingdom is also heretical. It is always turning the world upside down.

How does all this add to our understanding of mission? At a very obvious level, just as postcolonialism turns the spotlight on diaspora communities so mission can helpfully do the same.

Typically, diaspora communities are both needy and open. Many diaspora communities give the impression that they are doing very well! People who leave their own countries to work somewhere else (if it is voluntary) are often go-ahead and successful. Think of the way that members of the Indian diaspora have prospered in areas such as business and information technology. But the reverse is also true. Immigrant communities often fall behind in terms of education, securing jobs and business success. Natural disadvantages to do with language and culture (I mean that they are different from those of the majority) hold them back. So do the prejudices of the host nation. Some are lonely and isolated. They need help to cope with a challenging new situation. The openness of diaspora communities is also an ambiguous concept. Often the sense that they are being discriminated against, the feeling that they are in a foreign land, the all-prevailing newness of their situation leads to a very understandable 'closed' or defensive mentality. There is evidence, for example, that diaspora communities are more likely to emphasise their religious commitments, if they are different from those of the host population, than they were back at home. Being religious is now part of their identity that they need to emphasise if that identity is going to survive. (In this respect Christians who are concerned about the growing militancy of Muslims in the West should remember Aesop's fable about the wind and the sun. The contest was about who could get a man to remove his cloak. The more the wind blew the more the man clutched his cloak around him. However, when the sun shone he took it off!) On the other hand people do 'open up' when they are in new circumstances. They try new things. The fact that they are not being observed by what was likely a close knit community at home frees them up to do this. When moving to a new place they expect it to be different and expect to have to adapt to it. Some of the new arrangements suit them better than the old ones.

Diaspora communities are also part of the 'network society'. Networks are often more important to them than places. In this respect the communications revolution – in particular satellite telephone connections and the internet – suits them very well. Place is still a factor: diaspora communities tend to congregate if they can, but the ability to communicate with other diaspora members without necessarily seeing them face to face very often makes them less dependent on their immediate neighbourhood for social interaction and therefore more able to choose to relate primarily to other like-minded diaspora people. In the search for relationships, strange, and perhaps unfriendly, neighbours come second. Whether this is a good thing, is another matter. Similarly, easy communications with 'home' means that the strangeness of diaspora life is alleviated. It remains one of the ironies of the network society that networks both connect and separate. By definition, being on a network with somebody else connects you to them, but what if the person you really need or want to connect with is on a different network, one to which you do not have access? Or again, might not the multiplication of networks lead to fragmentation? As Brian De Zengotita puts it:

> The multiplication of niches [in our communication systems] has been so intense that the word fragmentation doesn't begin to describe it. What with these search worms and filters and custom advertising hooking you up with stuff you're already interested in – why, you can spend your whole life online and never leave your head. (De Zengotita 2006, 198)

There are a number of missiological conclusions that we need to come to here. One assumes that needy people are the church's opportunity, and that it is neither exploitive nor patronising to offer people friendship and help in these circumstances. Moving into a new culture, far away from familiar friends and family, can be a difficult process, and leaving people just to 'get on with it' is certainly not an appropriate response. Diaspora communities can live with a constant sense of being under threat, and Christians in their dealings with threatened minorities have a responsibility to do everything they can to alleviate that sense of threat, whatever its source. On the other hand diaspora people are usually hoping for something new. They have not come such a long distance only to remain the same people that they were before. In a very profound way the gospel offers people a new start, and maybe that is the newness they have been looking for all their lives.

With regard to the network society the important thing, no doubt, is to be on the same network! An organisation such as South Asian Concern, a UK based Christian enterprise, penetrates the Asian diaspora network for the gospel, precisely by means of the network of which they are already members by other means. It is an extension of friendship evangelism. We are rightly rather doubtful of the 'cold calling' evangelistic method which seeks to win people for the gospel with whom we have no other connection than that we want to win them for the gospel! It is the old story. Nationals are best evangelised by nationals, and diaspora people may be best evangelised by other members of the diaspora.

However, the responsibility of a right influence is for everyone. Among Christians in particular it is unacceptable that we should allow people to become divided into exclusive ethnic groups – even in the name of dynamic evangelistic methods. I am not in favour of homogenous churches (that is, by deliberate design) for example. The cutting edge of evangelism in any church may have to have a cultural element in it – young people evangelising young people, employing someone from an ethnic minority group as an evangelist to reach his or her fellows and so on – but one of the essential witnesses of the gospel is still that we are all 'one in Christ Jesus' and that as far as the Domination System is concerned we are all aliens and there is every reason for us to stick together.

Diaspora people are often keen to do something for their home country. This can have missiological significance, too. South Asian Concern, again, is a good example. Its 'concern' is not just for the diaspora. In fact Asian diaspora Christians are warmly encouraged to take responsibility for the South Asian sub-continent and its need of the gospel. Notice that it is in a good position to do so. Because a diaspora never loses contact with 'home', because of the network effect, there is constant traffic between those at home and those in exile, so to speak. The gospel can be part of that traffic.

This is one of the great joys of the postcolonial situation. Postcolonialism, to say it again, reminds us that we are living in a world that has been profoundly shaped by the colonial experience. There are so many bad outcomes of that, it becomes a dispiriting task to catalogue them. Yet the continued connection between, say, Britain and India seems, from the point of view of the gospel, an example of redemption. Not that it excuses the history of British imperialism, but it takes something which had much that was evil and exploitive and uses it for blessing – a process at which, if the irreverence may be pardoned, God is very good.

Fate of the indigenous peoples

The postcolonial approach

Postcolonialism wants to look at what has happened to the new nation states that have emerged as a result of the independence movements and the end of colonialism. Part of this, and a part which is often neglected, is reviewing the fate of the indigenous or pre-modern societies which were originally subject to the impact of colonialism and which continued to clash with the modernity of nationalism after independence. Postcolonial studies therefore reach back before the independence movements and consider colonialism and its effect upon colonised peoples and then ask the question: what has changed for them since independence? There are a number of possible ways into this discussion. One could begin with case studies, illustrating how some of these indigenous peoples are faring today? Anthropologists have often provided these, showing a keen concern for the preservation of fragile cultures and trying at the same time to describe how new ideas can be 'fitted into' vulnerable contexts without damaging them. One could look at the important work which has been done by people like Benedict Anderson and Partha Chatterjee to theorise the postcolonial nation state, a key player in the debate (Anderson 1993, Chatterjee 1986 & 1993). Gandhi, in the Indian context, wrote some very relevant material on this issue as he contemplated the change from colonialism to national independence (1997). In this chapter, however, we shall be looking at the issue from a missiological point of view.

Traditional and modern: taking sides

If there is a 'war' between modernity (usually today expressed in the form of economic nationalism or even economic globalisation) and indigenous values, on which side should the gospel stand? This is not an easy question. Historically Christian missionaries very often saw themselves as having a civilising purpose and found it difficult to understand that this might be a rather 'colonial' attitude. Not surprisingly many anthropologists, convinced that they needed to protect indigenous cultures, as we have just noticed, claimed (and still claim) that the missionaries were some of the people from whom these cultures needed protection (Stoll 1982)! On the other hand some missionaries would have agreed with them from the outset that indigenous peoples often needed protection. In the first half of the nineteenth century John Philip (1775-1851) in South Africa appealed to the British government to protect the Khoi against white settlers who wanted their land. Later in the same century a remarkable group of missionaries in central Africa (present day Eastern Congo, northern Zambia and western Angola) saw it as part of their mission to protect Africans from the influence of white traders and acquisitive European imperialist powers. Dan Crawford was the best known of these because of his best-seller *Thinking Black* (Sweetnam 2006, 15). Other notable figures in this story were C. A. Swan and F. S. Arnott. Much more recently we have the work of the *Iniciativa Cristiana* in the Argentinean Chaco (Sinclair 1980). Here the indigenous population were given weapons by the missionaries which enabled them to mount a very necessary defence against the inroads of an exploitive modernity.

Perhaps the missionaries and the anthropologists were always more allies than they realised. Certainly, over more recent years, because of a greater emphasis on contextualising the gospel, missiology has relied heavily on anthropological studies. Missionaries with skills and training in the discipline – Paul Hiebert or David Burnett would be examples – have provided invaluable insights into the way pre-modern societies function and how the gospel might be communicated within them. Despite the relative decline of anthropology as an academic discipline, this approach has by no means outlived its usefulness. Quite apart from the fact that there are still plenty of 'pre-modern' communities, and that the remote areas of our planet have not been entirely overrun by the messengers of modernity, the pre-modern *within* the modern seems, if anything, to be on the increase. Within modern states and cities, communities with their own distinctive ethnicity and culture are being multiplied at a great rate, usually as a result of a world increasingly subject to the migration of peoples. (See the chapter on 'Migration and Diaspora'). Also, where the nation state comes under pressure (think, for example of the former Yugoslavia) tensions tend to express themselves along communalistic lines.

From one point of view this can be seen as a sort of cultural regression. If it is accepted that the modern state, and beyond it globalisation, is the necessary way forward, then those who still want to play the 'communalism' card are, at heart, little more than deniers of the inevitable. In the end, or so it is said, we have no choice but to go along the pathway of modernity with its affirmation of progress, nationalism, secularism, economism ('you can't buck the market'), and globalisation. If indeed traditional communities have no future, then from a missiological point of view the necessary switch is from anthropology (the study of pre-modern societies) to sociology (the study of modern societies) as providing the necessary background to mission. I have some sympathy with this way of looking at things, though only some, and would certainly agree that missiologists today need grounding in the 'modern' sciences – economics, politics, psychology, media studies as much as sociology. Martin Ott, in a trenchant piece which he calls 'Leaving the Past Behind' about his own experience of mission in Malawi describes how his anthropological expertise had to be supplemented by other more 'modern' disciplines in order to understand what was going on in the Malawian context. He says: 'My field of interest in Africa has shifted to issues of poverty, democratisation, education, economic development and human rights. Traditional culture remains an important but no longer determining factor.'

Notice, however, that Ott still feels that the study of traditional culture remains important. He makes the point, at the end of his piece, that essential to any approach is 'to start with the people we are dealing with, not our preconceived ideas'. In this respect I am particularly impressed by the series of studies edited by Richard Werbner (Werbner & Ranger 1996, Werbner 1998 & 2002). The approach of Werbner and his team is to study contemporary African society without, I think, any attempt to categorise it as 'traditional' or 'modern'. (If these categories are used, then it rapidly becomes clear that traditional and modern forces are *both* at work, often in a way that creates something novel.) Let me give you some examples taken from the book *Postcolonial Subjectivities in Africa* (2002). All of the following are offered:

- Spirit mediums are supposedly empowered and validated by important historical figures from the past.

- Out of feelings of deprivation and loss, a Kenyan, Peter, and his friends create photographs which, so they say, are so beautiful that they cannot be Kenyan! They are 'transformed' into Americans , though not rich Americans, rather poor African-Americans, thus expressing a critical attitude to their own social situation.

- The Nuba and Gamsk peoples in Sudan both suffer oppression from outsiders. The Nuba have invested in armed struggle to survive, but the Gamsk in dream consciousness.

- Militarisation in Africa, especially the widespread availability and use of guns, has reshaped gender relations. Women are more than ever marginalised because not involved in military activities, but men are less able to protect their womenfolk and this leads to domestic violence and sexual abuse.

- Who does a child belong to in a society such as that of the Cameroonian grassland in which the relationship between the individual and the collective is in constant negotiation?

- The concept and practice of chieftainship has changed dramatically over the past thirty years. It stands somewhere between egalitarian citizenship and the traditional hierarchical exercise of power. Expectations are therefore contradictory.

- Serious illness in Eastern Uganda (AIDS is the obvious example) is approached through a deliberate tentativeness, an avoidance of the 'clinical' approach that only offers a final and perhaps fatal diagnosis. Instead the involvement of spirits and sorcery, which allows that there may be some remedy, is favoured.

- There is an ambiguous attitude to incest in Karambola (Madagascar). The web of connectedness is valued but the disadvantages of being shunned by other social worlds is also recognised.

While much of the above is the continuation of the 'old' anthropology – topics such as spirit possession, dream consciousness, traditional sources of authority etc – the studies also show clearly how the impacts of the traditional past and modernity are both at work to create new situations.

I would like to end this section by referring to a sort of case study from the cinema, the film *Rabbit Proof Fence*. The film has very much to do with 'the fate of the indigenous' and is based on true events in Australia in the 1930s. Its main theme is the strenuous attempts made by the Australian authorities to 'socially engineer' the 'Aboriginal question'. In essence the plan was to keep the two races – the Aborigines and the white Australians – apart. Where there had been miscegenation a division was made, based on skin colour, in order to place the children on one side or the other of the racial divide. Mixing was considered to be the problem. Both races were supposed to benefit by being apart. What was to be avoided at all costs was an 'unwanted third race'. The man in charge of the process (Mr Neville – a real historical person) is titled 'Chief *Protector* of the Aborigines'! He has the power to remove any 'half-caste' child from his or her family, and the three children in the film, who are of mixed parentage, are singled out, particularly at the moment when they might be reaching marriageable age. The fear is that they will compound an already problematic situation by producing children who are yet more 'mixed'.

In a sense Neville is the villain of the piece, but, although his attitudes are painfully and stereotypically racist, he is also seen to be an earnest man who believes in the rightness of what he is doing. He sees himself as taking on a necessary but thankless task and one in which he is poorly supported by society at large (he complains about the shortage of cash for the project). The public, presumably, would rather ignore the situation or even simply acquiesce in the destruction of the aboriginal way of life. And there we have it. Our hero thinks that he is *preserving* the aboriginal culture. Mixing the races, creating hybrid people, who do not belong to a 'pure' race or culture is, to men like Neville, the ultimate confusion. Of course, as in South African *apartheid*, there is something sinister going on at the same time alongside the logic of racial theory. The Aborigines are being kept separate, and sent to a special school, so that they can be assigned a permanently inferior role (domestic servants or farm labourers). Nevertheless the question remains. Is preserving 'pure' races and cultures what we want to do? If not, what consequences does this have when considering the fate of the indigenous peoples and cultures which is the concern of this chapter?

In the film a tracker, an Aborigine, works for the school where the girls are confined, mainly, it seems, to track down runaway students and return them to captivity. He appears to be 'in the pay' of the enemy, but this is probably unwillingly; his own daughter is in the school and he is clearly hostage to that situation. He is a key member of the outfit, it could scarcely do without him, but he is treated as an inferior – he is an Aborigine after all. He has joined the system, but he also undermines it, deciding on at least one occasion not to return the runaway girls even though he has successfully tracked them down. (In postcolonial terms he is an example of the way colonial subjects have always 'answered back' on their own terms without openly resorting to defiance.) I suggest that the tracker in some ways stands for a 'hybrid' solution (though not in terms of race) to the dilemmas posed by the evident clash of two civilisations. While the action centres around a dualism, with Aborigines on one side and white Australians on the other, the tracker belongs to both sides. He is clearly an Aborigine by race but, for whatever motives, has joined the white establishment. Though this brings him a degree of pain and humiliation, it does mean that he retains elements of power and choice that are available to nobody else. Whereas one side can only coerce and the other resist, the tracker follows a third way. While this analysis may seem too hopeful (and clearly compromise of this sort does not work where the coercive side has no good purposes at all, as in, say, a Nazi concentration camp) and many might simply put the tracker down as a collaborator or traitor, it does, I believe, go some way to illustrate the subtle ways that 'hybridity' might work in a situation which is otherwise hopelessly dualistic.

Questions about survival

Rabbit Proof Fence and the other historical and contemporary examples we have just described, raise all sorts of questions of a missiological nature, and because they are questions that span the pre- and post-independence eras in the Global South, they are postcolonial questions too. At base, most of them have to do with the issue of survival. First of all, *can* indigenous, pre-modern, 'tribal' societies survive? Is that a realistic goal? Secondly, do we *want* them to? Thirdly, do *they* want to, that is, do they want to continue to keep apart from modernity and what it has to offer? Is that what they choose to do? Fourthly, is there some half-way house where the good of the past is retained but newness is assimilated in a healthy way. Fifthly, is this anything to do with mission?

(1) Whatever we might wish, or indeed do, I suspect that indigenous people will have to change in the direction of more 'modern' lifestyles. This is partly due to a psychology of progress. Sadly, the old ways will pass away simply because they are judged to be old. Also, obviously, economic and social conditions change, and very often this happens without the victims of the change having any say in the matter. If the old hunter-gatherer way of life is irrevocably past, and if the rural economy is failing, how can you advise the young people of the village *not* to go to the big city. And once they are there, how can anyone prevent the change away from the values that previously ruled their lives? Even those who stay behind may find their lives profoundly disturbed. Perhaps some well-meaning organisation (sponsored by government, NGO, church etc.) has built a school in the village. Or satellite television has become a possibility. In more sinister mode, we might envisage a situation in which people are cutting down the jungle on which villagers' livelihood depends and there is apparently no way to stop them. Or worst of all the government (or somebody with government authority) is building a dam, and the village is about to disappear under the water (Roy 2002).

(2) But then, we may not feel that the survival of indigenous cultures is something worth striving for anyway. What, after all, are we trying to achieve? Some would argue that preserving a culture is like putting it in a museum and leaving it there. We may preserve it, but only by a sort of mummification. They would add to this humanitarian and utilitarian arguments. If 'scientific' medical help is available why not give people access to it? If plastic buckets are more efficient than earthenware pots (even if less aesthetically pleasing!) why not sell them some? So it goes on.

Even these apparently common sense examples need some discussion, however. Are humanitarian or utilitarian arguments necessarily the last word? Would, for example, the introduction of scientific medicine destroy the practice of local, indigenous medicine? Is the production of earthenware pots an important local industry, the undermining of which would prove a severe economic loss? More fundamentally, is the village way of life simply more healthy and more productive of human values. Ched Myers in his booklet about Sabbath Economics speaks of 'the primal value of the most basic human competence – hunting/gathering and local horticulture – the cooperative, egalitarian lifeway that sustained human beings for tens of thousands of years prior to the rise of concentrated agriculture, cities, and eventually imperial economics based on slavery' (Myers 2001,11). Notice that Myers is suggesting that there is a baneful progression here. Abandoning the economics of the village leads ultimately to slavery.

(3) Do the people in question themselves always *want* to retain their indigenous culture? At one level, something like radio or satellite television may be welcomed with open arms, particularly by the younger generation. At another, many missionaries bear witness to the gospel being received as good news (as it certainly claims to be) because it delivers people from fear and connects them to a larger spiritual hope. A book like Chinua Achebe's *Things Fall Apart* explains very well what people have lost with the advent of modern times; however, it does not do justice to what they have gained, or feel they have gained.

(4) Anybody who has to do with an indigenous culture largely untouched by modernity, whether they be government official, development worker, missionary or even an observant anthropologist, must think very carefully about the nature of the change that their presence (and what, so to speak, their presence uniquely represents) will bring about in the community. They should be asking themselves all sorts of delicate questions. Do I understand, really understand, what is happening here? If I mix my ideas with those of the people, what sort of mixture might that be – an explosive one, perhaps? And if I create an explosion, do I really know what might be destroyed? Furthermore, do I appreciate that the situation will not be straightforward or even-handed? When change comes, one gains perhaps, but another loses (Ingleby 1997, 183-7). Overall, the question remains (the one I asked at the beginning): if there is change will it retain the good things of the past, and contextualise the new things in a productive and healthy way? Here is the surprised lament of the missionary Frank Drown working in the Amazon.

> Some Indians from a different tribe in the northern jungles having learned Spanish in mission schools, were going to the coast to work on banana plantations. It seemed to them like a good way to make more money. I had heard many accounts of homes broken because only the men went out, never to return or perhaps to come back to die of white man's diseases. Would the same things happen to the Shuar we were training in our schools? Would the very help we were giving turn out to be a curse? I was shaken when I

heard that just such an experience had befallen one of our schoolboys (Drown 2002, 271).

(5) All these questions and struggles are profoundly to do with mission, because change is what the gospel is about. In some ways mission is an *exchange*. I have something valuable in the pack on my back – to use a homely illustration – which I am prepared to share with you and which I believe will enrich your life; but I realise that you have something valuable to give back as well – an exchange, in fact. However, this is not quite a simple swap when it comes to the gospel. The exchange is that I give you the gospel (it is 'new news' to you) but you then give it back to me enriched by your own experience and culture (in which God may have been already at work) so that I receive it as something which is new to me, in that I could never have seen it *in that way* before. (So that mission is both proclamation and dialogue, to use a familiar terminology.) The second phase of the movement, which we might call contextualisation or enculturation, is only possible if I give my valuable possession away. If I cling to it, insisting that the gospel must continue to be expressed predominantly in terms of my culture – there is a power issue here too – I cannot receive it back. Furthermore, the process of change is short-circuited or at very best deformed. Where there is change, it is the sort of change we associate with imperialism.

This process of 'change by exchange' applies quite as much to what we call 'development' (the NGO word) or 'growth' (the government word) as it does to Christian mission. Unfortunately it is not very common, in missionary or NGO or government circles. We are all too busy telling instead of listening. At a deeper level, we are deceived, as I have explained elsewhere (see the section on Postcolonialism and Development), by the commanding ideas of the Enlightenment Project with their baneful tendency to treat people of different cultures as the 'other', and to control and dominate them.

Let us return, however, to our main theme: the issue of the survival of threatened peoples. In an article I wrote some time ago about the fate of the Machiguenga tribe in Peru, I linked this question with Jesus' parable of the Good Samaritan. Thus:

> When a man is lying by the roadside in imminent danger of dying, what is the appropriate response? The answer is easy. Everything must be done, first of all, to make sure that he *survives*. All over the world small communities, local

cultures, tribes and peoples are struggling to survive. Is it not our neighbourly, Christian duty, to try and make sure that they do (Ingleby 2007, 20)?

Aiming at survival may be the first goal, the simple answer to our question, but everything gets much more complicated after that. To draw an analogy: in a famine situation, feeding the people – wherever the food comes from – is an entirely appropriate response. Thereafter 'food aid' needs to be carefully thought about, if only because making a community dependent on food hand-outs instead of their own agriculture is not an appropriate long-term response to conditions of agricultural vulnerability. Similarly, survival for a threatened tribal group may demand some initial separation of the group from its threatening context, but, long-term, separating it from the busy world around it may result in little more than creating an exhibit in a museum of ethnicity, as we have seen.

So perhaps there are two aims: helping threatened groups to survive and then helping them to integrate into the modern world (without, it is to be hoped, losing their identity, which would mean that they had not survived after all). This dual task seems to me to be immensely complex. Let me list some of the difficulties.

- The achievement of survival itself is increasingly problematical. The forces ranged against the 'little people' of this world are stupendous, and also very varied – political, commercial, environmental and indeed spiritual. The Domination System has a rage for uniformity (Revelation 13:16,17) and employs a large number of sophisticated means to make sure that we all want the same thing and ultimately, do what we are told.

- Even if survival is assured for the time being, there will have to be constant and vigilant negotiation. If I give away my language, my distinctive clothing, my celebrations, my family rituals, my food preferences, my work patterns, my rhythm of life and even my environment (going to live in the city, perhaps, instead of the village or the jungle), am I the same person? Nor does deciding what I can 'give away' necessarily tell me what new things I can take on without being overwhelmed by the newness.

- Of course, some would say that I have put matters in a way that is too stark. Instead of losing and gaining, why not simply see the process as gaining. While retaining the good of the traditional way, newness can be added where appropriate in a measured and non-threatening way. In the film *The Story of the Weeping Camel* traditional Mongolian culture is celebrated and there is little sense that new features from outside – the motorbike and satellite television, for example – are a threat, indeed they are largely welcome. There is a slight generation clash over this, but it is nothing serious. Everyone keeps smiling and there is certainly no sense of crisis. Having said this, I am convinced that even for this confident and well established culture there will be storms ahead, which the film chooses to ignore. As I see it, there is already a significant and dangerous challenge to the old ways, and these will need to be defended if they are to survive.

- It is a truism that traditional ways of life are supported by community. The new lives people are being drawn into, say in the city, may be much more atomistic. Though people often speak of 'my culture' the truth is that culture is always a shared enterprise. The moment someone becomes isolated is the moment that the destruction of 'their' culture begins. That is why, if we are talking about survival, we have to think carefully about anything that leads to dispersal. Years ago I worked in Malawi. In the villages the women and children and the old people had been abandoned by the young men who had gone away to South Africa to work in the mines. The only thing you could say about the villages is that they were dying in many different ways.

- The issue of identity is like a thread that runs through the postcolonial discourse and through missiology also. For example, identity issues are hugely important when thinking about hybridity or migration (see above). Suffice it to say that a group's sense of identity is crucial to their survival and a secure identity depends on many factors such as control of one's history, the ability of writers and artists to tell the community's story, confidence in the future, equal relations with neighbours (i.e. other communities), success in learning to live well within available resources and so on. (The gospel, of course, provides or enhances all of these, as well as introducing a new existential optimism and a resource when things go wrong.) My point is that if we are concerned, as part of God's mission, to affirm people's identity then we must be sure that the *way* we bring the gospel is not inadvertently working against that purpose. Much missionary work in the past, for example, ignored people's history or denigrated their writers and artists. By so doing, at a time when colonialism was already creating confusion over identities, missionaries became part of the problem rather than the solution.

- There is, I think, a spiritual battle going on (Ephesians 6:12). The 'new' has a glamour, a false seductiveness. People are taught to be impatient. Survival is equated with *economics*. 'The grass is always greener.' Contentment is seen as a vice. Reading the essays of Wendell Berry, as he laments the destruction of his beloved Kentucky countryside, I sense a sort of anguished bewilderment. How could a whole nation acquiesce in such a wholesale devastation in return for such ephemeral and meretricious gains? But as Berry himself would agree, that answer is not a rational one. He holds up the light of reason himself in his beautifully argued essays, but this appears as little more than a flickering candle in a very dark world, a darkness that cannot be explained by, and is not subject to, rational enquiry.

This last thought reminds me to say that what our threatened communities need is not simply survival but salvation. If I may refer again to my essay on the Machiguenga tribe:

> However important their identity as Machiguengas, it is not what defines them as the people of God (Galatians 3:28). What would define them as such would be an acceptance of Jesus as Lord. This would not only define them, but would *save* them. The tribal customs, stories and beliefs, beautiful and powerful as they are, are no match for modernity, as we have seen. But Jesus is (1 Corinthians 12:1,3). It was the Christians who successfully challenged the totalising imperialism of their day, the Roman Empire (Ingleby 2007, 18).

I truly believe that the gospel gives people the power and discernment not only to survive but to thrive in a world where the pressures to conform, and then to surrender, are formidable. Great Babylon swallows up the nations; New Jerusalem welcomes them, renewed and resplendent (Revelation 21:26).

The Postcolonial City

After all these years, after all these supposed evidences of progress, we have not yet learnt to live together successfully in community. A cool announcement that we are heading towards a 'planet of slums', the title of a book by Mike Davis (2006), that within thirty years every third person will be a slum dweller, gives the game away. We cannot really pretend, if that is really where we are heading, that such an outcome is anything more than an outright failure of our politics, our economics, our social engineering and for that matter our religion.

So here are the questions: (1) Is it true? Are we really in such a mess? (2) If it is true, whose fault is it, and even if we can answer that question, will deciding who is to blame make any difference? (3) What, if anything, can we do about it, or is this 'descent into hell' inevitable?

Are we really in that much trouble?

The overall purpose of this section is not to describe urban poverty or to calculate its extent, so much as to demonstrate its connection, past and present, with colonialism. Nevertheless something needs to be said about the reality of the case. I suppose this is a simple matter of statistics, observation and experience and the slightly more difficult matter of judging world trends. I mention 'experience' because it is possible to live a life so shielded from the harsh realities of the urban poor that they simply escape our notice. This makes it difficult for us to give them any weight in our calculations. Of course we can read the statistical evidence, but that may be no more to us than a row of figures. There is all the difference between an economics textbook and Jeremy Seabrook's *In the Cities of the South* (1996) with its sad and yet inspiring stories of personal struggle. Be that as it may, the statistical evidence seems compelling. I quote from a couple of recent books. 'One billion people – or one in three urban residents – now live in an urban slum, the vast majority of them in developing nations' (Kramer 2006,3) or looking ahead, 'At current rates, within a decade of this writing we'll have more than twenty cities in the world with more than ten million inhabitants, most of them in poor nations. By the 2030s, the number of people living in informal settlements could double to about two billion, and we've yet to find some programmatic panacea for urban blight' (199). Mike Davis, in the book already mentioned, *Planet of Slums*, reckons that by 2015 there will be at least 550 cities with a population of more than a million. City population will be something like 10 billion by 2050 (2006,2). Most of these people will be living in slums and most of them will be in the Global South.

How did it happen?

Urban deprivation is not a new phenomenon. It is as old, at least, as the industrial revolution. In searching for causes it is necessary to take into account both general issues of poverty and the more specific issues concerning cities as such. Are they simply places where it is particularly difficult to sustain good communities? This second question has received contradictory responses. Certainly a case has been made out in favour of the city. It is possible, it is felt, at the very least to *imagine* a good city. Examples would be David Harvey's *Spaces of Hope* (2000) or Richard Rogers' *Cities for a Small Planet* (1997). The culminating vision of the good community in the Bible (Revelation 21:1-22:5) is a city, the new Jerusalem. The 'image of the city' at its best, offers a vision of order, security, beauty and fellowship. It can be contrasted to the savagery of the jungle, the emptiness and barrenness of the desert, and the lack of sophistication that characterises country life. At another level the city offers us a community of choice as against the Nation in which we seem fatally entangled by blood and destiny (Williams 1958,92).

Yet a very different angle is possible. The countryside offers freshness, renewal, a nearness to nature, honest work, simple pleasures, a slower and therefore more reflective sort of life and so on. Have people really learned to live together in a happy and healthy way in the city? What about the pollution and crowding, the noise and haste, the extravagance and waste, the prevalence of crime and social disorder? Why is it that slums form so quickly in the modern city? Villages have people living in poverty, but they do not experience squalor in quite the same way. It may be quite reasonable to conclude that there is something inherently wrong with the modern city. Perhaps people are simply not designed to live so closely together. They need more territory. Perhaps the built environment as against the natural environment renews itself less easily. It is easier to exploit people in the city. If they are adrift, cut off from their roots in the soil of the countryside, then others can 'carry them off' for their own purposes.

It is fair to say, I suggest, that it is difficult, even if it is not impossible, to create and sustain good communities in an urban context. The city magnifies human failure. Behaviour which is manageable in the village is soon out of control in the city; contrasts, such as that between rich and poor, are more stark. None of this persuades me that we need to look very far beyond issues of wealth and poverty as we examine the advent of 'a planet of slums'. In most countries the crisis in our cities begins with the crisis in our countryside. They are not two separate problems, but tied together, and have an overarching cause. The countryside has been ruined and our city slums are full of refugees from this disaster. Rural and urban deprivation are two scenes in the same tragedy. Also, while this is an economic process, values and worldviews are factors which obviously transcend geography. We have inherited from the

Enlightenment an ideology which denies this tragedy, or at least, hides it. Part of the Enlightenment myth is the colonial idea that there is, and always will be, a metropolitan centre (good, advanced, civilised, active, rational and so on) and a periphery (bad, backward, barbarous, passive, irrational). Incorporated into this myth is city and countryside as *essentially* different. However much you strive to change the relations, city is where you 'get on', the countryside is where you stagnate. In the village your 'bright young things' are only waiting for the chance to get away to the bright lights. It is their natural milieu. Material products from the city, though often evidently inferior in quality, are preferred because they are 'the latest thing'. This reminds us directly of the days of high imperialism. The metropolitan centre was the source of everything that was desirable. People from the colonies wanted nothing better than to be there, however much they had to give up in order to make the trip.

The dynamics of city life are best understood, therefore, by a consideration of its internal and external *relationships*. How does the city relate to its rural hinterland? Who has moved into the city recently and why, and what ongoing links do they maintain with village or small town life? What are the nature and purpose of those links? (We can widen this and ask the same questions of international migrants.) Within the city the relations between the wealthy centre and the peripheral slums need to be examined. Many street children, for example, are migrants from the slums to the city centre. What emerges is that today's megacity is a *colonial* space in nearly every aspect of its relationships. Historically, of course, many of the world's great cities such as Kolkata and Mumbai in India, Shanghai and Hong Kong in China, or Nairobi in Kenya, were formed directly by colonialism. Like the great industrial towns of Britain which sprung up in the nineteenth century (Manchester, Leeds etc.) they grew with unprecedented speed as a result of a purpose which had very little to do with their surrounding countryside. Just to take one example, up to the nineteenth century India's cities were largely administrative centres (Delhi, Mysore), and though important, were quite small by modern standards. Cities with large slum populations had to wait until the arrival of the colonial trading city. The same pattern of growth is true, *mutatis mutandis*, of Europe's cities.

Thus, as we have said, an Empire essentially operates as a metropolitan centre with a subservient, contributing periphery (colonies). So does the megacity. It has a metropolitan centre where power and wealth reside and a 'colonial' periphery which can be either the rural vicinity or its own slums or both. Actually, it has a third 'periphery', a pool of immigrant labour, people who come to work in the city on 'colonial' terms and who have been 'produced' by neo-colonialism and its unfair economic and trading arrangements.

We can illustrate this in a curious way by means of the leisure industry. The 'colonies' are not just a source of cheap labour and cheap produce (are the farmers world-wide getting a fair return on their labour?) but a holiday destination for (wealthy) stressed-out city dwellers. We go to the countryside for rest and relaxation or to the ex-colonies as part of the ever-expanding international tourist trade. The exception here appears to be the slum areas. It seems hardly likely that these will become centres for rest and recuperation or tourist attractions! Yet even here there may be some connection. They do provide reserve *space* when wealthy city dwellers want to increase their leisure opportunities. So, in areas that are conveniently designated as 'needing development' (think of the areas where new buildings are planned for the London 2012 Olympics) we build stadia, golf courses, museums, concert halls, casinos, hotels and parks. This sounds good news, but these same areas often suddenly become 'desirable', prices rise, and the original (poor) inhabitants cannot afford to live there and are shunted on to find living space somewhere else. The same has happened, in Britain, to the villages. They have become dormitories and retirement homes for the incoming rich and the country folk have been displaced. They are now living in the poorer parts of the cities!

What can we do?

Rescuing the colonised (of whatever sort) does seem a good idea, but only so long as it means genuinely improving the life of the poor people who live there. So often 'development' (the current buzz word) means something else. It would certainly help the overcrowding in our cities if more people were able to live contented and prosperous lives elsewhere. But, as we have noticed, the re-invigoration of the countryside, the regeneration of our slum districts and the economic strengthening of nations in the Global South is a complex task, demanding not simply new economic arrangements but a new post-Enlightenment (postcolonial?) worldview.

Theologians and philosophers – see for example Gillian Rose (1992) – speak about 'starting with the middle' and indeed this seems a good place from which to understand and respond to the life of modern slum dwellers. We need to see them as people *in transit* so to speak. They have come from a different world and they are migrants, even refugees. But it would be unwise to think of their present situation as permanent. It is not for nothing that slums are called 'informal settlements'. Of course efforts are made by them to obtain more permanent status: title to the land they are occupying, houses that will last, connection to public facilities that are legal and reliable and so on. However, when they have these, they are no longer living in slums; their informal settlements have become permanent. They have 'moved on' and in a more satisfactory sense than if they had simply moved to another part of the city, or to work abroad under yet more precarious conditions.

We must ask these people who are occupying the middle what is their protology and their eschatology. Life in the slums is 'between the times' of initiation and consummation. This sense that they are still people 'on the move' who know that there is something better and that there is still the possibility of reaching it, may help them to see their final destiny as something other than that of being everlasting migrants, moving from the slums to the city centre, and perhaps from there to a destination overseas. They may then also come to see that 'in their end is their beginning' and vice versa, that the purpose of their move to the slums is not to abandon the villages or the cities of the South that they have come from, but to treat their present situation as a stage on the way in their mission to re-affirm and re-invigorate these very places. Some have even suggested that we should *encourage* the go-ahead elements in the village (global or otherwise) to head off to the big cities to make their fortunes, but also to encourage them to keep in touch and come back later. This is a distinctly 'diaspora' approach and another link with postcolonial theory (and the New Testament), which rates the diaspora experience highly.

As for the slum areas, we need to give them serious attention before the situation overwhelms us. At a purely technical level I suspect that our cities are so huge that the centre-periphery pattern needs to be replaced by a multi-centred, more networked one. I am no architect or town planner but I am sure that we can do better in this respect. Richard Rogers has some lovely ideas for the city of London in the book already mentioned, *Cities for a Small Planet* (1997, chapter 4). He is dismayed that we have not grasped our opportunities to do some serious planning. 'As a society we are shamefully ignorant of the positive impact that architecture and design of cities can have on our lives', he says, and asks for legislation to help to bring this about. Rogers' response to the woes of the city is part of the 'technological fix'. The idea is that if we could organise things better, we could live better. I am not at all blaming him for taking this approach (he is an architect and empowered to give us this perspective) nor do I deny his premise that better designed cities would have a 'positive impact'. But it is easy to overlook the issue of power. Of course we need legislation, but what if the legislators, speaking generally of course, simply wish to maintain existing relations which are to their advantage?

From a missiological point of view, the peripheral city space calls to us for two reasons. It is that final frontier, beloved of centrifugal mission: not Jerusalem, Judea or Samaria but 'the ends of the earth' (Acts 1:8). For those of us who live in the comfortable centre of power it is that place, a new and alien culture, to which we must 'cross over'. And of course, in a globalised world, that frontier might be just around the corner. Slums are everywhere – in the West and in the Global South. A mission agency like Servants For Asia's Urban Poor has got it about right. The new mission frontier is precisely the urban slum because slum dwellers are at the end of the line as far as power and privilege is concerned. They are the 'poor' to whom good news is preached. (There is no need to limit this to Asia however.)

To be a servant of the poor and to live among them by choice rather than necessity (a core value of the Servants organisation) is the answer to the power equation which keeps our slums in place. It introduces the values of the 'upside Kingdom'.

- People have worth wherever they live.
- Power and fulfilment come not from escape or self-preservation but from death and resurrection.
- People and situations can be *mended* (the lame can walk, the blind see, captives can be set free).
- This is a time of acceptance.
- There is no need to 'perish'. Re-cycling by means of eternal life is our destination.

These are the sort of values we have to smuggle into the whole discourse of urban renewal. It is not an easy thing to do. Consider the famous analogy which Walter Benjamin used in his 'Theses on the Philosophy of History':

> The story is told of an automaton constructed in such a way that it could play a winning game of chess, answering each move of an opponent with a countermove. A puppet in Turkish attire and with a hookah in its mouth sat before the chessboard placed on a large table. A system of mirrors created the illusion that this table was transparent from all sides. Actually, a little hunchback who was an expert chess player sat inside and guided the puppet's hand by means of

strings. One can imagine a philosophical counterpart to this device. The puppet called 'historical materialism' is to win all the time. It can easily be a match for anyone if it enlists the services of theology, which today, as we know, is wizened and has to keep out of sight (Benjamin 1999, 245).

The moral of the story is that while it is true that theology today is 'wizened and has to keep out of sight' it also remains true that social scientists, town planners and the like need some sort of theological rationale to inform their plans if they are to succeed. Rightly, the trump cards in many of our discussions about urban deprivation, are ethical and moral (i.e. theological) ones. 'Distribution of resources must be fair.' 'The arrogance of the rich must give way to justice for the poor.' 'Corrupt officials vitiate our best efforts at town planning.' 'Can we allow greedy landowners to evict their helpless tenants.' How many 'theological' terms have we used already? It seems unfair that these arguments need to be so much in the background; that we cannot be up front about the fact that it is God who requires us to 'do justice, to love kindness, and to walk humbly'. I am not too worried that this clandestine borrowing, remains a secret, however. It reminds me of Jesus' mustard seed parable, or of the story of the farmer who plants his seed in the field where it grows 'he knows not how'.

What I am really saying here is that effective action to rescue us from a 'planet of slums' has to be taken at the level of theology, worldview, and hegemonic ideology. In the widest sense of the term it is a matter of spiritual warfare. Until we 'change our minds' (Romans 12:2), and persuade others to do likewise, nothing much will happen. For centuries together slavery was an accepted part of the European worldview; so was colonialism. We learnt, slowly, to do better. Of course there is still slavery and there is still (neo) colonialism, but at least we do not accept them as a matter of course. They are not 'common sense' (i.e. what is commonly accepted as reasonable behaviour) as they used to be. We need to do the same for urban deprivation and the causes of it. If one of the causes is a global economic system which widens the gap between rich and poor by creating and sustaining an imperial centre against its colonial periphery (as I have tried to describe) then we need to see such a system as akin to the slavery or colonialism of a by-gone age, something which, when we look back on it in a later age (if there is one), we see for what it is – a monstrous injustice which we Christians should be fighting tooth and nail.

What About Zion?

I suppose if you asked the man (and woman) in the street in the Middle East what was the most important postcolonial issue, they would almost all say 'the Israel-Palestine conflict'. Oddly many Christians (particularly in the United States) might agree with them.

My father, who was a serious student of both the Bible and world affairs, once suggested to me that the prosperity of nations was tied to their dealings with, and attitudes to, the Jews. He put forward some Biblical evidence for this, and also a number of historical and contemporary examples. It was no coincidence, he felt, that Britain was at the zenith of her power when she had a Jewish Prime Minister (Disraeli) and that the Third Reich should have collapsed so spectacularly in the light of its anti-semitism.

I was very impressed by his arguments at the time, but have grown less so since. The arguments from Scripture now seem to me very 'Old Testament'. The New Testament, I feel, moves away from the idea of Jewish particularity when expressed in ethnic or nationalistic terms. As for historical examples, it is simply too easy to pick and choose from history in a 'historicist' way. Can specific events be linked so easily and so certainly to God's favour or disfavour?

I am still a sceptic about historicism and still convinced that my interpretation of the Bible with regard to the Jewish nation is broadly correct, but also now think that there is more to be said on the subject than is allowed by my rather reductionist approach. A good deal of my recent reading had been about the holocaust, not so much about what happened in the concentration camps as about the Jewish communities that ended up there. I am not sure where this interest came from precisely. It possibly began when I read W. G. Sebald's *The Emigrants* and the same author's *Austerlitz*. Vikram Seth's *Two Lives* also has a strong connection with the persecution of the Jews, as does Peter Singer's *Pushing Time Away* subtitled *My Grandfather and the Tragedy of Jewish Vienna*. A friend lent me a biography of Primo Levi and subsequently I read *Bad Faith* by Carmen Callil, an account of the life of Louis Darquier who was in charge of the deportation of Jews to the concentration camps from France. (I should also mention the film *Au Revoir les Enfants* directed by Louis Malle, which is likewise about French attitudes to Jews during the German occupation.) I have always been interested in Walter Benjamin, the German Jewish literary critic and philosopher, and this led me to several accounts of his time in France and his suicide which terminated his attempt to flee the Nazis.[15] *Three Women in Dark Times* by Sylvie Courtine-Denamy, a book specifically about a trio of Jewish women , Edith Stein, Hannah Arendt and Simone Weil, only one of whom (Arendt) survived the 1939-45 war, looked carefully at the relationship of all three to their Jewish identity.

All this, so to speak, was background reading. What really made me think again about 'how the Jews fit into history' was Edward Said's essay, *Freud and the Non-European* (Said 2003b) and two books by Jacqueline Rose, *The Question of Zion* (2003) and *The Last Resistance* (2007) especially the latter. Jacqueline Rose understandably wants to come to terms with the holocaust. She is a Jewess herself and an expert in 'holocaust literature'. She is deeply concerned about the human rights record of the current Israeli government. She was also a friend of the late Edward Said, himself a Palestinian and writer on the Palestinian question.[16] My point here is, however, that we all (we Europeans, anyway) have to come to terms with the holocaust and the Israel/Palestine situation. This is simply because they are political events and issues of such moment that we ignore them at our peril.

Rose's contention in *The Last Resistance* is that these events – the holocaust and the way the state of Israel reached its present form – are linked. Furthermore they contribute significantly to our understanding of colonialism, and therefore postcolonialism (this is my idea not Rose's). At a very simple level the attempt of the Nazis to essentialise their own culture and to exclude all those - Jews, gypsies, Jehovah Witnesses, and any other people they considered deviants or imperfect, has huge resonance for today in terms of our efforts to establish healthily multi-cultural or hybrid societies. The Jewish experience in Europe (up to the rise of fascism, that is) was marked by a tension between maintaining Jewish identity and assimilating to the European experience, including European nationalism. Such a tension is equally found in the postcolonial immigrant populations in Europe today. Again, the establishing of the State of Israel and its subsequent history are part of *colonial* history. The non Israeli population of the Middle East see the birth of Israel in these terms precisely. The ongoing support for Israel by the United States and her allies has confirmed the opinion. Nor has it been forgotten how Britain and

---

[15] An interesting fictionalised version of these events is Bruno Arpaia's *The Angel of History*.

[16] Rose wrote a reply to Said's lecture on *Freud and the non-European* published in the book of that name.

France carved up the Middle East after the First World War and that, as a part of that settlement, established the state Israel with Britain taking the lead.

Jacqueline Rose traces the way in which the experience of the holocaust led to an aggressive, militarised state of Israel. Her approach is essentially Freudian: the suppressed trauma of the holocaust resurfaces in powerful ways among an Israeli population who cannot even yet look at the holocaust steadily, particularly because it speaks of the Jewish people as helpless victims.

> For trauma, far from generating freedom, openness to others as well as to the divided and unresolved fragments of a self, leads to a very different kind of fragmentation – one which is, in Freud's own words 'devastating', and causes identities to batten down, to go exactly the other way: towards dogma, the dangers of coercive and coercing forms of faith (Said 2003b, 75-6).

Those trying to understand the reaction to colonialism in the Global South today might benefit from this insight, particularly with regard to the colonial subjugation of Africa and the Atlantic slave trade. Ziauddin Sardar wrote recently in the *New Statesman* (20 August, 2007 p. 21) (having just seen the museum exhibition 'Breaking the Chains' at the British Empire and Commonwealth Museum in Bristol):

> A couple of weeks later I met Joel, a black American university lecturer. We got into a heated discussion about the nature of colonialism, imperialism and their ongoing histories. The more I insisted the history of western attitudes to other peoples was one integrated process, the more irritated Joel became. Eventually, in anguish, he shrieked: 'No, Zia, your ancestors never stood on a block to be sold like cattle.'

Joel's cry of anguish is the cry of victims who believe that the wrongs perpetrated upon them outweigh those of any other victims, and therefore that their cry has a unique claim on our attention. I am not sure about this. Does this not place the crimes of the slave trade outside of history, which is where we do *not* want them to be. Also, and this illustrates my point well, there is one other group who could in fact demand equality of suffering with enslaved Africans, and that is the Jews. But here we see the problem writ large. Much of the failure of the state of Israel stems precisely from its demand that historic norms should not apply to it because of the holocaust. This allows them, they understandably believe, to lay aside the rules that apply to every other nation. A number of examples of this kind of thinking are described and critiqued in Rose's *The Question of Zion* (2005, 142). The results of this mindset have been disastrous. There is, in fact, no place outside of history where a nation can thrive. We are all rightly subject to its exacting demands. Neither the Jews nor black Americans nor anybody else should be accorded special status if that means that they are exempted from the normal laws of civilised behaviour, or that they can withdraw from the fellowship of those who are equally bound together with them in misfortune.

Having said that, it is clear that the trauma of colonialism in its many deadly varieties, remains, and that we Westerners have by no means paid our debt in full in this respect. We must not be surprised if we get a response of shrieking anguish from time to time. Sadly, Western Christians are largely unaware of this sort of reaction from Africans, or from, let us say, Palestinians, those who know, if they cannot always express it, that they have been victims of colonialism. In the latter case, matters are even more complicated because of the confusion caused by Christian Zionism. I suppose my father had a very mild form of this, though he would never have bought into the extreme versions that are common today, especially in the United States. While not wanting to get into detailed Biblical exegesis in this essay,[17] it surely needs to be said that the extreme forms of Christian Zionism are doing much damage to the cause of the gospel in the Middle East and elsewhere. Any attempt to give a theological rationale for injustice (specifically injustice of the land grabbing colonial sort) must necessarily do so.

One of the responses to the vexed issue of the future of Palestine, proposed by Edward Said and commented on by Jacqueline Rose, is the unitary state (the two state solution now being scarcely viable) with both Israelis and Palestinians finding common ground in their experience of diaspora (Said 2003b, 53). Whether this is practical politics is of course the issue, and Rose in her response, while honouring Said's optimism, wonders, as we have seen, whether the traumas of the past are not too deep, and whether the most usual response to trauma (following Freud) is to reproduce it. One thinks of colonial traumas such as partition between India and Pakistan, and how the animosities have been constantly renewed since then.

To return to all those painful accounts of the singling out of Jewish minorities in Fascist Europe – Germany, Austria, Italy, Poland, France after the summer of 1940, and many more nations during the period of Nazi political and

---

[17] My general approach will be clear from comments made above and I have put a more detailed account of my interpretive stance in Appendix 1.

military success – what we see here is the crucial failure of a policy of Jewish assimilation. Whether the Jews failed to assimilate (as some might say) or were not allowed to do so (as was certainly the case in many instances) what is certain is that issues were thrown up in ways that illuminate our postcolonial situation today. My point is that we ignore Jewish history at our peril and that it is right that we continue to agonise over the dreadful spectacle of the holocaust and ask 'what happened here?'.

Let me make some points that arose naturally from my reading. The first is that a shared culture will not necessarily make it possible for people to live at peace, if there are other 'identity issues' at play. David Oppenheim, Peter Singer's grandfather who is the 'hero' of *Pushing Time Away* (2003) was a truly eminent teacher and scholar in Vienna before the *Anschluss*. He was a lover and disseminator of German culture. Furthermore he had fought for his country, Austria, in the First World War and been wounded and decorated. He could not believe that his fellow Austrians would harm him. Nevertheless he ended up in Theresienstadt concentration camp. There were, of course, many similar stories. The obvious lesson is that while a shared culture is going to help people 'get along' (it is no doubt a good thing for immigrants to learn the language of their host countries, for example) it may not be the whole of the matter, nor indeed the most important issue that has to be attended to. I am thinking of a mission team largely composed of Europeans but also two Asians, a Japanese and a Korean. It was, rather ignorantly, assumed that the two Asians would bond together, and indeed they seemed to have much in common. However, the Korean had not forgotten what the Japanese had done to her people during the Japanese occupation. This led to some unexpected difficulties!

A second point is drawn from *Bad Faith*, Carmen Callil's account of the career of Louis Darquier (2006). Darquier, as I explained above, was the man the Vichy French government appointed to oversee the deportation of French Jews to the concentration camps. He was a thoroughly despicable character, but, perhaps the most depressing thing about the book is its revelation of the cooperation Darquier frequently received from 'ordinary' French men and women. Sometimes, no doubt, the motive was fear, but often it seemed much more like malice. There are other examples of this in the film, mentioned above, *Au Revoir Les Enfants*. The simple equation may be that in times of crisis the glue of common decency comes unstuck. This may seem little more than an all too obvious comment on the fallibility of human nature, but it is worth remembering that times of crisis present *particular* challenges to our Christian discipleship. Each day has its distinct challenge and that is the battle that we have to fight. In broad terms it seems to me that the particular challenges of our historical epoch have been fourfold – the struggle to end colonialism, the battle against fascism, the Cold War and the continuing presence of dramatic levels of inequality. (A fifth, the issue of global warming, may be upon us.) Especially in the first two the history of the Jews, as I hope I have demonstrated above, has been a central component. To this day, Christians need to remember the holocaust and what led up to it and what resulted from it. We also have to be involved in the politics of the Middle East. Much depends on the conflict there and attempts to resolve it, and in that conflict the future of the state of Israel and what happens in Palestine is probably the central issue. Not that Israel is God's favourite and therefore enjoys God's special protection. Rather Jewish politics in our day are something which demand important ethical responses from us which show us where we stand as far as God's justice is concerned.

Of all the accounts that I read of the wartime travail of the Jews, Primo Levi's was one of the few which actually described conditions in Auschwitz (1987). Levi strikes one as a great survivor, somebody who used his cool scientific intellect to protect himself from the personal cataclysm that had overtaken him. It therefore comes as a shock that he committed suicide some years after surviving the camp and returning to Italy. Most commentators believe that this was *not* a result of delayed concentration camp trauma (though who can say?) but it does simply remind us that life is a fragile thing and that here was a man who had experienced 'the slings and arrows of outrageous fortune' because he was a Jew. Given that we know that anti-semitism is not dead today, it is our Christian responsibility to show 'positive discrimination' towards a people still at risk. Again, my father was right. The Jews do demand our special attention – not for theological reasons, but because of the way that they have been persecuted. Despite the belligerence of the Israeli government, the Jew remains the man beaten up on the roadside and we Christians are called to be good Samaritans. The Jew is the man or woman next door who helps me to know how to be a good neighbour.

There is another way in which I think it is important to 'read' Jewish history when we attempt to make sense of the 'the world we're in'. From quite early in their history as a nation many Jewish people have experienced exile. The very word 'diaspora', so popular today in postcolonial discourse, originally referred specifically to the Jews living outside of Palestine. I have already mentioned that Edward Said once suggested that it was the Jews' bitter experience of exile that might help them to live at peace in the same country as the Palestinians who have also known what it is to be driven away from their land. My simple thought here is that the experience of being a migrant, an exile, a refugee, a member of a diasporic community is something which belongs to more and more people in our globalised, postcolonial world . In this field of experience the Jews are the experts. Notice that some of the characters in the New Testament – Stephen (Acts 7), the writer of the book of Hebrews – themselves diaspora people, actually celebrate their 'semi-detached' situation. If only we could catch the spirit of the Jewish exile who taught that the *shekinah* went with the people of God wherever they travelled, how differently we might see the fate of the exile.

Finally, I mention, with caution, the question of the end of the age. For many Christians the fate of the state of Israel is bound up with how history itself will end. [18]Again, I think this is half right. I have no interest in detailed timetables. I do not think the establishment of the state of Israel in 1947 was predicted in the Bible, indeed I do not think that the Bible says anything about contemporary history in that predictive sort of way. What we do have in the New Testament is a warning by Jesus of the potential disaster for the people of his own day which was based on certain trends clearly visible in contemporary events. (See, for example, Matthew 23:33-9.) Now consider this comment by Uri Avnery:

> In our days, historians wonder what folly took possession of the Jewish people 1,930 years ago, causing them to start a hopeless rebellion against the Roman Empire and bringing utter destruction upon the Jewish commonwealth in Palestine. A hundred years from now, historians will ask themselves what folly took possession of this people, causing it to elect [Ariel] Sharon, a bloody person who has not done anything in life apart from shedding blood (Rose 2005, 44).

What disaster is pending for Israel and for the whole Middle East? We cannot tell, but it seems certain that we cannot go on in the way that we are – there must be a radical change. Jesus is still the Jewish Messiah, rejected no doubt, but Messiah nevertheless. (It is not really for a Gentile like me to say this, but I may be forgiven as it is part of my overall argument about the Middle East.) We are still waiting for the moment when Jewish people say again 'Blessed is he who comes in the name of the Lord'. The people of Jesus' day were in a 'last chance situation' and their last chance was to recognise the true nature of the Kingdom of God and welcome the King. The same may be true today.

---

[18] For my own stance see Appendix 2 'Eschatology and mission'.

To put it more generally, any society, however near destruction or disaster, can take advantage of the 'healing' (Revelation 22:2) that the values of God's righteous rule imparts.

The New Authoritarianism

This section is not really about postcolonialism as such but about the postcolonial world and a sort of chain reaction which it sets off among Christians. Increasingly, for many of us the impression is – and we are not wrong about this – that we are living in a fragmented and confusing world. A typical response is a distrust of any idea that God might be at work in the world outside of the church, and a retreat from engaging with the world into a narrow and dualistic theology. This in turn produces a failure of nerve which leads people to abandon positive remedies and to exchange them for reaction and denial. Thus over the last few years the 'big issues' in the life of the evangelical church such as abortion, homosexual clergy and marriage, the gathering strength of Islam (and in the UK in particular concerns about the doctrine of the atonement and the nature of blasphemy) have been characterised by *reaction*. If we are not careful we shall be getting the same sort of reputation as fundamentalist Islam, as people who authenticate themselves only by being defensive, aggressive, irrational, and unable to put forward their own positive agenda.

I have no scientific evidence for this, but my impression based on anecdote, discussion, general reading and observation is that these reactionary tendencies are increasingly common. Also, their most usual manifestation is authoritarian leadership. A selection of our leaders are exploiting the general fear and anxiety which accompanies a failure of nerve; they demand loyalty to themselves and to inflexible theological positions and demonise those who disagree with them. As a result, congregations are being split, good people are being alienated from churches they have served faithfully for years, discussion is being stifled, and the wider concerns of the Kingdom of God are being neglected. Instead of confidently presenting the gospel, we are worrying away at what we see as an attack on our fundamental beliefs and Christian lifestyle. Of course, these *are* under attack, indeed always have been, but, as I say, our reaction has been to play into the hands of a certain style of leadership. Our fears, have been exploited by authoritarian figures, who have seized on the opportunity to become shepherds of a confused and frightened flock.

Something similar is going on in the world at large, I mean the world outside of the church. It is not an illusion that our freedoms are being curtailed and that the means of democratic expression are being subverted or are falling into disuse. Wherever we look the structures of a once living democracy are proving insufficient to contain the fears (or is it the disillusionment?) of people. The behaviour of Bush and the Neocons in the US was one obvious example. This was partly because of 9/11, but also because the globalisation of the labour market without the protection of the welfare state has made Americans much more susceptible to right-wing populism. In the UK the Labour government has largely disregarded parliament and public opinion in recent years. Putin and his successor in Russia have taken a more authoritarian stance. Elsewhere there are elected hardliners in Israel and the Palestine Authority alike, and we see the apparent failure of reform in Iran, despite revolutionary protest. Right wing parties in Europe, such as the BNP in Britain or the neo-Fascists in Italy, are certainly doing better than ever before. Even where this is not expressed in electoral terms, the polarisation in European societies (as typified by the reactions to the Danish cartoons and the murder of Theo van Gogh – just to take two examples) suggests a distinct tendency. There are an abundance of examples if we look at the global picture.

Christians reflect (as may be inevitable) wider trends which are already visible in society. While this is not necessarily a bad thing – there are good and bad trends in society – we have to be discerning. For example, the present concern about environmental matters seems to me a good trend. A tendency to describe everything in economic terms, indeed to make economic worth 'the bottom line' (note the metaphor) is a bad one. I think society's 'loss of nerve' leading to a distrust in its own institutions and ways of proceeding, is also a bad trend, indeed it is almost a pathology. Some of the symptoms are:

- the weakness of the organised structures of dissent (e.g. Trade Unions) – instead we have constant radio phone-ins, television voting, or opinion polls, where it is much easier to make a quick, unconsidered, prejudiced assessment
- hopes pinned on gambling
- consumerism – it was the fascists who believed that a society addicted to consumerism was susceptible to their taking power
- the way that *domestic* policies win or lose elections
- identity politics; the clash of civilisations has become a clash of ignorances
- terrorism and the normalisation of irregular warfare
- increased ethnic loyalties: community and race to the fore

- a disconnection from the political process, both local and metropolitan together with a pride in ignorance about such matters
- a victim mentality
- a fortress mentality (these last two go together often resulting in a sort of cynicism – 'you can't trust anybody')
- fear of the future and a search for security.

This last point deserves some elaboration. The search for security goes on, all too evidently, in the way that we are prepared to surrender our liberties in the hope that 'strong government' will protect us. It is also seen in the increasing popularity of what we might call 'fearful religion'. Some aspects of Islamic religion immediately come to mind in this context. However, Islam is relying on the sort of sanctions that secure many religious systems, including at times Christianity. Fear is a real motivator after all, and the idea that society can only be saved by fear is common enough. We are all afraid of chaos and even of freedom, and as Thomas Hobbes suggested, better a society ruled by fear than a society with no ruler at all. Or, in religious terms, better that we fear God, even in an abject way, than the moral anarchy of 'every man (and woman) doing what is right in their own eyes'.

The root cause of all this fear-filled behaviour is an anxiety brought on by loneliness and alienation, a feeling that I do not fit, and a need to search for an authority which enables me to lay such personal identity issues to rest. The content of this structure of authority is to some extent immaterial; the purpose is to create a structure where people can feel at home. I say 'to some extent' because it is not that these people do not know what they believe – they often spend a great deal of time mastering their particular belief system – but the purpose of becoming expert is precisely to defend or secure the system. Behind this lies the wider purpose: to ensure that nobody tampers with their all important identity refuge. Any tampering with the system, even open discussion of it, is fiercely resisted. It does not matter, however, what the shelter looks like (i.e. what the fundamentalism is) as long as it remains robust and therefore fulfils its primary function.

If a search for greater security is typical of our society, what then of the church? As I have already suggested, Christians are not immune. Let me refer back to a couple of issues, one relatively minor and one major, as examples of Christian paranoia. Recently, in Britain there were unusual, and unusually vociferous, protests over the showing of a programme entitled *Jerry Springer – The Opera*. The screening of this material by the BBC caused much outrage among the Christian public. On the face of it, these protests may seem to be a good example of Christians finally getting their act together and speaking out against something that was manifestly wrong. Indeed, much comfort was taken from the huge numbers of Christian people who protested.

There are, however, some worrying features about the protest. First of all, what does it mean to make a stand against blasphemy? Is it right that we need to defend God's honour? What we do need to be clear about is our own presentation of the *character* of God. So God is just and God is loving and it is 'blasphemous' to represent him as unjust or unloving. Similarly a blasphemy against God is when we treat other human beings, made in the image of God, and given to us by God as our neighbours, in an unjust or unloving way. This can be extended in many directions. Comments such as 'the poor are lazy', 'I wouldn't employ him because he's black' or 'there is no such thing as society' are not only an offense against my fellow but an offense against God. 'Taking God's name in vain' is precisely representing God and his world in this way. As for swearing and mocking, well I suggest that we leave God to defend his honour, if that is what he wants to do.

One approach might be that we would naturally defend a person we loved (say our wife or husband) if we heard someone else mocking them. In the same way God's lovers feel they want to protest when he is being demeaned. But is this really analogous? God is not someone I need to protect in that sense. He does not belong to me, rather the reverse.

In any case was *Jerry Springer –The Opera* really making serious theological assertions. Think of all the statements about the content of the Christian faith that we let pass by. Indeed from within the church we have people denying the resurrection or the uniqueness of Christ and nobody says very much about it.

It is extremely worrying, too, that because of the protests against *Jerry Springer –the Opera* and similar actions, we Christians are being seen as those who line up with other 'fundamentalists'. This extends to the way the protest was conducted. There was even a hint of violence in the protests. Threats were issued and some employees of the BBC had to have their homes protected. Frankly, this was a disgrace. But even more serious is the way that we Christians are defining ourselves as a party or faction in a world which is desperately competing for recognition and 'identity'. The Muslims burn books, the Sikhs close down plays (also a recent event in our cultural calendar) and the Christians (almost) stop TV shows. Is that how it is going to be? And then there are all the things we did *not* protest about. All those civilians killed by *our* bombs in Afghanistan and Iraq; all those children who died of malnutrition and preventable diseases because of *our* trade policies, all those weapons *our* government sold to oppressive regimes which have been used to kill and maim and torture innocent people – when did we protest with a concerted Christian voice about that? And then, lo and behold, along comes a tawdry opera on the television, shown as an attempted critique of a justly infamous 'reality show', and we all come out and protest.

No, the truth is that we were speaking up for ourselves not for those 'who cannot speak up for themselves'. And here is the main point. We were expressing our fear and bewilderment that we Christians are increasingly a beleaguered minority when once we had the power to be enforcers. But, an alternative approach might be that we have actually reached a *good* place. At last Constantinianism is coming to an end. We can now start 'turning the world upside down' again. Who, after all, wants to turn things upside down when they are on top? But we are not 'on top' anymore. So we have been set free to own 'another king' who is not Caesar.

Too often Christians say, in outraged tones, that other communities would not be treated the way that we are. Would anybody on TV get away with the sort of blasphemies that were aimed at Jesus if they were aimed instead at Mohammed. This may be true but should we not be glad, first of all, that we, as a society, are beginning to understand the sensitivities of our Muslim neighbours? Surely it must be a Christian thing to do, to give them the consideration and support that they feel they need. If something really matters to them, and it does not infringe on the liberties of others – say girls wearing the headscarf in schools – then we should rejoice that our society is sufficiently tolerant that it allows this to happen. After all, we would very much like the same freedoms to be extended to us as Christians. But you might say, that is just the point. The same freedoms are not being extended to Christians; we are being more harshly treated than other religious groups. There are a number of things that can be said about this. Firstly, Christianity has for centuries been the establishment religion in the West. It is still much established. We have some way to go before there is really a level playing field. Secondly, it may be necessary at the moment to be *more* sensitive to the needs of our minorities than strict justice demands – a sort of reverse discrimination. We should be pleased when this happens. It is a sign that there are still some Christian values about. Thirdly, Christianity is, or ought to be, adopting a servant posture. We cannot in the circumstances stand on our rights and expect to be able to call in the government to help us.

Then there is the even more contentious issue of homosexuality. The *Springer* business will soon be forgotten, but the issues surrounding homosexuality are likely to be with us for a long time. Of course, this is largely a debate *within* the church (though it has a much wider field of debate in the USA, I should judge) and therefore rather different from *Jerry Springer- the Opera*. Even so, it seems to me that the nature of the debate illustrates very clearly the current climate of Christian insecurity. I am not, I should add, judging the issue at this point. Let us assume that there are genuinely divergent views among Christians and that this is bound to cause debate and strong feelings. The question is: how are we going to deal with the matter?

My first question is a very simple one. Why is it so often matters to do with sex that get church people so worked up? We know about sex, do we not? We have not, I think, discovered something recently about it that we never knew before. We also know, as Christians, that we have a tendency to give it too much prominence. When people are accused of 'misbehaving' we usually mean sexual misbehaviour. Young people have been put out of church fellowship for 'living together' but nobody is disciplined for graft or greed or pride or anger. The fact that we hardly ever talk about sex in church – after the sermon people are more likely to chat about the sporting results or the weather than their sex life – means, I suspect, that it is something we are still rather frightened of. Frankly, it is this fearful and irrational promotion of sexual sins to a place of undue prominence in the league table of deadly sins that has made it so difficult for us to talk sensibly about the homosexual issue. Using the test I applied to the blasphemy issue, why is it that there are a whole clutch of potentially church splitting disputes – over such matters as the historicity of the resurrection, the uniqueness of Jesus, the authority of the Bible – and nobody much has said that it is time for us to go our separate ways? I am not, of course, suggesting that as things stand we need to split the church on any of these matters, my point is that we can sit down and take communion with people who have expressed doubts, it may be, on all of these issues, and yet we cannot with those who disagree with us about homosexuality. I know that some people have said that this is a matter of standing up for the authority of the Bible, but I think that is just playing a game. If we were so concerned about that, we did not have to wait until the homosexuality issue came along for us to take action. Questions about the authority of the Bible have been around since the middle of the nineteenth century.

Once again, we end up in a position which allows our enemies to feel that all their worst suspicions are confirmed. They always knew that we were hung up on sex. They have long suspected that we were more interested in our own respectability and 'purity' than in the things that should really make us distinctive as Christians such as loving our enemies and being with the poor. They see us as standing in the way of every progressive movement – the emancipation of women, freedom of speech, gay and lesbian rights – and doing this because we are part of the religious establishment which has always opposed change. Now this is a caricature. But there is enough truth in it to make us stop and think. I can only say the same thing about the issue itself. We need to stop and think about that, too. The dispute itself certainly has got out of proportion.

If the way that we handle protest and dispute is the symptom, what are the causes? Obviously these are many and complex, but in the context of this essay, I want to highlight one in particular. It is the speed of change (what Alvin Toffler called 'future shock') in this globalised and postcolonial world. There are several aspects to this, such as the weakness of the institutional church and its minority status, the end of denominationalism, a more multicultural society, the resurgence of other world religions, post-imperial realities, the growth of terrorism, global warming, employment mobility and the like. Many of these look like the 'usual suspects'. Global warming or terrorism would be on anybody's list of anxieties, but I want to apply this list to Christian people in particular.

I have already commented on our discomfiture that the church, certainly as an institution, seems to grow daily more peripheral to the concerns of ordinary people, is less able to make itself heard, is more legislated against, in a word is weaker. For the older generation (say, people over forty) who have thought of the church as at the very least a *respected* institution, this can come as a profound shock. Along with this goes the feeling, even among Christians, that church attendance is not such a sure sign of Christian belonging as it used to be. The so-called 'emerging church' is one symptom of this. So is the widespread feeling that church attendance is more like shopping at the supermarket: I go because I get what I need, but I do not really feel any great loyalty to one chain store rather than another; it is just a matter of sorting out what suits me best in terms of product, price and access. Denominational loyalties are also open to question. People, especially but not only young people, do not really care very much nowadays about denominational traditions. If these sorts of loyalties are breaking down, how do you *measure* people's depth of real Christian commitment. If the answer is that we cannot, this is also profoundly unsettling. One of the responses to this situation is to try to define ourselves more precisely. So, for example, evangelicalism becomes more fiercely evangelical, and of course this is precisely where the 'new authoritarianism' comes in.

It is a truism that our society is more than ever 'mixed'. This is an obvious product of postcolonialism and globalisation. Even our churches may be 'invaded' by people who come 'from the ends of the earth', and though we make a show of welcoming them, we often find this quite difficult. (In Britain, to our shame, we have often excluded these people, and certainly made little attempt to allow them to express their own cultures in our churches.) However, even where we have steadfastly retained the homogeneous nature of our congregation, there is a certain uneasiness about the fact that we are surrounded by people of different colour, belief and culture, and are not really doing anything about it. It is all very unsettling. We do not see the arrival of people in our neighbourhood from different cultures than ours as an opportunity so much as a threat. We cannot altogether ignore them but we do not know how to approach them either. It was much simpler when mission meant sending people overseas. Now the missiologists say that mission is 'from everywhere to everywhere' . There are even Christians from the Global South who have come to evangelise us! In some ways, our response to these new situations is our own Christian way of making the wider adjustment that people have had to make to the end of Empire and the postcolonial reality. Also we have to add in the religious dimension to the cultural one. It is hard enough to adjust to new cultures, but what about the challenge of religious pluralism? A simple question such as – how do I relate day to day to my Muslim neighbour? – can be difficult enough in the current climate. Working through the relationship of Christianity to Islam and other faiths is even trickier.

Terrorism and climate change have made us feel less physically secure, and here we Christians are in the same boat as everybody else. I wonder, however, whether Christians do not feel uniquely under pressure when it comes to explaining the bad news that all too often makes up today's headlines. In times of crisis when people are hurting and afraid, theodicy is a risky game. It is also full of possible miscommunications and misunderstandings. Recent attempts by some Anglican bishops to comment on the severe flooding experienced in the north of England have not gone down well in the media, for example. While we must honour these church leaders for not remaining silent (too often the church's approach) and can agree with them that there is a link between the West's greedy lifestyle and climate change, their singling out for particular blame the 'sexual orientation regulations' (see above on the church's fixation on issues of sexual behaviour) seems a spectacular mistake. Again, the fact that terrorism is so often 'Islamic terrorism' (in the press anyway) and that religion is seen (as in Richard Dawkins and his friends) as the problem rather than the solution, is also confusing.

Lastly, we are all on the move so much more, and that too affects us as Christian people, not just individually – though that is true – but in terms of our communities. I am not here referring to people changing church membership because they prefer another church in the vicinity, though, as we have seen, that is hugely on the increase. People simply have to move more often, usually for reasons of employment. Thus, the membership of churches is changing at an unprecedented rate, and for those who are trying to build a stable and effective community, this is a huge challenge. Not surprisingly, one response to this situation is to huddle together more closely in whatever ways that is possible. Huddling together can lead to a sort of 'fortress mentality' and that may be right in certain circumstances. But we need to beware that we do not turn our fortress into a prison.

Pedagogical and performative

The terms 'pedagogical' and 'performative' were originally coined as part of the postcolonial discourse by Homi Bhabha in the context of nation building. He writes of 'two incompatible opposites', the construction of an ideal image of the nation ('pedagogical') whereby it is seen as having an essentialist character, something to be discovered and passed on, and the idea of the nation as socially manufactured ('performative'), which enables all those placed on the margins of its norms and limits – such as women, migrants, the working class, the peasantry, those of a different 'race' or ethnicity – to *intervene* in the signifying process and *challenge* the dominant representations with their own.' (McLeod 2000, 119). Obviously this can be extended beyond nations to the family, the church or even team building. The 'pedagogical' approach would then mean that the appropriate authority will teach the true nature of the nation, the family, the church, the team; 'performative' would mean that we are together creating new forms of nation, family, church and team, which, because it does not appeal to irreducible and fixed norms, can include new elements in our performance. (Of course this does not mean that we ignore the past – this is also one of the elements in our performance.)

I am reminded here of the description of 'midrash' as currently understood by Biblical scholars. This is J. A. Sanders' description:

> The purpose of midrash was to call on Scripture to interpret contemporary life and history. When the ancients believed that what was happening to them was part of God's plan, and that God was acting in their day, they reported their belief and those events in scriptural terms. They engaged in re-signification of Scripture in order to understand themselves and what was happening to them. There was a two-way process: their context was signified by Scripture and Scripture was re-signified in its high adaptability to speak to many contexts (Evans 1989, 168).

Jacqueline Rose, commenting on her sister Gillian's work puts it this way:

> Against the vision of Judaism as 'unchanging, without history' she [Gillian Rose] offered us the early rabbis endlessly renegotiating 'knowledge and responsibility under their historically and politically changing conditions'…The key to Talmudic argument resides in its complex relation to a rationalism which is interrogated but never left behind, 'a rationalism which constantly explores its own limits without fixing them' (Rose 2007, 226).

This Talmudic approach contrasts with a more 'scientific', propositional and Enlightenment way of interpreting history or Scripture and this is a possible explanation for something which has puzzled me recently. In a theological discussion on the Trinity I was surprised when a Chinese colleague of mine indicated that such a debate would have little currency among Chinese Christians. They were happy to accept a Trinitarian theology in broad outline but the real question was whether the debate contributed to a more meaningful praxis. How did the idea of Trinity work out in daily living? Another colleague who had worked for many years in Africa agreed that a similar approach would have been likely there. Perhaps this also relates to the 'pedagogical' and 'performative' paradigms. The former leads to an attempt to make 'once for all' statements that we can all subscribe to, to refine a series of propositions that exclude error and draw precise boundaries. The latter moves on from the propositions to praxis. How, so to speak, can we 'perform' the doctrine of the Trinity in daily life?

Another way of looking at these two contrasting approaches is through Zygmunt Bauman's legislative and interpretive reason. Bauman, a sociologist, suggests that sociology at its best is seen as an interpretive skill as against a legislative use of reason. Social study, on this view, should be embedded in a particular 'life-world' or 'communal tradition'. (There are many of these and it is not sociology's purpose to reduce the number.) The strategy is to discern the meaning of the tradition from within and then to translate it with as little damage as possible into a form assimilable by one's own tradition. This is supposed to be a process of mutual enrichment. Interpretive reason also accepts that the job of community building is never-ending. It is a process rather than a blueprint. David Harvey, in drawing up a list of what he describes as 'the basic framework' of the social process, speaks not of 'elements' but of 'moments'. He says 'I use the word "moment" in order to avoid, as far as possible, any sense of prior crystallisation of processual activities into "permanences" – things, entities, clearly bound domains, or systems'(Harvey 1996, 78).

This overall approach – performative, interpretive, processual – has consequences. First, it involves an inevitable attack on power hierarchies which are by their very nature attempts to subsume and foreclose the argument. As has often been noticed, an absence of contingency, a claim that there is no other future but this present, is a necessary weapon for total systems. Interpretive reason is also an attack on 'privileged' knowledge, that there is a 'true' interpretation which can declare all other interpretations invalid. A second consequence is that plurality is known as a blessing not a curse. Indeed it has become the constitutive feature of being as such. Human existence is inevitably ambivalent and contingent. Thirdly interpretive reason refuses to position itself outside of the inevitably local and particular discourse and to seek grounds other than those which that discourse provides. It accepts as inevitable its own 'insidedness' and defiantly believes that it can turn that to its advantage.

Both Homi Bhabha and Zygmunt Bauman clearly favour one of their two options. Bauman is making a pitch for interpretive reason and Bhabha for the performative. There is a balance to be maintained, however. As Paul Ricoeur would have it, in every situation there is both a need to be willing to listen and a need to judge (the latter is the famous 'hermeneutics of suspicion'). He calls for both 'a vow of obedience' and 'a vow of rigour', an openness to symbols and a doing away with idols' (Thistleton 1992, 344). If we are building, for example, a new inter cultural team, we must both listen to the cultural wisdom already available to us through the experience of the team members and at the same time be aware that not everything that has the sanction of past experience is helpful or suitable.

The overall framework of 'pedagogical' and 'performative' provides a number of opportunities for missiological reflection. It might be an opportunity, for example, to sort out the proclamation/dialogue debate which has been going on for such a long time in missiological circles.[19] Again, the very word 'pedagogical' reminds us of Paolo Freire's approach to education (1996). Freire's idea of 'conscientisation' is precisely the opposite of a pedagogical approach whereby the teacher is seen as the infallible 'guru' handing down wisdom from above. This is a familiar theme, but that does not mean that it is something which we have dealt with adequately in Christian circles. Much of our approach to teaching and preaching remains highly authoritarian. Freire's idea of 'generative themes' whereby topics for discussion arise out of the experience of the community, and then generate open-ended debate is still little heeded, except perhaps in some development circles. In some ways the value of debate and discussion is at the heart of the postcolonial preference for performative rather than pedagogical solutions. The pedagogical has something 'military' about it.

I am reminded here of Salman Rushdie's humorous parable about the two armies in *Haroun and the Sea of Stories* (1991). The armies in question were notable for their different attitudes to authority. The Chupwala army was characterised by grim silence and unquestioning obedience to orders; the Guppee army was famous for its tendency to discuss everything, even orders that came down from the highest authority.

> 'What an army', Haroun mused, 'If any soldiers behaved like this on Earth, they'd be court-martialled quick as thinking.' 'But but but what is the point of giving persons Freedom of Speech', declaimed Butt the Hoopoe, 'if you then say they must not utilise same? And is not the Power of Speech the greatest Power of all? Then surely it must be utilised to the full?' (119)

In the event when the two armies came to battle the Guppees were immediately victorious. The Guppees fought with a common purpose.

> 'All those arguments and debates, all that openness, had created powerful bonds of fellowship between them.'(185)

The Chupwalas, however, proved to be a rabble.

---

[19] See above p. 133 for an initial attempt at this.

> 'Their vows of silence and their habits of secrecy had made them suspicious and distrustful of one another. They had no faith in their general, either.'(185)

This may seem an unlikely, even foolish, story but many a Christian organisation might benefit from it. Of course as Christians we are rightly taught the value of obedience. A friend of mine used to have on his desk the verse 'Whatever he says to you, do it' from John 2: 5, a text which might be thought to imply that it was Jesus' role to give the orders and ours to carry them out, however unreasonable they sounded. Somebody once remarked that the verse did not say 'Whatever he says to you, *discuss* it.' But even there, we have to be careful. Think of the number of times that Jesus' teaching consisted of asking questions. Think also of the way that Paul appealed to his readers to work through difficult issues, even, perhaps at the expense of his own authority. ('I speak to sensible people; judge for yourselves what I say.' 1 Corinthians 10:15) Also, we do not have the direct link to authority that the gospel writers had. Like it or not we are interpreters.

Above all, from a missiological point of view the preference for the performative links up with the theme that has constantly recurred in these pages: the 'construction' of the Kingdom of God. The task which awaits us is the discovery of new inclusive forms which reflect the 'wisdom of God in its infinite variety' (Ephesians 3:10) and enable us to pursue God's mission in God's way.

Chapter Four

What next for mission?

Can we be optimistic about mission from a postcolonial perspective? Let me sketch out the scenario as we might like it to be. At the beginning of the modern missionary movement Christianity was largely a European affair. Then, as a result of the efforts of thousands of missionaries, Christianity began to grow and thrive in other parts of the world, notably Latin America, sub-Saharan Africa, Oceania and parts of Asia. Now the centre of world Christianity has moved from the West to the South. This is particularly significant because Christianity in the West is beginning to decline. Many are conjecturing that the only way that the West can be saved is if it is re-introduced to the gospel, and that this could happen by means of a reverse flow of missionaries from the South.

Why might this, rather simplistic, description be described as a 'postcolonial perspective'? At the heart of postcolonialism is the understanding that the colonising and colonised worlds are still bound together by their colonial pasts. The large number of European citizens who have an African, Middle Eastern, Latin American or Asian origin is just one sign of this. The extension of Christianity to the South as a result of the modern missionary movement is part of the South's colonial experience – a good part, we might argue, but colonial nevertheless. The re-evangelising of the West by the South (if that is what happens) will be an example of postcolonialism, analogous to the way that Asian and African writers have successfully mastered various

Western academic disciplines, a sort of 'The Empire strikes back' scenario. Postcolonialism began as a field of literary study. My suggestion is that we should now add to postcolonialism the field of missiology.

The modern missionary movement

There were, almost from the start imperialist and elitist aspects to mission. Let me illustrate this from the Indian context. Alexander Duff, a leading light in the missionary community from the 1830s onwards, belonged to the era when missionaries were beginning to be respectable in the eyes of government, and their agenda was a 'civilising' one. They were feeding off the attitudes of men like Grant at the India Office and Bentinck in Calcutta (today's Kolkata) who were Enlightenment style reformers. Thomas Macaulay's famous educational programme of Anglicisation[20] fitted Duff precisely. Duff quite deliberately targeted the wealthy and influential Indian classes in the hope of winning them over to Christianity, and his 'trickle down' approach remained a feature of much Indian mission, particularly educational mission, thereafter (Ingleby 2000, 56).

Duff and his colleagues give us just one example. The pattern, as I have suggested, applies to the modern missionary enterprise as a whole. Here are some of the typical ingredients.

a. A link with commercial expansion, which was not always reprehensible but which certainly often had a dubious moral foundation. (The link with the opium trade in the early days of Chinese missionary enterprise, for example, is particularly worrying.)
b. More seriously, the whole drive towards cultural imperialism, often with apparently good motives, but with a clear admixture of racial pride, was an aspect of much missionary work. Can missionaries like Alexander Duff be exonerated here?
c. Whatever the motives, what about the damage done? Consider the evidence from the South Sea Islands and Latin America in particular. In general, was the missionary attack on other cultures, say in India, a part of the process which made secular values (rather than Christian ones) the currency of the future (Ingleby 2000, 291-4)?
d. Mission became stuck in the role of self-styled 'benefactors' (Luke 22:25). The missionaries were too rich to help the poor.

---

[20] See above p. 51

The truth is that the gifts bestowed on the new born missionary movement mostly came from a malevolent past – Enlightenment thought, venture capitalism, a Christendom model of Christianity, denominationalism, authoritarianism, patriarchalism, and alliance with State violence. There was some hope, of course, that some of this baggage would be thrown away when it became evident that it was useless – like explorers who jettison cargo in order to lighten the ship – and this did happen from time to time. There is evidence, for example, that missionaries in India were far less worried about denominational differences than their supporters at home. Sadly, however, in most cases missionaries not only took their baggage with them but were unable to let it go and then passed it on to their successors. This failure to contextualise was depressingly common. The modern missionary movement was a God given opportunity to start something new, especially to undo the religion of power which Christianity had become. On the whole, this never happened. The dreary catalogue – commercial attitudes, cultural and linguistic imperialism, theological insensitivity, racial superiority, identification with the powerful, unwillingness to relinquish control and so on – anything but humble service of the servant Jesus – remained in place, even among the high-minded.

As an example we might take Henry Scott Holland and his well-known hymn, 'Judge Eternal'.

> Judge eternal, throned in splendour
>
> Lord of lords and King of kings,
>
> With thy living fire of judgement
>
> Purge this land of bitter things;
>
> Solace all its wide dominion
>
> With the healing of thy wings.
>
>
> Still the weary folk are pining
>
> For the hour that brings release;

And the city's crowded clangour

Cries aloud for sin to cease;

And the homesteads and the woodlands

Plead in silence for their peace.

Crown, O God, thine own endeavour;

Cleave our darkness with thy sword;

Feed the faint and hungry heathen

With the riches of thy Word;

Cleanse the body of this Empire

Through the glory of the Lord.

Scott Holland was a Christian socialist, a founder of the Christian Socialist Movement, and a prolific writer on social affairs at the turn of the nineteenth and twentieth centuries. He was also a Christian imperialist. I am not trying here to describe the sort of behaviour which we all know characterised Western imperialism. It is easy to see now that that had a very dark side – from the Atlantic slave trade to the Opium Wars to Leopold's Congo. There were those, like Scott Holland, who gave imperialism a brighter aspect. Who could not hope that 'this land' would be purged of bitter things and be healed? People in city and countryside alike were crying out for renewal and only God himself could dispel the darkness, feed the hungry, cleanse the nation. Should we not cry to him to do so? Look a little closer, however. Where are the 'wide dominions' mentioned in the first verse, who are 'the faint and hungry heathen' in the third. Doesn't the word 'empire' in the second last line come with a slight sense of shock? In fact, Scott Holland is unashamedly asking God to bless the British Empire! And this was a persistent theme of Victorian and Edwardian Christianity. It is God who has given us our Empire. He gave it to us for a purpose, so that the new day of civilisation might dawn and the light of the gospel might spread. The Cambridge missionary, H. C. Carlyon, working among the Jats of the Rohak district, showed no embarrassment in linking the success of the British in seizing India with the claims of Christianity. For example, 'Is it not strange that a handful of men from a distant country could conquer your country when it was protected by the three hundred and thirty million gods that you believe in' (Ingleby 2000, 314)?

Many mission histories bear a proudly remembered record of the way that the missionaries 'handed over' to the national church. Well – better late than never! But the question is: what did they hand over? Is it not possible that they handed down to their successors much that hindered them; that they preached the good news of the Kingdom, but systematically demonstrated worldly values; that social transformation was accompanied by far more powerful social reproduction? 'I received from the missionaries, what I now pass on to you.' Much anxiety has been expressed that the church of the South should remain 'true to the gospel' by which we in the West mean that they should agree with us. It would be a happier situation, I suggest, if they were *less* like us.

We white Westerners forget too easily. We would like to sweep the issues of colonialism, racial prejudice and slavery, with its accompanying tale of destruction, exploitation, greed and cruelty under the table. But that it is because we were the perpetrators and have become the inheritors and beneficiaries. We must remember to ask the victims what *they* think. If you ask a mixed group from the West and the Global South about what have been, in their opinion, the most important events of the last fifty years, I suspect that the Europeans will mention such matters as the fall of Communism and the environmental crisis. However, in my experience, those from the Global South have different memories and will invariably nominate the end of Western colonialism. *They* have not forgotten. The right sort of memories matter hugely in mission, as in every other sphere of life, and they need to inform any meaningful attempt to create a missiology for today. Much of our thinking about mission history and therefore about mission is still too triumphalistic, too Eurocentric, too androcentric – in a word, too colonial.

At the heart of the debate lies the question which haunts every aspect of our Christian ministry. Do you start from a position of strength or of weakness? There is a paradox here, as we know. We almost invariably start out from a position of superiority, thinking we have something to give. We believe ourselves to be 'benefactors', but Jesus had something to say about that (Luke 22:25, 26). In a larger sense, this is the Enlightenment and also the Development fallacy. There is a permanent exhibition on the Enlightenment in the British Museum. Looking at it, it does not take long to realise that the Enlightenment was an organisational power game. There was a rage to put things in order and thus to control them and to control those who were supposedly disorganised. How do you subvert, Jesus must have asked himself, a system as well organised as the Jewish debt and purity systems by which the Jewish leaders of his day controlled the people to their own advantage? Beyond that, how do you subvert something as formidably well organised as the Roman Empire? Well, we know well enough that the mission of the church was born in weakness.

> He, the Servant, grew up before Him (Yahweh) like a young plant, and like a root out of the dry ground. He had no form or majesty that we should look at him, nothing in his appearance that we should desire him. He was despised and rejected by others; a man of suffering and acquainted with weakness; and as one from whom others hide their faces he was despised, and we held him of no account...By perversion of justice he was taken away. Who could have imagined his future? (Isaiah 53:2,3, 7a)

We have to consider the possibility that it is better to do our ministry from the bottom. I was in Southall in West London, recently and the Bishop of Willesden, Peter Broadbent, reminded his congregation that in Southall Christianity was only the fourth largest religious group, after the Sikhs. Hindus and Muslims. He suggested that there might be some advantages in witnessing to their faith in this 'non-imperialistic' (his words) situation.

I suspect that we are still practising a sort of Western cultural domination today. Consider the sloganeering that went with the 10/40 window, people groups, sort of approach. Consider also what might be styled 'conference Christianity' or even 'conference mission'. This is part of a managerial approach to mission which fits in well with the global managerial culture but bypasses the costly demands of enculturation and incarnation. A friend of mine reported her recent conversation with a North American missiologist who was happy to state that the responsibility of the West is now to 'manage mission'. By this he meant offering expertise, finance and direction but doing it at a distance. It seems that we can all stay 'in Jerusalem' after all.

Of course, I do not wish to denigrate in some wholesale fashion the way that mission thinkers and leaders in the West have responded to the collapse of European colonialism. For some time now, there has been an earnest effort to get away from 'the bad old days' of 'the West to the rest', to divest ourselves of an Enlightenment centred theology with an uncontextualised gospel, and of churches controlled by the missionaries instead of the nationals: this is all very familiar, and not very radical any more, though it still needs working at in some cases. My question is whether events have not once more overtaken us. As mission responds, albeit slowly, to the changes in the world's climate of thought (a process which is both good and bad and to some extent inevitable) are we being dragged into a 'new missionary imperialism'? Let me advance some propositions, some of which I have mentioned already.

- The significant action in mission remains in the West. Financial resources, technology, educational opportunities, publishing opportunities, conferences etc. are still predominantly Western controlled. Why is this the case? There should have been changes by now.
- Tricontinental Christian leaders have been co-opted into this Western dominance, as described in the section on 'the inheritors' above[21]. I see this as an increasing trend.
- At a more profound level there is evidence that the *model* for Christian practice is increasingly North American, even in the churches of Africa, Latin America and Asia. I can mention the following: (1) big rally events with healings and dramatic manifestations largely reminiscent of revivalism and tele-evangelism in North America. (2) a disavowal of the past, of tradition and sometimes of accumulated experience and wisdom (for example the rejection of the leadership of elders) (3) a prosperity gospel (4) cultural styles in worship that are 'western' rather than indigenous (though not 'classical' i.e. not necessarily those inherited from their missionary past).
- There is a huge increase in short term mission or 'mission trips' with young people visiting 'mission locations' for a few weeks during vacations. Mission of this sort can be all too easily reduced to 'Christian tourism' to exotic locations. The new missionary remains the privileged outsider, the voyeur Westerner, the representative of a superior civilisation. There is no need to struggle with the difficult and humbling task of learning language and culture. There is some raising of awareness ('I never realised how these people lived') but little recognition that *their* poverty is mostly *our* fault. This may seem to be a bizarre comparison, but I am reminded of the difference between the old colonialism and the new. 'Old colonialism' became settler colonialism and, to some extent, integrated into the new society. There were wars of conquest but the purpose of these was to make it possible to stay and 'civilise'. New imperialism however is in for the 'quick fix' (think Afghanistan). 'Staying on' is precisely not on the

---

[21] See above p. 30

agenda. Hit them quick and get out. Is short term mission little more than another way of expressing the ephemerality of our globalised postmodern culture where we no longer invest in long term relationships and have a pick-and-mix attitude to cultural experience? Cultural exchange rather than personal change is now the order of the day. We do often say about the young people who go on short term mission that they are changed by the experience, and it is probably this belief that encourages us to invest so much in the process in the first place. But changed at what level? Equally those who welcome them are also introduced to a new world. The danger is that they may see the visit of short termers merely as an opportunity to link with generous foreign donors, or to open up the possibility of a return visit. This may seem a rather cynical description, but in fact it is simply one aspect of globalisation – cultural exchange with the economic power lying in the West.

- The 'globalisation of mission' sounds good, but the de-territorialisation of mission (as of international politics) too often simply empowers those who have access to the networks (the gatekeepers) and we all know where they live.
- American theological preoccupations and debates still (perhaps increasingly) dominate world-wide theological agendas. Here are some examples: (1) the concentration on 'people groups' in mission (2) the inerrancy debate – long past its 'sell-by date' (3) trying to separate the gospel into evangelism on one hand and social concern on the other (4) an emphasis on a particular premillennial eschatology linked with concerns about the state of Israel, despite the fact that there is a great deal of doubt about the Biblical interpretation that the premillennialists espouse. Even among premillennialists there is much disagreement. American Christian leaders should look around and understand what difficulties they are creating for other Christians in mission on an issue which, in terms of world Christian belief, they are a minority. Eschatology, at that level of detailed interpretation, is not, after all, a fundamental belief. All that the great creeds of the church say is that 'he (Jesus) will come again to judge the quick and the dead'. It is a form of American theological imperialism to force eschatology so high up the agenda.
- There is still much racial prejudice among us.
- We treat other cultures as 'exotic', ours as normative. The West is metropolitan, the South is suburban or rural.
- We are still beset by 'orientalist' stereotypes: black people are lazy; Orientals are devious or 'inscrutable'; Arabs are oppressive of democratic values; Muslims are terrorists; foreign governments are usually corrupt (especially in Africa).

- We (Europeans) believe that all immigrants are illegal or a threat to our way of life, except when we need them to *maintain* our way of life.
- The 'fashions' of the West – its managerialism, consumerism, economism, progress-driven ideology – are still held up as desirable models.
- Worse still, we Christians have used our faith to bolster our sense of superiority. We know that we are superior because God has demonstrated his favour to us in an unmistakable way. Otherwise how do you explain that we in the West are prosperous and powerful and others are poor and weak? Actually you could argue almost the reverse. God started to become distant to us just as we became wealthy and powerful. It is not the poor who need us so much as the wealthy who need the poor. We the non-poor need the poor so that we can understand how God works in the world without the distancing and distortion that wealth brings. Christianity has declined in the West (Europe i.e.) *because* of the way that we tied Christianity to imperialism. Callum Brown has demonstrated (Brown 2001, 195 and *passim*) that effective Christian piety migrated after 1800 from the public masculine sphere to the home and the feminine sphere, a necessary way of marginalising religion in the 'real' Britain because at the time we were engaged in the essentially unchristian enterprise of capitalism and world domination. To put it crudely, the captains of British commerce and their military allies found Christianity an inconvenient partner in their imperialistic ventures, and decided to leave it at home with the women. This may not have damaged institutional religion, but it may have 'killed the faith that gave it meaning' as Karen Armstrong has suggested.[22] Thus it was that in many cases where Christianity was exported after 1800 it reflected its increasingly institutional character. Even at home, I suspect, the godly left their values in church while they colonised and exploited their own people in the nation's mines and factories. I am not saying, of course, that Methodism and the Evangelical Revival had no influence on public life in Britain and elsewhere, but I am saying that the practice of successful commerce through empire and industrialisation seems, largely, to have been exempt from these influences! I should add that Empire builders are permanently at this sort of disadvantage. It is characteristic of imperialism that it is frequently pious in its discourse, but ruthless and corrupt in practice.
- Finally, we have transferred *colonial* Christianity to the Global South by means of an insufficiently contextualised gospel – a *Western* Christianity at a fairly deep level, leading to a syncretistic response. This process

---

[22] See 'That's Us in the Corner, Losing our Religion' a review of Brown's book in the *Independent*, 21 December 2000

continues. Despite the apparent failure of the secularisation theory, secularism remains a powerful force and one of the West's chief exports!

These points are only a sample. I truly believe that the world is a sadder and more dangerous place today than it was, let us say, twenty years ago. Then we lived in hope that the end of colonialism and the fall of the Soviet system would together bring us to a new era of freedom and *shalom*. Instead we have fallen into a new imperialism. All too often Christians in the West have gone along with this 'new world order', and this is reflected in our defective mission life and practice. We still believe that God is on *our* side, that *we* are the 'channel of blessing' that God has chosen to use. We offer others pity, salvation, and even service, but not, I think, equality.

The South and the West

So what about the good news that, despite the failures of the West, the church in the Global South has grown and prospered and may yet prove to be the missionary church of the future? I should say at the outset that I am by no means as optimistic as all this sounds. Crucially, it is very difficult to take the colonial out of postcolonialism, or to put it another way, we have no choice but to write the history of the modern missionary movement under the heading of colonialism, and this has its consequences. Postcolonialism is certainly a better place to be than colonialism, but the former quickly shades back into the latter and the ill effects of the colonial era are not that easily shaken off.

The Churches in the South

First of all, have the churches in the South been fully redeemed from their colonial origins? At this point I can imagine an angry response. 'Who gave you, a Westerner, the right to ask this sort of question? Is this not just another example of colonial attitudes?' I have two initial responses to that. Firstly, you will notice that I am not trying to excuse colonialism, as tends to be the fashion nowadays, quite the reverse. I think that colonialism is an almost unmitigated evil. I think that if Christianity had come to the South more often 'under the sign of weakness' as it did to, say, the Roman Empire in the first three centuries of Christian growth, then that would have been better. Instead it usually came 'under the sign of power'. The initial growth of Christianity in

Latin America (under the sign of the *conquistadores!*) is the most depressing example of this, but there are many others we could give. Secondly, I find that when I accuse the church in the South of ongoing colonial attitudes, then many Christians from the South agree with me. To draw an analogy from another field, we could cite Chinua Achebe's *Anthills of the Savannah* (2001), a critique of modern Nigerian politics and society in the form of a highly readable and beautifully constructed novel. Achebe is trying to re-constitute African society by means of a re-assertion of some of the values of African traditional ways. As a natural corollary to this he is suspicious of any idea of an Africa which might flourish by means of modernity, and even the best of the moderns in his story fail to escape the perils of western-style elitism. This postcolonialism of Achebe does not, however, allow him to excuse the failure of African leadership simply because it is African, indeed he fiercely attacks contemporary African political culture. In doing so he is predictably contemptuous of the behaviour of corrupt Westernised politicians, but he does not rely entirely on traditional wisdom either, rather on a mixture of revolutionary passion and concern for ordinary people. So the situation is complicated in a postcolonial way. In the same way, Christians from the Global South are often far less starry-eyed than many Westerners about the way that the church in the South is developing.

Let me be forthright and mention some of the ways that I think that the church in the South remains colonial in its thinking. I am generalising, of course, and can, myself, think of exceptions to every one of the points I am about to make. That does not make the generalisations untrue. After all, to speak about 'the South saving the West' is also to use a very generalised term.

As I have already said, many of the problems that have been bequeathed to the church in the South are simply to do with the bad example set by Western missionaries. If I speak about the church as being hierarchical, patriarchal, territorial, insufficiently contextualised and yet culturally determined, legalistic and more concerned with membership than discipleship, then the first thing to say is that the church in the West, the 'sending church' of the modern missionary movement, displayed all these characteristics. It is not that surprising if some of this has rubbed off! It may be, of course, that some of these same characteristics are found in the Southern churches because they have inherited them from their own cultural background rather than the missionaries. It may be. But we need to examine one thing at a time. Was the 'missionary inheritance' always something positive? I can give a political analogy. When one looks back to decolonisation there is a proud record of power being transferred. 'Freedom at midnight' in India for example. Very often the claim is that this was voluntary (not true!) and that we, the British, handed down the very best of our heritage (also not true): superior technology, parliamentary democracy, an efficient and honest civil service and so on. But why should our successors really believe that that was what we valued when we demonstrated quite *other* values when *we* were in power? We had certainly not ruled democratically in India. Indian industry and technology were not allowed to thrive if it competed with ours. Indians were not allowed into the top jobs in the Civil Service.

In many ways 'democracy' is a test case. In the case of the British Empire, there was, I think, a more or less sincere attempt to bequeath democracy to ex-colonies as the Empire collapsed. Since then there has been much sorrow expressed that the ex-colonies have, in many cases, turned away from democracy. But should we Westerners really be surprised that some autocratic, hierarchical, not to mention corrupt, ways surfaced after de-colonisation? After all, whatever we said about democracy and the like, our practice when *we* were in power was completely different. The way we ruled colonies was certainly autocratic and hierarchical and often corrupt. In like manner, in colonial days, in many cases missionaries ran the churches, controlling church government and church finance and systematically taking the credit for the work of others. There was often covert racism and contempt for unfamiliar cultures.

I am not simply saying here that Western missionaries sometimes behaved badly. There is no new news in that! What I am saying is that this had consequences which may reach down to the present. I am also saying, more controversially, that for this reason as well as some others, we cannot simply accept that the churches of the South have got it right, even if they appear to be growing and successful. Let me describe in a little more detail some of my concerns about ways in which the church is developing in the South.

a. Hierarchical

The Western church has a poor record in this respect. From very early times leadership roles that were fluent and charismatic in New Testament times hardened into hierarchical institutional structures that were solidified even further by Constantinianism. The Reformation was supposed to address this issue (and there were those like the Anabaptists who certainly did) but overall it never went very far and authoritarian and hierarchical church structures remained the norm. Though there were radical protests, it was the voice of a very small minority. The modern missionary movement carried with it not only the conservatism of establishment Christianity but also the sense of intellectual and cultural superiority that came from the Enlightenment, and, sadly, a fair degree of racial pride. Some of this has been passed on, indeed, in my experience, nearly all the churches in the South with which I am familiar struggle with this issue.

b. Patriarchal

I remember a well-known British Anglican feminist rejoicing publicly when, at the Lambeth Conference in 1999, the African bishops took a strong stand (as they are doing today) against what they called 'homosexual practice in the church'. She used this as an instance of the way that the Southern church could come to the rescue of wayward Westerners, with the added thought that we did not like it very much when they did. However, when asked about patriarchal attitudes, also displayed by the Southern leaders at the Conference, she was more reticent! When the day comes that 'the Empire strikes back' we may not be able to pick and choose. The struggle against patriarchy in the Western church has been a long and at least partially successful one. Despite pockets of resistance in the Church of England and elsewhere, it seems likely that the admission of women to the ministry was the really big revolution. I cannot see the Western church wanting to go back to a more patriarchal stance. But what if the churches in the South see feminism, even if it is a Christian feminism, as another example of a damaging Western secularism, clearly contrary to the plain teaching of Scripture? On what grounds will that be sorted out?

c. Territorial

For centuries together European Christianity was hopelessly territorial. Christendom was a place. The post-Reformation solution was to have different places – Protestant Holland but Catholic Spain – for different sorts of believers. The Edict of Nantes in France was revolutionary because it agreed that Huguenots could be loyal Protestants and loyal French citizens at the same time; but the Edict of Nantes was revoked. Roman Catholics did not get decent civil rights in the UK until the nineteenth century. The churches of the South have followed suit. Thus, territory and property are the marks of a successful church, one that is beginning to take root. According to this view, government, local and even national, exists to reflect the wishes of the Christian majority. Christian hospitals are not so much a means of outreach or 'to show the love of Jesus to a suffering world' but something for the Christian community. Christian schools are to give 'our people' the educational opportunities which will help them to succeed. Christian territory in this sense is to be defended, certainly in the law courts and through the ballot box, but if necessary by force, particularly if it is threatened by those of another religion. A good deal of the fierce conflict that takes place between Muslims and Christians today in Africa (Muslims to the North, Christians to the South) partakes of the same ideology. One big question is: how will these attitudes translate to a multicultural society such as we have in the West?

d. Insufficiently contextualised and overly culturally determined

It is a truism that the missionaries struggled with the whole issue of contextualisation. They did not, many of them, really understand the local culture; they thought that Western culture was superior anyway. They introduced Western ways into the churches of the South which were culturally inappropriate but which survive nevertheless till today. Where churches in the South cling on to these Western ways they may still be insufficiently contextualised. Since independence, matters have not improved greatly, and we Westerners have been complacent about this. For example, we have used our money and influence to perpetuate Western forms of theology, particularly by putting a high premium on Western style training and qualifications. We have, again in some cases, offered new and exciting versions of mission – huge rallies, prosperity teaching, charismatic personalities – as an alternative to the patient and genuine efforts made by (some) church leaders to continue the very necessary process of contextualisation. It is ironic that the missionaries believed that their Southern brothers and sisters were trapped in an alien culture and needed delivering from it. The truth so often was that it was the missionaries who were culture bound. They could not see that they had brought with them a Western worldview from which they found it very difficult to escape. Unable as they were to see things differently, they had no choice but to invite their converts to join them by seeing things as they did. Everybody else's culture must change except theirs. We know now that this was wrong, but did we manage to pass on the virus? Evidently, everybody prefers, in both senses of the word, their own culture, but we also know that all cultures are under God's assessment, and that all cultures are part good and part bad (with bits in between that are neutral). The challenge is to decide which parts are which, and not to think that ours is better than somebody else's just because it is ours. Equally, it is not right to 'take on' somebody else's culture wholesale, just because we wish to be politically correct or are sensitive about our own cultural imperialism in the past.

What I am coming round to is that Southern Christians, having rightly learnt to defend their culture against Western cultural imperialism, also need to learn the difficult lesson that *their* culture is not some sort of universal norm either. People say that they do something 'because it is our culture'. This is fine, but not if that means that it is therefore *necessarily* right behaviour and beyond question. Missionaries from the South need to learn the difficult lesson, which we Westerners took so long to assimilate, that the cultural grammar they bring with them to the West is an inadequate statement for humanity as a whole. They are going to find this difficult, the more so because when they get to the West they will find others who have arrived before them who share their culture, and the tendency will be to cling to them and enjoy their approval. This is natural behaviour but it will not make them successful missionaries. It will mean that we have churches in Europe composed of culture sharing immigrants, but equally that these churches will be in a ghetto situation. It is easy to say this because it is exactly what happened to Western missionaries when they did not enter into the local cultures and preferred the company of their own folk. All too often they opted for attendance at an 'international church' in a capital city where the majority of the congregation were missionaries, diplomats and foreign businessmen and everybody spoke English.

In other words, being insufficiently contextualised also means being overly culturally determined. We cannot enter somebody else's culture because we are unwilling to abandon in some measure our own. Also an unwillingness to 'judge' our own culture means that we are trapped in it. We cannot see it clearly enough to abandon what is bad. Thus Western missionaries often made a virtue of things of which they should have been ashamed. The emphasis on task rather than relationship, for example, was put down to efficiency and discipline, when often it simply denoted a superior attitude and lack of human relationship. In reverse, Southern Christians often laud their sensitivity to the 'spiritual' (knowing about demons and the like) when in fact they are struggling with fear and superstition.

e. Legalistic

The substitution of law for grace is the normal process that attends the movement from freedom to control, from charisma to institution, from love to power, from gift to merit. What we have on offer in mission today is all too often a glorification of zeal, of drivenness, of an 'I must try harder' work ethic, of success. Western missionaries certainly tried this out – many of them got full marks for 'trying harder' – but the Kingdom of God grew despite their zeal not because of it. We have sadly passed on the baton. If I have prayed enough, studied hard enough, preached sufficiently enthusiastically, filled up my diary with enough appointments, neglected my family enough, then I have proved, at least to my church back home, that I am a missionary. Not all Southern missionaries are infected by this disease, of course, and it is worse in some parts of the world than others. (I leave you to work out which parts.) But, wherever it comes from, it will not win the West. We have had enough of this sort of thing.

One of the saddest by-products of legalism is the feeling legalistic people have that they are owed something. 'All that effort I put in and what was the result? They were not even grateful.' There is also a sort of bafflement. 'I did all the right things, in the right order, and I did them with all my might, but nothing much happened. It must be the people I was working with. They were so hard, so fickle, so superstitious.' Have you encountered missionaries who talk like that? Similar bafflement has been expressed to me by missionaries from the South trying to come to terms with the indifference of people in the West. 'There was no response. People here do not want to listen. People are too interested in the easy life.' But the truth is that the 'formulas of zeal', when they interrupt the 'formulas of grace', simply do not work in the West. We Westerners tried that in the past, but it did not satisfy. We know about 'muscular Christianity', about duty and church attendance, about prescribed 'quiet times' and not going to the pub, and we need somebody to call us back to grace. In some ways I think we need a *quieter* approach. More shouting, more enthusiasm, more flag waving and drum banging certainly turns up the volume, but we are looking for a different wavelength altogether.

f. Membership not discipleship

It is difficult to accuse people who are zealous in their Christian behaviour of being weak on discipleship. They could quite justly point out that they are much concerned with discipline and 'discipline', after all, is from the same root word as 'disciple'. Yet the zealous or legalistic frame of mind has one other characteristic, and that is a need for visible success. It is akin to the 'territoriality' already mentioned, the need to see concrete, institutional evidence that I am becoming established. As a result it is often possible to keep my Christian life in two compartments. The one that is visible – everybody can see that the Kingdom is being built, and that I am contributing significantly to this process by my hard work and enthusiasm – and the invisible world where I confront myself, my fears, my ambitions, my loves, my hates, my real desires and my secret actions, the things that I do when nobody is watching. So it is quite possible that I am, apparently, 'zealous for good works' in attendance at the prayer meeting and the doing of evangelism, but secretly I am racked with guilt because I cannot resist watching pornography on the internet every night.

It is an additional twist that the visible side of my Christian life may have real benefits – it may win me esteem, may get me a job, may promote me to leadership. So a gap can open up between what I call 'membership' – an open belonging to the cause – and 'discipleship', by which I mean allowing God into my inner life so that he can control it, and then living with the consequences. I am not saying, of course, that 'real' Christianity is all 'inner' and that what I do in the 'outer' world does not matter. In fact, I am saying the reverse. That a renewal of our inner life leads to real discipleship in which we put aside impure motives and 'membership' is no longer a sufficient expression of our faith. At this point it is likely that sacrifice becomes part of the picture: we see that our own success or thriving is not what this is all about, but something else, something more costly. So, if I am a Christian Hutu in Rwanda, then my 'membership' is transformed into a costly discipleship which makes me refuse to attack my Christian Tutsi brother.

What I do wonder is whether it is possible to progress from one to the other – from membership to discipleship – indeed whether this might not be a natural progression. I think I can best explain this through 'stages of growth' theory. According to this theory, Stage 1 (this is a simplified version of the theory available from a number of authors) is our human experience of chaos in which life is out of control or meaningless. Stage 2 is when we are offered and accept structure in our life in order to achieve some aim not otherwise obtainable. The structure is imposed upon us and we submit to it precisely because it prevents us from slipping back into chaos. People who have committed themselves to church membership are usually moving into Stage 2. Stage 3 is when the values and beliefs imposed in Stage 2 are interiorised and are something we are prepared to live by because we perceive them to have intrinsic worth. We do things not because we are expected to do them, but because we want to. We become, in the terms already discussed, disciples rather than members. Stage 3 can seem rather 'selfish'. These are *my* values which *I* approve, and I do not need others to make them effective in my life. There is also, however, a Stage 4. This agrees that 'I would do this even if nobody was watching me do it' but adds that it is still necessary to take my values and re-connect them to others. This is the moment when discipleship becomes costly discipleship.

I have two points based on this analysis. Firstly, if people often move from Stage 2 to Stage 3 and then Stage 4, as a sort of natural progression, it is clearly worthwhile moving people from Stage 1 to Stage 2 *in the hope that* they will in due course move on. In other words, membership is not to be despised if only because it *may* lead to discipleship. Having said that, we need to be careful that membership and discipleship are not confused as the same thing. The tendency to measure effective Christian life in terms of church membership is confusing in this way.

I can think of many examples of this movement from Stage 1 to Stage 2 and indeed the whole history of 'conversion' – of a person or a group or a people – may illustrate it. The conversion of the English as described by Bede in his famous history, is one such example. If it is true, and I think it is, that the churches of the South are still largely at Stage 2, they will not get very far with people who are at Stage 3 or 4. Of course, people in the West have not necessarily interiorised the right values. But that is not the point. The point is that it is not possible to treat people who live in a post-Christian society as if they were living in a pre-Christian one. To put it in the form of a question: do Christians from the South understand the post Christian West and can the methods that they have successfully employed in the South, and which have admittedly led to dynamic growth there, succeed in the West?

This is where I have my doubts about the thesis that Philip Jenkins advances in his book *The Next Christendom* (2002). Jenkins, having rightly identified that the world church is 'shifting southwards' suggests that the new churches of the South are a more authentic expression of Christianity – one closer to primitive Biblical Christianity – than the current Western ones. This explains their rapid growth and impressive demonstrations of power. (Re)appropriation of the Church's first century praxis is precisely what the West needs.(See, for example, Chapter 9 'Coming Home'.) I remain unconvinced, for the reasons already stated. The phrase 'the next Christendom' suggests to my mind all the wrong ways of thinking that we have been struggling to quit ever since

Constantine. I also believe that the twenty-first century Church needs to get away from its inherited West-South, South-West paradigm (itself a product of colonial thinking) into a more 'hybrid' pattern. But I have already made this point.

As a coda to this section I want to mention two other characteristics of the churches of the South which are also the result of colonialism. The Western missionaries all too often taught their (the possessive is significant) churches to be dependent. That dependence, sadly, is still too often a habit of mind which needs to be broken. It continues to be fostered by the fact that the West has largely retained economic power in a neo-colonial way. We have to face the hard fact that economic dependence almost invariably leads to other sorts of dependencies. If we want the South to help the West then we are going to have to hand over economic control as well as other sorts. This is broader than just seeing to it that we do not give 'with strings attached'. It means going back to David Livingstone's idea that 'commerce and Christianity' go together. Fair trade measures which allow, for example, a Malian farmer to export his cotton crop successfully, or a Latin American coffee farmer to get a decent price for his crop, may be more important for the life of the global church than we can easily imagine.

The other postcolonial reality that I think harms the churches of the South is the belief, on their part, that they continue to be victims. This may be another sort of dependency, but, in any case, it needs to be replaced by something more positive. Poor self-esteem, self-pity, resentment are not 'missionary' virtues. The West has its own examples of people who have fallen into dependent mentalities and feel themselves to be victims. We have a hard time coping with them. Ask any church leader. If we are looking for help from the South then we are looking for people who are quietly confident that they have something to offer in their own right. Endlessly reacting to the injustices of colonialism, real as they were and are, will not build the Kingdom. The injustices of colonialism should not be forgotten, but it is *Westerners* who should be recalling them and doing something to put them right.

Western retention of power

If there is going to be a serious move to enlist the South to 'save' the West, then this has implications for the Western church which may be uncomfortable. Being a 'receiving' church has its responsibilities, too. Also the whole process suggests that there will need to be a significant power shift, and it is my impression that we in the West are still very carefully retaining the power in our own hands. Furthermore there is collusion. Many Westernised Southern elites are accepting this situation, so long as they are allowed to buy into the action. This has always been a danger. The inheritors of colonial power – both in the state and the church – were faced from the start with the huge temptation of simply stepping into the power structures abandoned by their former colonial masters. If anything, recent events have made matters worse. Globalisation was initially seen as a promising sign, and recent publications on the world church speak approvingly of global mission. Manuel Castells writes of 'The Network Society' which might be thought to be aimed at undoing the 'us' and 'them' of the colonial era. But, as Castells admits, there is also the possibility that we have simply created new power structures not much different from the old. So, in mission circles, we hold our big conferences in the Global South (Manila rather than Lausanne – the biggest ' Edinburgh 2010' event will be in Cape Town) but it is still the wealthy and well-connected that attend. And we are still measuring success in the same way – all going to the same international conferences, and having degrees from Fuller, and using laptops. Our international conferences – and I have been to some – are rather too much like the Davos forum, that annual meeting in a pleasant Swiss resort where the good and the great decide how the rest of us will live. Davos is certainly an *international* event, but it is not the feast of the Kingdom. You do not see many people there from the highways and the byways. It represents not 'whosoever will may come' but another exclusive, elitist network. If mission in the past has been too closely tied to a commercial model (the trading company model, agencies rather than churches etc.) then we must be careful not to continue the partnership. Global mission – supposedly the replacement for the Christendom model, though that terminology tends to get categories confused – is, in my view, the widening of the business model which we, the beneficiaries, are unwilling to abandon. Just as globalisation *sounds* attractive, in that it (theoretically) supersedes Western political and economic domination and brings a more international mix to the market place, so global mission *sounds* as if it has replaced 'the west to the rest' model. In both cases there are hidden agendas, however. Significant action remains in the West, and with those whom we have licensed in one way and another.

I went to see a play recently put on by the Royal Shakespeare Company called 'Believe What You Will' by Philip Massinger. It was set in the period when Rome was steadily building its Empire, though there were a number of cross-overs to the current world political situation. Rome offered her clients all sorts of supposed benefits as long as they were subservient, that is, they played by the Roman rules. She was the stern parent who knew best. The great crime was to say that you knew better, even if you were well aware that ultimately the rules of the game were drawn up to serve Roman interests. Rebellion led to harsh consequences. On these terms it came down to a 'lesser of the two evils' equation. Better peace with Rome even at a humiliating and unjust price, rather than war with Rome.

All this reminded me of the centre-periphery structure that we are still operating, certainly in the world at large but often in mission as well. Better to cosy up to the system than to fall out of it. Better to write in English than not to be published at all. Better to have a Western theological qualification than one that nobody really recognises and that keeps me permanently at the bottom of the church's hierarchy.

So, in summary, the West is hanging on to the power, though it is prepared to co-opt outsiders if that serves its purpose.

Southern alternatives

Whoever is at fault, it complicates the situation that truly 'Southern' alternatives have been slow to emerge. The Western overlay is, perhaps, simply too strong for the time being. Way back in the early years of the last century the great Indian missionary C. F. Andrews refused to allow his Indian theological students to study the history of the church after the early period and before the modern period because he simply wanted to protect his students from the assumption that theology came from Europe! Sadly, perhaps that is still the assumption. I know that theologically some good work has been done – Liberation Theology from Latin America, Indian Christian Theology, books and articles from scholars such as Mbiti and Koyama, but I also get the impression that these contributions are seen as passing fashions and little more. Theological power also remains in the West.

Where Southern alternatives *have* emerged, we are, frankly, uncertain of their meaning. I refer here to a recent article by David Martin in the *Princeton Seminary Bulletin* (2006). Martin begins where we began, with the history of the expansion of Christianity from the West to the South. He is quite negative about this. For example, he is caustic about the way that Christianity originally spread to Latin America.

> The mass conversion of the New World was carried out in the name of a faith already deeply infiltrated by syncretism

> in the Old World. It then joined itself to all the religious varieties of its new environment. Latin America today exhibits a spectrum of practices all the way from virtually unreached tribes to smouldering and confused memories of solar and chthonic faiths, and thence to exuberant spiritism and orthodox Catholicism (111).

Referring to the whole period since the arrival of Christianity through the *conquistadores* he concludes 'Half a millennium and twenty generations later the meaning of Christianity is still only dimly appropriated' (111). Further, he suggests that this process – the transfer of an incomplete version of the faith 'deeply infiltrated by syncretism' – is still going on, although the influences are now from the United States rather than Spain and Portugal. He calls this 'a religious version of the market in American goods'. His big example is Pentecostalism, the major Protestant grouping in Latin America, though, to be fair, he sees the possibility of two traditions, two contested meanings of the Pentecostal experience.

> Of course, the inevitable tension arises between the older more populist Pentecostalism which values humility and acknowledges suffering and the danger of riches, and a softer, smoother Christianity illustrating precisely those dangers in tendencies to authoritarianism, personality cult, display and greed in its leadership. (120)

This is a good description. The question is: is this latter, the 'softer, smoother Christianity' authentic, and do we want to re-export it, as it were, to the West?

Let me give a couple of brief illustrations of what I have called 'inauthentic Christianity' currently developing in the South. The first is similar to the comments I have already made on 'territorial' Christianity. The spread of Islam was a cause of great concern to European statesmen right up to the end of the nineteenth century for largely colonial reasons. In the missionary movement its spread in sub-Saharan Africa in particular was viewed with suspicion. Ludwig Krapf a CMS missionary in East Africa, for example, proposed a string of missionary stations from the east coast of Africa to the west to 'hold back' the Muslim tide, and for a while this was taken up seriously by the CMS (Pirouet 1999, 72). Notice the military and territorial emphasis. Much of our thinking about Islam remains 'territorial' to this day (witness the paranoia about mosques in Britain) a power game in which Christians must gain the advantage if God's Kingdom is to be established and God's people protected.

The carry-over of this worldview in a country like Nigeria or Indonesia is that Christians must secure 'their' territory by almost whatever means. We know that in northern Nigeria Islam and Christianity are locked in an often-violent struggle with the Christians sometimes as violent as the Muslims. The former president of the Christian Association of Nigeria, Sunday Mbang, has commented that 'most people who kill people come to church'; and 'they will walk very holy and shout holy, holy, and you don't know them'. This has many repercussions. As Giles Fraser has suggested, Archbishop Akinola's concern about a gay bishop in New Hampshire no doubt stems from the fact that, in his opinion, it hands a propaganda coup to the Muslims keen to depict the Anglican church as part of the sexually decadent west. He also suggests that Akinola needs to realise that it is playing a dangerous game of poker, trying to outbid fundamentalist Islam with fundamentalist Christianity (Fraser 2005).

Another example of inauthenticity is the increasing popularity of the 'prosperity gospel', or at least, a theology of power, deliverance and healing which promises God's people release from their alien circumstances. You may say to me – what's wrong with a ministry like that? For a start people are flocking into the churches, which can't be bad. Of course, I am not saying that power is not attractive, indeed popular. When Jesus fed the five thousand (we read that he was sorry for the people because they were sheep without a shepherd, harassed and helpless) soon enough there was another crowd that wanted to be fed. What a marvellous way to build a ministry! But when he preached to them instead of feeding them, and warned them about their greed for the miraculous, they left him in large numbers.

Let me pause here and take a longer look at the so-called prosperity gospel. As we have been saying, the church in the Global South that was the product of the missionary movement may be viewed as having a colonial origin and this is relevant to our understanding of the way that church has developed. We might add that this applies to church in the West as well as the South. In the nineteenth century the church (let us say in Britain for the sake of illustration, but the points made here would apply to any of the Western missionary sending countries) even before it began to send out missionaries, was frequently colonial in many of its attitudes, reflecting the attitudes of society at large. Working men and women in Victorian cities were colonised along with the inhabitants of distant lands, and sometimes with greater ruthlessness.

In another respect too the church in the Global South had a colonial origin, in that most nineteenth century missionaries had very little idea of contextualisation. The churches they founded were expected to reflect the missionaries' western culture. This was an unquestioned assumption: the missionaries would not in the main have thought of 'culture' in the way that we do, and when they did they believed that their British culture was inherently Christian and therefore normative. This meant that the form of church life was as near as possible a copy of the British original and so were the ethos, the value system and the patterns of thought. You have only to worship with the Church of South India to realise that that is the case. What is perhaps surprising, however, is the health of many of the same churches. Wherever you go in the Global South you can come across 'missionary' churches which are apparently doing well, or even very well. The Anglican church in Nigeria, for example, is certainly prospering in terms of numbers. It is also doing considerably better than the colonial churches back in Britain. The colonised working people there tended to abandon the traditional church just as soon as they could get away with it. As a result the British working class today are largely unchurched, indeed alienated from the Christian faith altogether. From a missiological perspective, it is interesting to speculate as to why there is this difference. One possibility might be that in the West the church remained an instrument of power, representing the establishment. The missionary presence in the South, whatever the Victorian attitudes of the missionaries themselves, was by comparison weak and non-threatening. Missionaries were vulnerable; many scarcely coped with their new environment. They struggled to learn a language different from their own. They were cut off from their families. Though they were often better off than the local people, they were not usually extravagantly or arrogantly wealthy.

Nevertheless, world-wide, we certainly do see some sort of negative reaction to missionary churches. In Africa we call this movement the 'African Independent Churches'. These usually emerged from situations in which charismatic African leaders could no longer tolerate being infantalised by the missionaries and determined to strike out on their own. They often added a desire to revive some of the African traditions that had been lost in the missionary churches. These two features: the revival of African traditions and the assertion of indigenous leadership clearly constitute the African Independent Churches (and others like them in other parts of the world) as contributors to the anti-colonial movement which swept through the Global South in the twentieth century.

Postcolonialism is, shall we say, *interested* in this situation. It embraces the rather confused situation by which, in the colonial period there are already anti-colonial churches and in the era after independence there are still 'colonial' churches. It also makes space for what I am going to call, rather controversially, 'neo-colonial' churches, and here I am getting back to the subject of the 'prosperity gospel'. Churches with a 'prosperity' approach (again I am referring to one scenario, Africa, but the descriptions would be equally applicable elsewhere in the Global South) are characterised by a tense relationship both with their own traditional African past and with the missionary churches. Their youthful iconoclasm has encouraged them to cast off what they would consider to be the dead hand of their forefathers' ways, and the more cautious and accommodating ways of both the mainline churches and the independent churches have also been rejected. Their natural affinity is with the global culture, in particular the youth culture, and with a more demonstrative and even spectacular form of the faith. They are also attracted by foreign models, though not necessarily by the networks which are still in place as a result of the missionary connection. Instead they look to a worldwide movement, usually associated with the more 'successful' societies such as the United States, and to the big-event Christianity of well-known evangelists and healers. There is a tendency to socialise the gospel (that is to put a higher value on its social than its doctrinal implications) rather than to contextualise or indigenise it. In the same way that the global culture homogenises and fragments society at large, so these churches share common characteristics – not least the 'prosperity' angle – and yet manifest themselves as multiple mini-denominations, usually reflecting the personalities of their charismatic leaders. I call these churches neo-colonial, because their source of inspiration seems to me to be found in the West rather than the Global South itself. This is not, of course, old style colonialism. How could it be when the churches are firmly under indigenous leadership? It is, however, an ideological colonialism, and like neo-colonialism in society at large, it offers the promise of global connection and global 'success' but with little real prospect of either. Only a quite small elite benefits, and they do so, often, at the expense of those they lead.

Once again, postcolonialism, I believe, gives us a lens by which we can examine the whole phenomenon and see it as yet another feature of a world shaped by its colonial history. So let me take that examination a little further. The Christianity of which I am speaking is rather like Coca Cola. Coke is a widely consumed and popular foreign product which appears to give a taste of a wider and more exciting world, but in fact only presents an illusion of connectivity: drinking Coca Cola will not make someone a successful person, whatever the promises. It is difficult to see how Coca Cola is 'the real thing' as it claims. It also has very little nutritional value and it usurps the indigenous products that do. Try telling that to the younger generation, however. What teenager wants to drink milk when he or she can have an ice-cold Coke? After all 'things go better with Coca Cola' don't they? To draw the analogy: it may be difficult to discipline a Christian congregation to the more mundane and exacting features of discipleship when they are being offered a diet of exciting and spectacular events in the church next store, particularly as the latter is linked to the promise of an easier and more prosperous life.

There is a certain mechanism here which is deadly. People are deeply attracted by the hope of a lucky strike, a 'magic bullet' (like the millions who spend money on the lottery). They are in Lenny Cohen's terms 'waiting for the miracle to come'. Cohen expounds this theme very subtly in a couple of his songs, for example in 'The Stranger' when he speaks about the poker player who is waiting for a card 'which is so high and wide, he never needs to deal another'. It is difficult to blame people for keeping hope alive when their lives are so oppressed, but the truth is that this is just another form of exploitation. People are prepared to pay a great deal of money for hope, particularly if they are close to despair. The answer to people's need however is not this sort of hope, but the Kingdom Of God. When people's needs are met in and by the just community, then the prosperity gospel will be seen as the counterfeit it is. This community is a sharing community in terms of economics, it is hybrid in terms of culture, it is a community for others in terms of mission, it is a community of equals in terms of government. It is not colonial or anti-colonial or even neo-colonial. It comes by accepting the rule of Christ and joining the company of others who do so too.

The right stance for the Western church today is not to seek to go back to yesterday's (apparent) triumphs. Frankly, we would say to our brothers and sisters in the South, please do not help us to do so. We do not want a revival of Constantinianism, we do not need more power, bigger numbers, greater prosperity. And if that is what you have learnt from us as the true meaning of the Kingdom we beg you to lay it aside. Of course some will say: who are you to lecture us, you Westerners? You were happy to tell us how it should be done, but once we learnt to do it better than you, you are telling us to stop! Rather like Westerners backing off 'progress' now they have got what they want out of it.

I see all that as very understandable, but no answer to our needs in mission. I am looking for a paradigm of mission not a way back to former glories.

What about post-Christianity?

Another question which is preoccupying Western observers is: have the Southern churches really worked out the true nature of the task as they set out to evangelise the West? If Europe – and to some extent the United States – is post-Christian, it does not need evangelising but re-evangelising. Europe has passed through the age of enchantment to the age of dis-enchantment and now needs re-enchantment. As I have already mentioned, it used to be fashionable to describe Western Christianity, with its numbers declining and influence diminishing, as in difficulties because of the onset of secularism. There is obviously some force in the idea that Europe's churches are in decline, but not, I think, primarily because of secularism. Perhaps an analogy with OT Israel might be helpful. We are like Israel in exile. Apparently thriving under the early monarchy, Israel goes into spiritual decline during and after the reign of David. Division and infidelity to the covenant, spiritual complacency and social injustice, all take their toll. The next stage is exile, and, on some views, despite Isaiah 40-55 and the work of men like Nehemiah and Ezra, that is where Israel remains. Some Biblical scholars such as N. T. Wright have even suggested that that is what the story of the Prodigal Son is about: the true Israel is still in exile while the stay-at-home elder brother is the Palestinian establishment. What if the Western church were the Prodigal Son of the twenty-first century, once in a place of privilege, now in 'the far country', in exile?

Or we could give this a more positive spin. Exile (or the wilderness) is the proper place for the church to be, though it often feels that it would like to be somewhere else. We want our own territory, somewhere we can control, something more secure. But it may not be part of the agenda to go back to a place of territory and power. Think about Matthew 4 where Jesus was offered the chance to head up a new exodus and restore the nation. It sounded impressive but Jesus saw it as a temptation. Reviving the church does not mean going back to the Christendom model. We were there once, in this country, and not so long ago. The churches were full. A man like Spurgeon in Victorian London drew huge crowds. But Victorian London was a terrible place. The churches may have been full but the real church was in exile, having decamped to the slums and pitched its tent there with the Salvation Army and the Christian Social Union.

Conclusion

Let me ask my question again: 'Can the South save the West?' and let me say again: 'I don't know. It is too early to tell, the history has not been done, the West is not ready for it and possibly the South as well. Meanwhile there are warnings that can be uttered:

- The South does not have to make the same mistakes that the West did; everybody makes mistakes, of course, but they should make their own!
- The West's supposed successes are not as impressive as one might think, certainly not as impressive as we have made them out to be.
- The South cannot necessarily trust *their* successes either.
- The culture of the West is unique – something never seen before. It is post-Christendom and perhaps even post-Christian. This culture will have to be understood on its own terms. Cultural work is hard work. It takes time, but it is essential. The jewel of mission is always contextualisation, putting off the clothes of my own cultural preferences and washing the disciples' feet. Contextualisation in this sense is the opposite of empire. It means putting off my demand for power and control. It is the Philippians 2 mode. We all need to keep this lesson close to our hearts. Did Western missionaries give the South the right model? Sometimes, perhaps, but not often enough.

The West invented the West-South divide. It is one of the products of the Enlightenment. Can we go beyond this whole paradigm of West to South, and South to West, and start again? How could we do this? How shall we describe the people of God?

Chapter Five

The Great Economy

If we are dissatisfied with the communities and organisations that are typical of our globalised world, do we have any alternatives? What might be the nature of 'the Great Economy', a term which, as we have seen, means much the same thing as the Biblical idea of the 'The Kingdom of God'.

Three preliminary considerations

Before we start to dream, to imagine some possible ways that we might live peaceably and joyfully together, I would like to suggest three guiding principles in our investigations.

First of all, our communities must be built in solidarity with the past (see above on the need for tradition). It is simply not possible to begin from scratch when it comes to politics. Of course what elements of the past we are in solidarity with, will have to be decided. For example, in my case I believe that we can dispense with the institutional church as a model (what a relief!). The church in its present institutional form too often stands for little more than a validator of the Domination System. (This has been going on from at least the time of Constantine.) We cannot, however, dispense with the Bible and its witness to Jesus and his witness to the truth. Our task is 'faithful improvisation', to use Tom Wright's phrase. 'Faithful improvisation' is the idea that we are writing a scene of a play in the light of four and half acts that have already been written – creation, fall, Old Testament history, the Christ event, New Testament and church. We are in scene two of the fifth act. We must therefore take notice of the earlier action: characters, examples, principles, stories, commands, but write our own story in the light of Scripture by means of the resources we have been given. These include the Holy Spirit, conscience, tradition (especially that of the church), philosophy and logic (Wright 1991, 18). To change the metaphor, the Biblical witness is like a foundation on which we need to build. The church is not a free floating organism, it is based on the apostles and prophets, with Jesus Christ being the chief corner stone.

Similarly the Great Economy of the twenty first century must in some ways be continuous with faithful expressions of it in the past. This is hugely important. We simply cannot expect to build good communities without some sort of pattern, and the obvious place to look for it is in the historical record of the experiments in 'good living' that have been handed down to us by our forbears. Let me give an example from the nineteenth century. William Morris, poet, artist, philosopher and socialist was one of a handful of men and women who attempted to resist the ugly tide of industrialisation and urbanisation that characterised their era (in Great Britain). He believed that he could do this best by drawing up a new pattern of society and he looked largely to the past to provide it, for example to historical contexts such as Iceland and pre-industrial Oxfordshire. About the way Morris perceived the Icelandic model, Fiona MacCarthy writes:

> Thingvellir...was the place of the first democratic parliament. Here in 930, soon after the colonisation of the island by the Norsemen from Scandinavia and Celts from Britain, the Althing or General Assembly had been formed, a gathering of thirty-nine independent chieftancies. The Althing continued without any central executive authority until Iceland came under Norwegian rule in 1262. This Parliament met at Thingvellir for two weeks every summer. Besides the official procedures of the legislature, there was what amounted to a national festival of sports, verse-readings and trading. Craftsmen set up their stalls and sold from them. A large proportion of that early population made its way to Thingvellir each year.

MacCarthy continues.

> Morris found much to admire in the primitive democracy of Iceland. So much so that he would explain it in laborious detail to his Socialist audiences of the 1880s, making the implied comparison between Victorian Britain and this orderly and equitable social system which respected the personal rights of all free men.

Apparently he was much impressed by the lack of crime, the high value put on manual labour and the liberated status of women (MacCarthy 1994, 306-8), all features of the utopia he describes in his novel *News from Nowhere*.

Morris was also captivated by the society formed by the numerous little villages surrounding his home at Kelmscott Manor in Oxfordshire. Here is Fiona MacCarthy again:

> Morris's view of the countryside roamed further outwards from these grey stone villages of Oxfordshire and Gloucestershire to all the variations of land and architecture that made up the texture of England as a whole. It was now that one of his most influential concepts, the ideal of the network of small ruralist communities began to surface. Here are the origins of garden cities. Morris wrote in those early Kelmscott years: 'but look, suppose people lived in little communities among gardens and green fields, so that you could be in the country in 5 minutes walk, and had few wants; almost no furniture for instance, and no servants, and studied (the difficult) arts of enjoying life, and finding out what they really wanted: then I think one might hope civilisation had really begun.' (MacCarthy 1994, 314-5)

'I think civilisation might have really begun' says Morris. Perhaps he was wrong. Perhaps he was foolishly utopian. No doubt he did not envisage the effect of the motor car on our society. Nevertheless how much we need people who can 'dream' in the way that Morris did. Nor is it a coincidence that this particular dreamer was so much in love with the past.

Secondly our communities must demonstrate God's justice. To put it another way, they must be communities built on an adequate understanding of the character of God. When Israel in Old Testament times attempted the task of nation building, the stress on law and covenant and the condemnation of idolatry (as, for example, in the book of Deuteronomy) did not have to do with some sort of tribal loyalty. It claimed, rather, that only by clinging to the revelation it possessed of the unique character of Yahweh, would it be possible for the nation to be a flourishing community. This is what Jesus is saying in his discussion with the Tempter in the desert. 'Human beings cannot live on bread alone, but need every word that God speaks' (Matthew 4:4 quoting Deuteronomy 8:3). If we look at the context of the Old Testament saying that Jesus is quoting here (the whole of Deuteronomy 6-8) we see that the discussion there is precisely about how to achieve 'the Great Economy'. The temptations in the wilderness very naturally follow on Jesus' dramatic realisation at his baptism that establishing the rule of God is precisely his mission.

Thirdly, the future invades the present and the community begins to experience, and anticipate (in both senses) the coming rule of God. Worship, in particular the eucharist, illustrates the character of this community. The eucharist helps us to remember the founder and the foundation events, and links us to the apostolic tradition. It reminds us that we belong to one body and that we therefore cannot discriminate in an unjust way amongst ourselves (which would be failing to 'discern the body'; see 1 Corinthians 11:29), and it also reminds us that what we are doing is until Christ comes, when we shall feast with him in the coming Kingdom. It *proclaims* the death of Jesus; it is a 'meal for missionaries'. Furthermore, it is a feast which takes place in the New Jerusalem which is always 'coming down out of heaven', re-forming itself in each generation and culture. The gates of the New Jerusalem are always open and the 'leaves of the tree' (on main street) are for 'the healing of the nations'. I find these elements – memory, justice, anticipation, mission, healing – all too often absent from our worship, and therefore from our communities. After all, worship is when we identify what is really important, try to see it as God sees it, and give him the glory for it.

Government

All this may seem rather dream-like. Is it really possible to construct something in the world of our street and our neighbourhood and our nation that is plainly to do with the Great Economy? I believe it is.

A Just Society?

As we have already said, at the heart of any consideration of the Great Economy is the ideal of justice. This is obviously a central idea in Jesus' teaching (Matthew 6: 33). I was at a meeting of the Campaign Against the Arms Trade recently. There was much (worthwhile) discussion about ways and means. However, there came a moment when it needed to be said that, even if it meant people losing their jobs or the nation (Britain, in this case) being weakened in its international influence, it was simply not *right* to sell weapons at a profit to people who might misuse them. But, in fact, it was not said, and indeed is not being said, or not clearly enough, even by Christians. So let us at least raise the question: is there anything about present global arrangements that make it difficult to achieve justice in our public arrangements?

At a very simple level it would seem that not everyone benefits from our present economic arrangements. There are still plenty of places where the global economy means very little, in the sense that they may have never heard of it and even if they have, they have no means of influencing it. As we are talking about something which is described as 'globalisation' this is a sobering thought. Even now, a vast section of humanity is effectively written out of the equation.

Further, being 'written out' of economic global economic arrangements may actually mean being their 'victim', or to put it another way, *unequal* development remains a constant, whatever else is happening. World trade has always been carried on in ways that advantage the wealthy nations, and there seems little evidence that the present economic difficulties will change that fact. Even within apparently wealthy countries like the US, there are more poor people than ever. Whatever the cause of the gap between rich and poor, and whatever the best way to close it, there is little debate about the present reality. There is also one particularly unnerving feature of this gap. By contrast with the 'high noon' of industrial capitalism, when manufacturing businesses needed a large workforce, the new rich no longer need the new poor in the way they once did, and so it becomes increasingly difficult to even out the differences between them. Also with the demise of the power of organised labour, there is no framework in which this conflict can be resolved. A growing gap between rich and poor, and no legitimate mechanisms to resolve the situation, spells trouble, particularly as the rich seem less and less willing to bear the cost of welfare regimes which were seen, at one time, as a suitable response to disparities of wealth (Held & McGrew 2000, 27-9). If this is an accurate description – the increasingly marginalised poor with no means of redress – then the policies which lie behind today's world are leading us to disaster, if only because blatant injustice will not be tolerated forever. It is noteworthy that the recent G20 crisis meeting in London (April 2009) – over which there was a certain amount of rejoicing – hardly considered the question of unequal development or for that matter the equally urgent and related issue of the environmental crisis. What is was concerned to do was to rescue the existing system. Of course it did say that the existing system would have to be more carefully regulated, which means, it seems to me, little more than that we can all go over the precipice more carefully. Is there nobody out there able to propose something radically new?

An alternative to capitalism: the politics of security

The big debate at the moment ought to be whether we can find an alternative to capitalism. We know perfectly well that if we give large sums of money to clever people they will use it to try and make more money, without much feeling that wealth should be shared. We know now also that they will take inordinate risks in order to do this, particularly if the consequences of failure are largely borne by other people! This means not only that society constantly teeters on the brink of crisis and even collapse, but, more fundamentally, systematic exploitation of people and the environment goes on unchecked. Is our political system about 'growth' or is it about people? If it is the latter, then a prime consideration is *security*. People need a safe place in which they are not forced to go into survival mode. They need the basics. In those rather harrowing programmes about survival, when people get lost in the Australian outback, or some such inhospitable place, it is instructive how quickly priorities change when there is a real threat to life. All of a sudden matters of taste, cost, convenience, choice and the like are ruthlessly subordinated to the single question – can we survive?[23]

The same question should be at the heart of our political and economic life, or to put it another way, the essential task is to create a human-friendly environment. I wonder whether we are in danger of forgetting this. I am not suggesting that humans should be satisfied with having their basic needs met and have no other aspirations, but I am saying that people will only thrive when they reasonably certain they can survive. So we have to provide societies where people are not vulnerable to forces which can, and therefore possibly

---

[23] I am not referring here to 'security' in the sesne of security from terrorism, but rather something that ensures people are free from constant economic insecurity.

will, deny them their basic needs. Good government might be described, in part, as a hedge against undue vulnerability.

What in fact threatens people, makes them vulnerable? First of all there is 'big government' itself. Government was designed, as I understand it, to protect us, but it is clear that it can become the problem rather than the solution. The American and French revolutions and their like assumed rightly that human welfare depended fundamentally on freedom. Arbitrary behaviour by governments meant that people were not safe in their own homes. Government's task should be precisely to make sure that they *are* safe in their homes – by defending the country's borders and providing just laws adequately enforced. But if the government becomes the 'enemy', then a citizen's security is radically compromised. We have seen too much of that in the history of our recent past for me to need to describe it any further. Right wing and left wing dictatorships, of course, both play the 'big government' card, often involving ideologies such as nationalism, or utopian socialism used to *increase* citizens' vulnerability.

The second major factor in our society that creates vulnerability is 'big business', or indeed the whole mechanism of wage labour. If I work for someone else in the sense that my livelihood depends on him or her, then I am at risk. Factors which have nothing to do with my ability or my conscientious discharge of my duties may result in my losing my job, and not being able to find another. Furthermore, and this is the really damaging reality, the company's policy may be deliberately to make me vulnerable, to keep me vulnerable, and ultimately to take advantage of my vulnerability, in order to serve its own purpose. In doing this the director of the company will be right to behave in this way if the *company's* welfare is threatened. (This is very close to the argument of 'socialist' dictatorships that one person cannot be allowed to threaten the interest of the state.) Self-employed people can also find that circumstances turn against them, even to the point that they lose their livelihood. But it is different all the same. For the self-employed person profit (in the sense of maximising the business effectiveness of the organisation) and personal security are the *same* goal. Employees are vulnerable in a way that the self employed never are. These principles are worked out in the Old Testament under the rubric 'Every man will sit under his own vine and under his own fig tree'. The saying significantly ends with the assurance, 'and none shall make them afraid' (Micah 4:4).

Responding to insecurity

This is all very well but we in fact live in a world in which both big government and big business are an ever present reality. Is there anything we can do about it? I think there is a great deal that can be done.

As a general principle we need to put human security – political, economic, social, psychological – at the top of our list. This means that it comes *above* economic growth, and of course above other considerations such as national prestige or consumer choice.

With regard to *big government* we can:

- Encourage devolution, decentralisation, local government and participative (rather than representative) politics.
- Value freedom in the present more than states of limited freedom in the name of some supposed future good.
- Encourage small businesses run by independently minded people.
- Support government initiatives that disempower the over powerful (e.g. use the honours system differently).
- Put a ceiling on election expenses so that 'small people' can get into politics.
- Reverse the trend towards 'big party' politics.
- Reverse the trend towards 'presidential' politics.
- Favour small political combinations by introducing Proportional Representation.
- Make the intelligence gathering and defence establishments more accountable.
- Pay more attention to 'freedom of information'.
- Tax enterprises that have nothing to do with human security (e.g. the entertainment industry) more heavily. Use the money for health and education.
- Make small business people the prime political 'movers and shakers'.
- Regulate political lobbying.

With regard to *big business* we can:

- Put a ceiling on company growth and an embargo on mergers, take-overs and the like. If necessary break up existing conglomerates.
- Regulate our commercial systems so as to limit the risk to a reasonable level and punish exploitive and greedy practices
- Encourage small businesses run by independently minded people.

- Where economies of scale are essential then go for co-operatives rather than big monolithic companies.
- Actively legislate against social trends that 'drive the little man to the wall'; for example forbid planning permission for out-of-town superstores.
- Be particularly sensitive to media monopoly; legislate against this.
- Give tax breaks to those involved in providing essential services to the community.
- Break up government monopolies too; but this does not mean creating 'private' monopolies instead.
- Encourage NGOs of all sorts.
- Promote 'fair trade' which puts human security before profits; give tax incentives for fair trade products.
- Re-introduce a serious wealth tax; if our 'best people' defect, accept the consequences.
- Re-introduce personal liability in business ventures.
- Introduce the Tobin Tax.

What are some of the arguments against these arrangements?

Some have suggested that the nation which adopts these measures will 'fall behind' – they mean fall behind economically of course – as a nation. Perhaps this is true, but this is something that I have factored into the equation. We may have to accept that GNP will fall compared to other nations. On the other hand I believe that our 'security level' will increase nation-wide, that the *distribution* of wealth will be more even, and that the nation will be more *involved* in its own politics and business in a way that will ultimately result in actual greater prosperity. I know that the dreaded 'unemployment' word will be raised at this point. For example, if business conditions discourage investment from overseas, will more jobs go? Clearly, I am looking for people to be more involved in work rather than less so. If big businesses break up, I am expecting little businesses to be run by people who are more enthusiastic and committed because they are 'minding their own business', so to speak. In any case has big business such a great record as far as employment goes? What about the effects of the 'credit crunch'? As I have said, it is partly because people are wage earners in businesses over which they have no control that they suddenly find themselves out of work.

Others have suggested that there are a number of businesses that can only be run as big businesses. Again, perhaps. Many big businesses could be broken up, with beneficial effects. Even where 'big is beautiful' co-operatives are often possible where the contributors are joint owners of the enterprise, rather than a system of management, waged workers, and shareholders.

There is also a suggestion that smaller businesses would mean less choice. For example, the small grocery store could not hope to stock the variety of products found on the shelves of the supermarket. Obviously this is true, but there are mitigating factors. A number of small specialist shops can often offer even greater choice, and certainly better quality, than supermarkets, and there is also the question of access. For those without cars for example, the closure of local shops (because they cannot compete with the local 'chain' stores or supermarkets) is often a real threat to their security. Food might become more expensive, but then we would be paying for better access and more personal service and for the environmental gains of not using the car so much. This might not be a very popular argument with some, but in a way it is my *fundamental* argument. Matters such as choice and even the need to pay more (more for my food and more taxes perhaps) are *not as important* as human security.

Again it might be argued that some people (e.g. pensioners) might actually find themselves more insecure if the cost of food went up. There are at least two answers to that. The pensioners are the very people who are likely to benefit from local shops and secondly, and more fundamentally, it should not be beyond our wit to envisage societies in which there are fewer pensioners in the first place. In many parts of the world the family business is run by the extended family. My idea of many more small self-owned businesses includes using the extended family as part of the work force. (If mum is running the shop, gran is looking after the children.) Asian families, who run so many successful small enterprises, are already working on this basis. Using families in this way extends the productive life of older people and keeps business costs down. This could be exploitive, but not necessarily so. My point here is that small business are *communities* based on the excellent principle 'from each according to his or her ability, to each according to his or her need' and that in itself provides a degree of social security which the impersonal state finds hard to match. The unit I have in mind then is the extended family/ small business/ community of equals with a shared purpose, providing employment and social security.

In the New Testament the disciples of Jesus complain about their lack of social security. They remind Jesus that they have left everything – families, jobs – to follow him. Jesus' answer is very simple. You *do* have the community, and that will provide more than you could ever need (Luke 18:28-30). As we have already seen, when Jesus said 'seek first the rule of God and his justice and all these things (material needs) will be provided for you' (Matthew 6:33) he meant that those who joined the community of the rule of God with its just ways (that is, a community which shared its wealth) had no need to fear want. The early Jerusalem church proved this in practice (Acts 4:34-5). People in the West who 'lose' jobs or families often have precious little to fall back on. We need to create a society where it is simply not possible to 'lose' your community, because you are part of an organic entity which needs you as much as you need them.

Finally, some will say that I have just described socialism and given it another name and we all know that socialism does not work. We certainly know that state socialism does not work, but, as I have said, that is just another form of 'big government'. The small businesses, indeed communities, I have tried to describe are socialist within, but entrepreneurial without, because the family as a whole is investing its skills and resources in making money and hoping to make a modest profit as a result. On the whole this model has not been much tried. Where it has had a thorough going exposition (as for example with the *Bruderhof* in the States and Britain) it has worked very well (Kovel 2002, chapter 9).

Advocacy

The challenge to big government and big business is one that urgently needs to be made and indeed I suspect that most people know in their hearts that good government includes intervention on behalf of the weak and marginalised against their oppressors.

There is a clear mandate to that effect in the Old Testament; King Lemuel's mother (who was probably not an Israelite), understood the principle perfectly well (Proverbs 31:1-9). We know next door to nothing about King Lemuel, but we do know that his mother had a big idea, one that had a truly global reach. Concerned, it seems, that her son might forget what being a king was for, she gave him strong advice about women and strong drink. Too much indulgence might weaken his grip on affairs. Surprisingly, this was not so that he could exercise power more effectively, but so that he could 'defend the rights of the poor and needy'. In the immortal words, he was 'to speak up for those who could not speak up for themselves'.

But where do we actually see this in practice? Currently most advocacy work is being done by Non Government Organisations (NGOs) such as *World Vision*, *Greenpeace*, and *Oxfam*. These NGOs have become very much a part of our global scenery today – and a good thing too. There has been a tendency recently to question their legitimacy. Who are these do gooders in *Amnesty International* anyway? What gave them the right to circle the globe pointing out human rights' abuses? Those folk in *Medicin sans Frontières*, who permitted them to do away with frontiers? But 'speaking up for those who cannot speak up for themselves' is everybody's right – and responsibility.

It is also the responsibility of governments. A king [in the Old Testament] is deemed to be a good king because he represents the interests of the weakest and most disadvantaged members of the community, usually described as widows, orphans and strangers (Jeremiah 22:3), that is, those who have nobody to stand up for them in the normal course of events. In doing this the king actually reflects the character of God (Deuteronomy 10:18). It is worth adding that this is what we should rightly call *strong* government, not some tough 'law and order' regime. Our natural inclinations are to give in to the powerful elements in our community, and to make room for their interests, simply because it is much easier to give in to them than to resist them. But, of course, these are the very people who can look after themselves, and who do not need special favour from those in authority. By contrast there may be those who are economically weak, or inexperienced, or powerless for some other reason, and it is all too easy for them to lose ground against the naturally powerful. Simply to allow these forces free reign, and to preside in a loose sort of way over a supposedly inevitable pecking order, is in fact *weak* government

Big organisations (such as the TNCs) do not understand this principle. In even more sinister fashion, there are supposedly no visible organisations running our world, just some sort of 'invisible hand'. How do we appeal to this non-entity to 'do justice', to be on the side of the poor, to help the weak? In fact, I am not sure I believe in this quasi-metaphysical entity, but I do think we can identify the 'powers' involved. They are the corporations and banks and insurance houses whose logos we see every day. Whether they want to listen to the message of 'good news to the poor' is another matter.

Government close up

Meanwhile, small is important and so is *local*, especially in matters of government and control. It is the unaccountability and 'distance' of so many of the 'powers' that control our lives in this global era, which make me, more than ever, an exponent of government which is as near as possible to the people governed. In this area too I have some practical suggestions, which I think Christians could adopt.

In essence I want to suggest small, 'low-level', local, political associations, based on personal relationships which would provide a tier of 'government' (co-operative local action groups) between the citizen and 'big government'.

We already have examples of this sort of association in our society today. Helena Norberg-Hodge speaks of 'a range of small, local initiatives that are as diverse as the cultures and economies in which they take place' (Goldsmith 2001, 242). Just to list a few which come to mind: environmental protection groups, housing associations, Neighbourhood Watch schemes, parent teacher associations. These tend to be specific to some particular cause however, and what I had more in mind were associations which have a more permanent basis and a wider remit, perhaps something like the village elders in a rural economy, or those who 'sat in the gate' in Old Testament times.

What might be the constitution of these associations? Here is a list of features:

(1) Clearly they must be participatory, as mentioned above. They should involve the maximum number of citizens as is practicably possible. A political elite is ruled out; indeed the membership may have to be those who have never taken the lead in society before. Certainly it would be important to avoid the big party political organisations, because of the way that they stereotype the participants. Yet some existing local groups could be used effectively as agents of political change. The leaders of a big church for example might have such a role, or if that were too unrepresentative a group, the leaders of a number of churches in the one locality, already perhaps organised as a minister's fraternal or the like. City wide church initiatives have been successful in promoting evangelism: why not add a political agenda?

(2) They should be responsible in the ordinary sense that they are accountable to those who have given them their mandate, but not necessarily representative, in that the divisions in our society tend to be all too easily replicated in our governments through a system of strict representation.

(3) They should represent the traditional concerns of the neighbourhood, or to put it another way, they should be rooted in the local culture. The trouble with 'global' or even national solutions, because they are usually imposed from a distance, is that they all too often ignore local factors which are essential to a proper understanding of the situation.

(4) A similar point is that a system which is local would promote 'people government' and guard against the impersonality of global institutions, big government and a distancing bureaucracy. 'Presidential' government which deals through the media and the communication network, is precisely what we do not want. I realise that the spread of an intrusive media culture seems inexorable, with increasingly sophisticated media technology and people on more familiar terms with the characters on their TV screens than their neighbours. But in a sense small associations are the alternative and therefore the solution.

Here I would like to add something about consumerism, building on the familiar work already done by so many groups and individuals to work for 'fair trade'. Certainly 'consumerism with an ethical face', as it has been called, might work to the advantage of associative politics. What do I mean by 'with an ethical face'? Essentially this would be consumerism that was not an end in itself, a move away from exchange-value and towards use-value. It would be the opposite of the Eighties' philosophy that 'greed is good', that unrestrained consumption was better for everyone whatever sort of growth it represented. A number of voices, not specifically Christian, have been raised against this philosophy. An article in the British paper, the *Independent* says, among other things:

> ...decades of research have confirmed that such things as good health, stable social networks and relationships – which are also important in keeping people healthy – are far more important to happiness than income or consumer choice. ('Money doesn't make the world go round' in *Independent*, 27 February 1995)

In other words, there is nothing wrong with consumer choice, but it is not necessarily the most important value. We Christians, in particular, need to mount a practical demonstration that there are values in our lives which are more important than our standard of living or our income or our possessions. We must insist (as the article in the *Independent* says) that money doesn't make the world go round – actually according to Dante it is love that makes the world go round – that money can't buy you love, that the love of money is the root of all sorts of evil, that people are more important than possessions and so on. Fundamental to a sense of well being (I mean *my* well being) is justice. I need to have a good conscience if I am going to live the good life. When the Apostle Paul thanked God for his good conscience, he was not referring to the fact that he was more morally scrupulous than others, or even that he had a better religion, but rather that he was at ease with himself because he was being true to his convictions. There was nothing that he could accuse himself of, at least at that particular moment in his life. This is where fair trade comes in. How can we live at ease with our conscience if we are knowingly living the good life at the expense of others?

To chime with our previous theme this consumerism needs to be expressed *locally*. The politics of our local supermarket may be more important to us than the policy at Washington or Westminster, or better still, we can act so that the policy at the centre takes second place to local decision making.

I admit that all this sounds rather utopian, a simple wishing that the world was a different place, even a regression to 'the good old days'. Yet there is something which can be said about this. Trends can be accurately identified and described. Are they therefore irreversible? Do we need to have such a socially determinist world view?

Two models

In order to keep moving from theory to praxis I have selected two specifically Christian models of the sort of local associations I have in mind. The first is the East Harlem Protestant Parish as described in Bruce Kenrick's *Come out the Wilderness* (Kenrick 1962). Another rather different model is provided by the *Iniciativa Cristiana* in the Argentinean Chako (Sinclair 1980). The issues that these organisations addressed arose out of their respective contexts. Clearly the needs of tribal groups in the Chako and of dwellers in East Harlem, New York, are different, and different again from those arising from, say, the average suburban context where one might expect such issues as schools and hospitals, the disadvantaged, green issues, law and order, housing and the like to be prominent. However, it is the structures rather than the issues that I want to deal with.

The East Harlem Protestant Parish was the initiative of three young men who responded to the evident need of a particular locality. They constituted themselves as an interdependent 'Group Ministry', accepting various disciplines (devotional, economic, vocational, and political) and involving themselves in the district's social needs. They attacked such issues as housing, heating, refuse collection, police brutality, drug addiction, and debt - a familiar litany of woe. They saw themselves as motivators and facilitators of anyone who wanted to work for change. They worked with local government agencies and were critical of them when necessary. They educated, informed, protested and organised. They were soon joined by others who wanted to do the same work. Very important was what they were not. They were not big government. They were not representing particular interests. They were not from 'outside'; they lived and worked in the locality.

The *Iniciativa Cristiana* was a programme set up by the *Mision Chaquena* in the Argentinean Chako in an effort to promote the social development of the Indian communities of the area, particularly at a time when Indian traditional society was deeply threatened by the onset of modern 'development' sponsored by government agencies. This tended to subordinate the Indians if not politically then certainly economically. The *Iniciativa* had to do with education, new employment opportunities, the preservation of communities through participatory politics, and a health initiative. Again, this is familiar ground for those in 'development' situations. The point is that what was needed was some sort of corporate action below government level, but more organised than individual initiative and protest, operating in the space between government and society at large. In practice in this case the government was sometimes sympathetic to the plight of the Indians and more often on the side of the enemy, siding with the business interests that wished to 'develop' (i.e. exploit) the district. On the other hand, the Indians were not able, as individuals, to resist this onslaught, and their existing community structures were not adapted to the modern world. So a new initiative was needed (the *Iniciativa Cristiana*) which was participatory, responsible, locally based and locally relevant.

Consequences and conclusions

What does all this add up to? Let me summarise my arguments again. We desperately need new structures of government, based on a theology and philosophy which accept and promote good human relationships and which counter the dehumanising effect of economic globalisation. The appropriate 'practical' response is the formation of 'small, low-level, local, political associations', which are rooted in the community and resistant to the pressures of 'big government' and economic globalisation.

There is nothing to hinder us setting up these associations right away, but also we must not be anxious if our attempts to establish the rule of God begin with smallness. Isaiah 11:1 starts small with 'a shoot out of the stump of Jesse', but ends with a global vision, 'for the earth shall be filled with the knowledge of God as the waters cover the sea.' Similarly when Jesus describes to his disciples the nature of the rule of God, one of his descriptions is the mustard seed (Matthew 13:31,2). There is only one tree in the New Jerusalem but, as we have seen, it is intended for the healing of the nations (Revelation 22:2). The key point about the community is its rootedness and fruitfulness, not its size.

Finally, let me try a little 'thought experiment'. If we could 'bring in the rule of God' and there were no barriers to our doing so, what might it look like? I suggest the following, in no particular order.

- It would be for everyone who wanted it. ('Whosoever will may come.')
- People would be accepted because they are people. In other words, arrangements would be fair. Nobody would be at a disadvantage for any unnecessary reason. Equality means, at the very least, equality of opportunity and equality before the law.
- People would have what they needed, not just to survive but to thrive.
- People would contribute in any way that they could and should be empowered to do so. Creativity and enterprise would be encouraged, talent recognised. Sharing would be the norm.
- Power would also be shared - no 'big bosses' of any sort.
- The ruling motivation would be love rather than fear.
- A healthy environment would be preserved by all means possible.
- Education would be for everyone, for ever.
- Freedom of expression would be jealously guarded.

Does this sound impossible? Let me ask Christians reading this a simple question. Is this how your church operates? Are they impossible goals as far as a church is concerned? I hope not. Let me run through the list above and apply it to a local church.

- The church doors should be open for all.
- Everyone who comes must be treated alike in the sense that there
- should be no discrimination.

- People should be 'built up' in every possible way and encouraged to contribute to the good of the community in every possible way, in particular by using the good gifts that God has given them.
- We may have 'big bosses' in the church, but we certainly could do without them!
- 'Little children love one another…perfect love casts out fear' sounds like a text we could put on the wall.
- People thrive best when they are treated as fully human. The community of the church needs 'shalom' in its eating, clothing, holidaying, partying, housing, working conditions, worshipping conditions, use of space (I could go on) as in every other way.
- We do not need any brainwashing, thank you; nothing that savours of mental coercion or intellectual blackmail. People can come and go as they please.
- Finally, people need to learn new things all the time. It is the community's responsibility to see that they have the opportunity to do this.

Notice that I am not talking about 'the perfect church'. I am talking about a reasonable goal for any church.

One criticism of this vision is that we seem to have forgotten that Christianity itself has a universal dimension. The narrowness and isolation of small communities may be necessary in times of hardship and persecution but are there no alternatives for those of us who live in better times? Can we not retain our integrity as communities, but at the same time, as part of a worldwide fellowship, demonstrate the scope of the rule of God? Possibly, but we are certainly going to have to change. At one end of the spectrum our churches are insufficiently integrated into local communities ('the community in the community') to make much of a stand against the global forces which are destroying them; at the other end, we have little real concept of the church universal and how it should shape our behaviour. For example, if our church's budget does not take into account anything but our own, local needs, how can we talk about global fellowship? At the very least we need to begin to reflect on the economic gap that exists, and is getting wider, between us and churches in the developing world. What structures are required to allow the claim that we live in a community transcending the economic, geographical and cultural borders between churches in the US and Europe and, say, Africa?

The Biblical Witness

For Christians the above thoughts on The Great Economy may seem too 'secular', something out of a discussion on politics that you might have with fellow members of a residents' association or local political party. My contention is that these are the contexts in which we should indeed be discussing politics, but also that in every context we can bring to bear the Biblical witness.

The testimony of Deuteronomy

We can begin our search for the Great Economy in the Old Testament. Here I am particularly drawing on the thought of Gordon McConville, Professor of Old Testament in the University of Gloucestershire.[24] In the Old Testament in general, power, properly exercised, has a human face. Thus, in the book of Daniel, God's 'empire' is given to 'the son of man' (Adam). By contrast, in the Exodus account power belongs to the chaos monsters, where chaos in the political realm means a self-legitimating power. In Egypt 'monstrous' power belongs to the Pharaoh because there is no power beyond Pharaoh. Just as in the creation story the forces of chaos are defeated by Yahweh, so political creation begins with the subduing of chaos. In Deuteronomy (see especially 16:18 – 18:22) it is envisaged that, under God and the law (*torah*) the supreme political power is exercised by the people (Deuteronomy 16:18,19). '*You* shall appoint,' Yahweh says. There are leaders – prophets, priests, judges (kings are an option though not a very good one) but it is the people who are addressed, not any hierarchy. It is certainly not a theocracy in the traditional sense with priests and kings claiming the divine authority. Also there is a *division* of powers, although all are under the Law. *Interpretation* of the law is vital, and it is the people who decide, though they may need some help from the judges, priests and prophets. The 'people' here means a people or nation, not a tribe or an empire. It is a unified people living within borders, not racially or ethnically defined, but living under one law: notice the accountability to strangers (Deuteronomy 14:28-9). The key metaphor

---

[24] Most of the ideas concerning the political testimony of the Book of Deuteronomy that follow come from notes which I took on the occasion of Professor McConville's inaugural lecture at the University of Gloucestershire. He has since published these insights (along with others) in his book *God and Earthly Power, An Old Testament Political Theology*. The details are in the bibliography.

is brotherhood (Deuteronomy 22:1-4). The individual is addressed as part of the whole (Deuteronomy 15:12-15). Memory is part of this. ('Remember that you were slaves in Egypt.') This is the key role of the *prophets*. They are there to act as the nation's memory, as a counter to forgetting.

So here is an exciting start to our search. Human government as a resistance to empire, as order, democracy, the rule of law, facilitative leadership, the division of powers, nationhood, brotherhood, and as creatively drawing on history are all mentioned. And people say that the Bible is not about politics.

Utopian imaginations and the Song of Songs

I have always thought it necessary to retain some sort of utopian politics, even when the disasters of our civilisation suggest an unrelieved pessimism. Obviously we need to avoid sentimental wishful thinking, but I am impressed by the spirit of John Lennon's *Imagine*, and even more impressed by something like William Morris's *News from Nowhere*. Morris's fable starts at a place where many of us have been. Walking home from a discussion with his friends about 'what would happen on the Morrow of the Revolution' the hero of our story (Morris himself) mutters sadly 'If I could but see it!'(Morris 1984, 183-4). But then Morris takes us to a place where none of us have been. Next morning he wakes up to find that it *has* happened. History has moved on and the New Age has dawned. Morris knew, and wants us to know, that we need some such vision if we are to struggle on in dark times.

The Song of Songs is a love poem which inhabits a utopian space, though there are also elements of realism. Thus, in an overall idyllic framework, the lovers nevertheless experience disappointment and even danger at times. The woman is frustrated in her search for her lover (3:2) and on a second search is beaten and wounded (4:7). Amid all the gorgeous spring time imagery, such as the blossoming of the vineyards, there is the image of the foxes which must be caught before they spoil the grapes (2:15). 'Love in the open air' is celebrated on a number of occasions, but there are also some disadvantages in spending the day outside in the fresh air and strong sunlight (1:6). Along with the description of the physical perfections of the lovers, we encounter a little sister who has no breasts (8:8) and amid all the frank exhortations to love and erotic engagement (1:2 and many other examples) there are also moments when the electric current of sexuality needs to be turned down (3:5 and parallels). The poem is therefore not entirely devoted to an ideal world in which lovers are perfect physical specimens or in which it is perpetual springtime and the whole world is on their side. In the great climax of the poem in chapter 8, love is as strong as death, but there is still death (8:6).

Having said this, the poem is rooted in reality only inasmuch as it constructs its own world which convinces us that it is possible and believable. Compared to what we know about contemporary Israelite society and the Ancient Near East, and indeed what we know about 'life' more generally, there seems no doubt about the utopian nature of the world of the poem. It is not so much that the lovers are such perfect specimens (in their own eyes, anyway) or that they are living in such a beautiful place, or even that they find so much unspoilt pleasure in their love making – after all, there *are* beautiful people, and lovely places and pleasurable exchanges. But it is difficult to accept that they would have 'got away with it' in real life. As far as we know there was no space for their sort of behaviour in a society which supervised courtship, arranged marriages and generally attempted to control with an iron hand the sexuality of its young people. The poem seems to operate outside the norms of society altogether. There are no significant family ties that will, so to speak, slow the lovers down, no ceremonies (no 'lah-de-dah' as Jake Thackeray might have said). There are also no worries about the woman becoming pregnant, indeed about anything to do with the responsibilities of family life. Furthermore, where do we see an example, outside of the poem, of the equality between the sexes which is such a surprising feature of the Song?

Yet, perhaps, we might say that whereas society would not have allowed this sort of behaviour, it may have wished that it could be free enough to do so. Perhaps there were people who said about this state of affairs too, 'if I could but see it'. They may have felt that though in a fallen world there was a need for rules, yet it would be possible to live differently – more freely, more equally – in an unfallen world. Song of Songs, I think, expresses that feeling, and celebrates a better, if for the time being unattainable, world. In that sense it is a pre-lapsarian fable. It is a reminder of a lost world, though not in a nostalgic way – there is no nostalgic feeling in the poem – rather with the effect of something almost to hand, which might still be a possibility. I am reminded of the Levellers in the seventeenth century Puritan revolution in England who used their little tag about life in the Garden of Eden, 'When Adam delved and Eve span/Who was then the gentleman?' as a critique of contemporary hierarchy.

The pre-lapsarian elements in the Song are not overwhelming. Images from Solomon's court (3:6-11) are used to convey the opposite feeling of luxury and sophistication, for example. Nevertheless the general sense of perpetual springtime and of the lovers, placed like Adam and Eve alone in the garden (4:13,14 etc.) gives a sensation of paradise.

So what has all this got to do with the Kingdom of God and the twenty-first century? First of all, the utopian vision of two lovers in a Spring-time garden fits very well into the vision of the New Jerusalem in the Book of Revelation, that last and best description of a time when God makes 'all things new' (21:5) as he does every springtime. Main street New Jerusalem is a garden with a tree (22:2,3). There are two lovers – the Lamb and his bride (21:10). There is no ceremony (21:22), only face to face relationship (22:4) and anything that might spoil or defile has been banished (21:27). My point is that we can see all these elements in the visionary world of Eden, the Song of Songs and the New Jerusalem. Somehow, therefore, we have to incorporate them in our understanding of the Kingdom of God. If we are only offering a civilisational scaffolding: a temple instead of a garden, ceremony instead of the unfettered expression of overpowering love, covenant and law instead of face to face experience, the responsibilities of marriage instead of two alone in the garden with nothing to hide, then we shall never really be able to eat the fruit that satisfies, nor dispense the leaves that heal (22:2). And of course mission begins with the good news of the Kingdom, of its fruitfulness (Colossians 1:6) and healing (Matthew 4:17, 23-5). Have you noticed also that in Jesus' teaching about the Kingdom there is a strong question mark placed against ceremony, temple, law and even familiar family relationships?

Admittedly, postcolonialism – the main theme of this book – is another matter. I include this meditation on the Song of Songs and its relation to the Kingdom here because, it seems to me, the postcolonial discourse is just one more attempt to prize us loose from the discourse of Empire. In doing so it needs all the help it can get! Like so many movements for change, it is good on analysis but not quite so good on vision. In a small way I think the Song of Songs can provide this.

Isaiah's testimony

Another example of the idea of the Great Economy in one particular setting is provided by the thinking of Isaiah of Jerusalem. In representing to his compatriots the sort of society which he believed Yahweh wanted, he also contrasted it with the actual existing arrangements, including the ongoing temptation to follow foreign models of politics and economics.

All of the following were featured in Isaiah's message as a mixture of desirable, and possible objectives:

- A systematic attempt to convert military hardware into peaceful and productive tools as a prelude to the cessation of war (2:4)
- A refusal to allow foreigners to dominate local trade (2:6-8)
- A commitment to justice and righteousness, as against violence and unanswered cries for help (5:7)
- A warning against the catastrophic effects of greedy capitalism (5:8-10)
- A warning against corrupt practices (probably in the law courts) (5:23)
- Intervention on behalf of the poor and humble (11:3-5)
- Ecological harmony (11:6-9)
- Justice in the courts and courage in times of conflict (28:6)
- Scientific agriculture (and all the other technologies) practised in open acknowledgement that they come from Yahweh (28:29)
- Good teachers (30:20,21)
- Better lighting (!) (30:26)
- The possibility of healing – a national health service(30:26)
- Government understood as primarily a source of security (32:1,2)
- The possibility of better communications (32:3,4)
- The need for good values to be seen to be good values (32:5)
- Cheats and exploiters to be named for what they are (32:6,7)
- Noble purposes encouraged to thrive (32:8)
- The possibility of freedom from enemies (33:18,19)
- Security as a goal and possibility (33:20-22)
- The disabled to share in good things (33:23b)
- Healing and forgiveness the norm (33:24)

A few disclaimers about this list: it is by no means complete. Also, I may not have got the exegesis right in every case, and if there is any unity of emphasis it may come from the editor of the book rather than Isaiah himself. Of course the description reflects a particular historical period and culture and some of it may not apply to other circumstances. Nevertheless, in my view, it does demonstrate something quite important. Isaiah (or the person who collected these Isaianic oracles) was not just a doom sayer, but somebody who believed that something constructive could be said about arrangements in the real world. He was not just 'pulling down' but 'building up', not just 'plucking up' but 'planting' (Jeremiah 1:10).

Apocalypse Now

In addition to a more careful reading of the Old Testament we need a re-birth of apocalyptic if we are going to think creatively about the Great Economy. This may come as a surprise to those who, understandably, associate an interest in apocalyptic with a thorough-going retreat from the 'real' world. We have probably all encountered people who have taken up apocalyptic passages in Scripture – in particular Daniel, parts of the Synoptic gospels and above all the book of Revelation – and used them as a seed-bed of wildly imaginative futurist constructions – I am trying to put this politely – which effectively distance us from the complex story of our own times. All I can say is: 'God defend us from all such'. Humankind appears to have two incurable itches: one, the world of the para-normal – the occult, Satanism, ghosts, spirits and the like, and the other, the unknown future. Fascination with either or both means, nine times out of ten, that we are trying to get away from the 'real' world and its challenges in order to escape into a fantasy world which we find much more exciting and which brings with it no responsibilities and hard choices. (An aside: I am not against fantasy. Fantasy can be read responsibly, too, as in the Narnian books, or Philip Pullman's *Dark Materials* trilogy; or it can be read for fun as in Harry Potter. Why not?) This is no substitute for hard political and social analysis and a sober application of Scripture. Biblical apocalyptic, as I understand it, gives us a God-perspective on this-worldly events. If we believe in God at all, that would seem a helpful thing to have. It is not about what is going to happen in the future, but about what is happening now, *if only we could see it*. So, Jesus on trial before the Sanhedrin, speaks about the verdict in apocalyptic terms. The earthly tribunal condemns him, but in the heavenly court he is vindicated. This is anything but escapist: it gives him the 'vision' to carry on and see the matter through. When Jesus dies, it appears that the evil powers that are against him have won. He dies, apparently abandoned, watched by his enemies, with his disciples scattered and defeated. And then we have an apocalyptic moment. The veil of the temple is torn from top to bottom. So it is not just the death of some poor innocent, the victim of another political 'fix'. In fact, if only we knew (and now we do know) the whole politico-religious temple apparatus, with its laws of exclusion and assertion of privileged power, has come to an end. Something has happened which will change history forever.

John in the Apocalypse says 'I saw heaven open'. Precisely. That is what we need to experience when we read the news and watch the images on TV. We need to know what God's 'counsel' is. For an Old Testament prophet that was his 'claim to fame', the authentication and vindication of his prophetic ministry, that he stood in the 'counsel of the Lord', that he had been there in the heavenly committee when the discussion was going on, and had overheard what was being said.

How does apocalyptic work for us today? We must get back, on a regular basis, to the cosmic battle. The present world order, in which we are involved as citizens, employees, voters, activists, and which we rightly examine through the lens of our reading, discussion, academic study and the like, is a world which, of itself, is subject to fallen, alien powers. In that sense 'the whole world lies in the evil one', and we are right to describe 'the world' (the usual Biblical term) as 'the Domination System'. This does not mean that there are no good people and even good organisations in the world, but its general tendency is first to forget God and then to organise itself in opposition to God, not necessarily deliberately, but as a sort of inevitable reflex action. The world's ideologies, organisations and associations become 'powers' and as fallen powers they serve themselves and enslave people.[25] As we have seen, one of their 'natural' tendencies is self-aggrandisement. They are empire builders. Many of these empires are highly impressive. But we Christians are called to struggle *against* them.

Apocalyptic gives us this conflictual viewpoint, but also hope in the struggle and the means to overcome. Confronted by the grandeur, and indeed the ruthless power of the Roman Empire, John on the island of Patmos, might have thought that Rome was everywhere and everything. But John had a secret, and his secret was the secret of the universe. It was 'the Lamb who had been killed' who was in fact the universal Lord, and not Caesar.

In viewing our own world, this sort of apocalyptic insight can work in two ways. First of all it tells us that the world systems, which may for the time being look mightily impressive, are in fact ephemeral. We must not be fooled. Where is the Third Reich or the Soviet Empire now? How quickly a huge, apparently fabulously wealthy, business corporation like Enron can crash. Is our whole economic system about to implode? The other side of the coin is that mustard seeds , though very tiny, grow into big trees. Apocalyptic may help us identify those small life-giving energies that the Domination System does not recognise, indeed would want to crush if it did. Again, John of Patmos, with his prophetic vision could see that seven fallible churches in West Asia Minor, struggling to keep their heads above water amid a torrent of imperial propaganda and persecution, were in fact God's New Jerusalem.

---

[25] See the fuller discussion above, p. 14ff.

It makes a huge difference when we read the news and are able to tell ourselves that the big battalions which seem to be carrying all before them, are not the inevitable future, that however free they seem to be to do as they please, their day of accounting will come. Equally, it is very exciting to feel the stirring of God's Spirit, to catch hold of a man or a woman, a movement or a moment, through which God is beginning to work. Apocalyptic blows like a cool wind on a sultry day, breathes like a current of fresh air into a stiflingly hot room. I have friends with whom I go and talk apocalyptic talk when I get discouraged, and I always come away reinvigorated, ready to renew the battle. Apocalyptic also has to do with worship. John, in Revelation, regularly pops through the door into heaven for a spot of praise. Worship, as we have said, is discovering what God is worth, and then telling him what we have discovered. Now that is an antidote to the diseases of Empire! Apocalyptic helps us to grow the tree of life in the middle of our Babylonish captivity and to find again that 'the leaves of the tree are for the healing of the nations'.

Let me try and fill out some of these ideas in more down-to-earth terms, by citing various apocalyptic moments in my own experience. I am not writing here about times when God has spoken to me about my own Christian life. Rather these are occasions when I was trying to work out what something in 'the big bad world' meant, and why it troubled me, and then I was able to see it in a new light, indeed I thought I could see it in God's perspective.

(a) *Edge of Darkness*

Edge of Darkness, the television serial written by Troy Kennedy Martin and starring Bob Peck was a fiction which dealt with the nuclear industry and its dangerous tendency to change from a supposedly peaceful and energy producing enterprise into a more sinister military one. It showed that the industry lived within, and in turn generated, a 'security' complex, supported by both big business and government, which allowed it to defend itself by illegal and violent means. It also promoted a sort of global *hubris* with talk of a new 'space frontier' and a new habitat for mankind to replace this 'tired worn-out earth'. Against this is pitted the resources of the GAIA organisation, a tiny group of committed scientists willing to take on the establishment at great personal risk. All this spoke powerfully to me of the Empire and the New Jerusalem. GAIA seemed to me to be the place where we Christians ought to be, and usually are not. Fact or fiction (and the author claimed that there was a great deal of truth behind what had been written) the film provided for me a reminder of true Kingdom praxis in the midst of a fully functioning Domination System.

(b) Where Satan has his throne

Though most apocalyptic images have to do with conflict, this is not always the case. The New Jerusalem, for example, is a garden city with a river running through the middle of main street and 'on each side of the river, the tree of life'. When I was teaching for six months at a secondary school in London I encountered the harshest employment conditions I have ever known, before or since. This was partly because of the physical context – dilapidated buildings, uncared-for poorly-designed plant, asphalt play spaces disfigured by graffiti and rubbish. Worse than that – much worse – were the social dynamics. The students were bored, scarcely under control, bullying and bullied, racist, and deeply competitive. The staff were anxious, frightened, divided and in survival mode (except that most of them did not in fact survive). Wherever you looked the Domination System was in full force. I remember that I was constantly on the look-out for some sort of (good) apocalyptic perspective. It never came. Personally, I was wounded by the Empire. For me Babylon had fallen, and I was going down with it. My only chance was to get out.

My next stop was teaching at a Christian College in West London. On my first day at work I arrived early and went for a brief stroll around the extensive garden. One of the governors of the College was a horticultural expert from the famous Kew Gardens. He had personally supervised the college grounds, both their lay-out and the choice of plants. On that late summer morning it seemed like a paradise to me and from that moment I could feel the healing begin. (For those of you who are familiar with *The Lord of the Rings* it was like being in Ithilien instead of Mordor.) It was the New Jerusalem instead of Babylon. Remember that in John's *Revelation* the New Jerusalem is 'always coming down out of heaven' (a present continuous tense). In one sense it is a place you can live in while Babylon still exists. So it was that I found my apocalyptic community, even though each day I motored past my old school and realised that I had escaped from a place 'where Satan has his throne'.

(c) The Great War

A relative of mine has told me that he went to a performance of Benjamin Britten's *War Requiem* and decided he never wanted to go again – it was all too disturbing. I know how he felt. The music by itself is haunting, and combined with Wilfred Owen's war poetry the effect is overwhelming. For British people the Great War has a particular resonance. I suppose it is partly because every town and village has a war memorial where the list of the dead in battle is so long that we have to struggle to disengage ourselves from the sheer depth of the human tragedy involved. The War itself, now frequently described as 'meaningless' – what, after all, was all the bloodshed *about*? – has become horrific for that very reason, because of its futility. In that sense it is the opposite of an apocalyptic moment. The point about apocalyptic is that there *is* a meaning; another perspective emerges which allows us to put purpose into the events we have witnessed. Britten's *War Requiem* struggles to do this, but does not succeed. He is building on the foundation laid by Wilfred Owen whose poems come out of the darkness and who can see no reason for allowing any light into the picture. One of Owen's best poems is called 'Futility' and that is no surprise. Britten had an opportunity to change this. For one thing the work was commissioned for the inaugural ceremony of the rebuilt Coventry Cathedral – a sign of hope after the Second World War. For another, in the work itself there is a 'heavenly choir'. You might say that the arrangement of the musical forces has an apocalyptic form. A form, but not a message – the voices from heaven do not offer any revelation or even relief. They are purposely remote and disembodied. As Christopher Palmer writes in the programme notes to the famous Decca recording: 'At a still further remove [than the full choir] is a chorus of boys' voices and organ suspended in limbo: innocent and pure sounding, but totally divorced from breathing human passion…They represent a zenith (or nadir) of remoteness.' At the other extreme the two chief protagonists, a German and British soldier, discover as a finale that they are in hell, and that their best prospect is the oblivion of sleep.

If the *War Requiem* is, as I have said, a profoundly anti-apocalyptic work, why introduce it at this point? Part of the answer, as far as I am concerned, is that the Great War demands some sort of response that goes beyond Owen and Britten. (I am not, of course, trying to suggest that there is anything lacking in the *art* of either man – they are both supreme artists). The very depth of the pathos they evoke makes me want to re-engage with the feeling I have, shared I think by many, that helpless incomprehension is not the only possible response. Notice the way that we want to go on *remembering*. Quite apart from official commemorations such as Armistice Day, the war graves are visited as much as ever. Books about the Great War, like Sebastian Faulk's *Birdsong* and Pat Barker's *Regeneration* trilogy still reach out to us powerfully.

This brings me to Vera Brittain's autobiographical *Testament of Youth*. Nobody could accuse Brittain of any attempt to glamorise or minimise the horror of the Great War. In that way she is fully in the Owen tradition. She was fiercely opposed to the jingoism which so disfigured public opinion during the war years, and remained deeply sceptical of any value-added meaning in the post-war years to do with patriotism, heroism or martyrdom. But there is something else. It might be difficult to prove this, but the way that the War tore Brittain savagely from her roots was what gave her life direction. She herself knew how important it was for her to get away from the claustrophobia of her small-town upbringing in Buxton, and even her university education at Oxford. Had she married Roland – the fiancé who was killed in the war – would the story have become less interesting? She herself wrote of what she called 'handicaps' – 'the Victorian tradition of womanhood, a carefully trained conscience, a sheltered youth, an imperfect education, lost time, blasted years' as something which urged her on.

> Dimly I perceived that it was these very handicaps and my struggle against them which had lifted life out of its mediocrity, given it glamour, made it worthwhile; that the individuals from whom destiny demands too much are infinitely more vital than those of whom it asks too little. (Brittain 2004, 602]

In any case, it is a function of apocalyptic, as I am describing it, that crisis, disaster, persecution and the like, open up the possibilities rather than close them down. The Great War was truly Vera Brittain's 'apocalyptic moment' in this sense.

Reading her book was also an apocalyptic moment for me – to compare small things with great. It gave me a new perspective on this particular story of human suffering analogous to the 'open door' which the seer offered to the communities to which he was writing in the book of Revelation, communities which, like me, were struggling with the meaning of a hostile world. Neither Vera Brittain nor John of Patmos wrote their books in order to *explain* history. That is not how apocalyptic works. What they had was a revelation. They understood that sacrifice – crucified Saviour and sacrificed friends – empowered rather than diminished their lives.

Perhaps I am overloading *Testament of Youth* with personal significance. It may just have been a rather moving book which I read at a difficult time in my life. Perhaps Vera Brittain would have denied that there was any revelation, or any connection between her manifest sense of purpose after the catastrophe, and the catastrophe itself. Maybe so, but it is still of significance to me that Brittain helped me to see the Great War in a new light, as a beginning as well as an end. Other troubling events have not necessarily found a similar 'apocalyptic moment'. Take, for example, the holocaust. I have read a number of books about it, but nothing has altered the feeling that this is an end with no beginning, not apocalyptic but catastrophic pure and simple.

(d) Walter Benjamin

Though I find the holocaust an inexplicable aporia in the historical process, the same is not necessarily true of the Jewish experience as a whole under fascism. I am helped in this by the Jewish literary critic and philosopher, Walter Benjamin. Benjamin committed suicide when he thought, probably wrongly, that his attempt to evade arrest and incarceration at the hands of the fascist authorities, had failed. He knew enough to be sure that if he did end up in a concentration camp he would not survive. He left behind him a number of writings that have ensured his lasting reputation, indeed he is now more honoured than ever. Benjamin was a Marxist and a materialist (of sorts) but he was also a Jew who knew his theology and had been exposed to Jewish thinkers such as Martin Buber. Stephen Bronner describes him as 'a messianic materialist'. As Bronner puts it: 'A messianic hermeneutic renders whole or gives cohesion to what has become fragmentary and redeems the suffering of the past. Utopia, previously conceived by Marx as immanent within history, is now transformed into an external standpoint with which to judge progress.' (1994, 137-8). What this meant in practical terms was that Benjamin did not have to believe in 'inevitable progress', which was just as well for him because when he surveyed the history of his time he saw nothing but one pile of wreckage upon another. On the other hand his apocalyptic stance enabled him 'to confront the linear and teleological view of history inherited by Marxism and the Enlightenment' with 'a new view of the past which is open and capable of constant reconstruction' (137). For Benjamin, 'opening the past to reconstruction' meant that he could include all the losers. As he put it himself 'only for the sake of the hopeless, is hope given us'. Think again of apocalyptic. In John's Revelation we have all these elements. The world catastrophe ('Babylon is fallen'), wreckage upon wreckage, and the need for an interpreter, someone with 'a new view of the past', someone not committed to the inevitability of Empire. This someone finds hope by identifying and promoting the 'losers' who are to be the eventual invitees to the party. As Benjamin says: 'Those who are alive at any given time see themselves in the midday of history. They are obliged to prepare a banquet for the past. The historian is the herald who invites those who are departed to the table.' (Bronner 1994, 144). Or as John might say: 'Blessed are they who are invited to the marriage supper of the Lamb'.

In what sense was reading Benjamin an 'apocalyptic moment' for me? Briefly, it allowed me to question my heritage as 'a child of the Enlightenment'. I grew up with the relentless myth of Progress, which seemed more and more as time passed to be simply untrue. By the time I had finished my university studies (mid-1960s) I was convinced that I had to find something different. I was as committed as ever to following Jesus and was attracted to certain elements in Marxism (or at least to something which demonstrated more social concern than the churches I went to) but needed a way to bring it all together. I floundered about for a long time – Liberation Theology helped at one stage – but I never really felt at ease with my own worldview until I encountered the Critical Theorists and, in particular, Walter Benjamin. Up to this point I had avoided Biblical apocalyptic because it seemed to me escapist (and still seems so in the form in which it has been embraced by many in the church). Benjamin and co, as I have described very briefly above, enabled me to return to it. Of course at that point I found that many others had returned to it too. A friend of mine was doing a PhD on Ernst Käsemann whose most famous phrase in this regard was 'apocalyptic is the mother of all Christian theology'. Strange that I, a Christian, should have to come to apocalyptic through a Marxist materialist. In fact the Critical Theorists were more theological than they allowed, as we have seen in the case of Benjamin. It was another Critical Theorist, Theodor Adorno, who said: 'The only philosophy which can be responsibly practised in the face of despair is the attempt to regard all things as the way they would present themselves from the standpoint of redemption' (Myers 1994, 395) – an apocalyptic commentary if ever there was one.

It was all such a relief! To quote Ched Myers: 'Critical Theory helps free theology from its self-imposed obligation to *rationalise* reality by answering questions to *problematising* reality by questioning answers' (1994, 33).

(e) Two recent films: apocalyptic and the nature of 'failure'

The film *The Painted Veil* is based on a novel by Somerset Maugham. The chief protagonists are an ill-assorted couple, Walter and Kitty, who get married in England and set off for a posting in China, where the young wife falls in love with another man and has an affair with him. The furious husband insists that the only way forward is for them to go together to a dangerous and harsh situation in the interior of the country where he has been asked to help with a serious outbreak of cholera. As far as he is concerned there is no question of reconciliation. If not exactly revenge, at least it is a 'lesson'. Desperate, Kitty learns, for the first time, that she can relate to people – to the nuns who are caring for the sick, to other imperfect people like herself that she meets, and to the children she offers to look after. Finally, out of her growing self-knowledge, she is ready to challenge Walter. She is to blame, but so is he. Why had he married her when he had known what she was like? What had he unreasonably expected from her? In what way had he insisted that she conform to his needs and desires? If she had failed, so had he. He, at last, sees this. As he says: 'It was silly to look for qualities in each other we never had.' Out of their mutual failure comes understanding. It is only when they are able to lift

>...the painted veil which those who live
>
>Call life: though unreal shapes be pictured there

and move beyond the 'twin destinies' of fear and hope that they are both able to realise that they are looking for love in the wrong place. (Perhaps I should add that I am referring here to the film; the book is much more doubtful about the possibility of understanding, indeed there is no reconciliation in Maugham's original version.)

Apocalyptic is like that: it asks us to 'lift the painted veil' but also to accept that the next step is not necessarily going to be a triumphant conclusion. It does usher us into greater reality, but that reality may be a deeper experience of human failure, of suffering or death. Too many readings of apocalyptic have left this out. The great apocalyptic moment of the New Testament is the cross. In John's Revelation the conquerors are the martyrs. I came away from watching *The Painted Veil* saddened that it had taken me so long to learn that lesson.

The *Constant Gardener* returns to the theme of the Domination System: big business, supported by government and expressed, in this instance, by Big Pharma. Though once again a fiction, John Le Carré, the author of the novel on which the film is based, assures us that 'the half has never been told' as far as the wickedness of the pharmaceutical industry is concerned. The film, otherwise excellent, is less tough than the novel, contriving some sort of happy ending. Against the Domination System (as in *Edge of Darkness*) are the few: Tessa, the passionate protester, the African doctor, Arnold and in the end, the 'constant gardener', Tessa's husband, Justin. They all get killed for their pains and (in the novel) appear to achieve very little by means of this ultimate sacrifice. Another failure, you might say. The world goes on its way. Despite this dismal ending, the plot draws us in, however, simply because we could not possibly want to be on the side of the Empire. All this loss and dying and apparent failure seem so much more *attractive* than what the Empire has to offer. It is not just a question of doing good, of standing for justice, but of wanting to belong, even when we have a sneaking feeling that it would take more courage than we ordinarily possess.

Most of the best apocalyptic stories end with a feast, a celebration. Not just any old party, of course, but a feast of memories. People are there, in part, because they have made it through the tough times and are being offered the opportunity to remember what that was like. An appropriate image might be a regimental dinner, after a protracted and dangerous military campaign.

> Do you remember...?
>
> Of course I do.
>
> We were holed up in that trench for twenty-four hours; I thought we'd never get out.
>
> I thought we were going to die.
>
> So did I.

Of course, if there has been no campaign, no action, no terrifying moments, no loyalty, then perhaps there is not much point in having a celebration either. When Jesus said to his disciples at the Last Supper that he would not drink wine again until he drank it with them in the Kingdom, we can understand the words as a vow as well as a prophecy. He was promising them that he would see it through to the end: then, and only then, the time of feasting would begin. 'Blessed are those who invited to the wedding feast of the Lamb', precisely because they have shared Christ's sufferings and seen the battle through to the end (Philippians 3:10,11). In the apocalyptic world (the victors are the martyrs) it does not necessarily mean that 'seeing it through to the end' means victory – not in this-worldly terms. On one view, Tessa and Justin and Arnold in *The Constant Gardener* were losers. It is just necessary to be faithful, to be constant.

(f) Puddleglum and *The Silver Chair*

Puddleglum is one of those attractive characters who always forecasts disaster but is a rock of fortitude when things actually do go badly wrong. His 'apocalyptic moment' occurs when he and Jill and Eustace are in the greatest danger. Trapped in the dark, underground world, they are invited by their captor, the Queen of Underland, to view their situation as an all-encompassing reality. Their memories of Narnia – a world of sunshine and fresh air, of colour and movement, of joy and freedom – are simply fantasies. There is no such place as Narnia.

Puddleglum comes to the rescue.

> Suppose we *have* only dreamed, or made up all those things – trees and grass, and sun and moon and stars and Aslan himself. Suppose we have. Then all I can say is that, in that case, the made-up things seem a good deal more important than the real ones. Suppose this black pit of a kingdom of yours *is* the only world. Well, it strikes me as a pretty poor one. And that's a funny thing, when you come to think of it. We're just babies making up a game, if you're right. But four babies playing a game can make a play-world which licks your real world hollow!

Apocalyptic is, as we have seen, about coming to terms with destruction and disaster, of 'seeing through' the 'fashion of this world' but it is also about 'the fair beauty of the Lord'. From time to time we *are* invited into that world.

> My windows open to the autumn night,
> In vain I watched for sleep to visit me;
> How shall sleep dull mine ears or dim my sight
> Who saw the stars and listened to the sea.
>
> Ah, how the City of our God is fair!
> If without sea, and starless though it be
> For joy of the majestic beauty there,
> Men shall not miss the stars, nor mourn the sea.

I do not think that Lionel Johnson, the author of the poem, needs to miss out on the stars and sea. We are promised a redeemed creation. However he is right about the beauty of the New Jerusalem. The point is that 'dreams' are better than this world 'realities'. Apocalyptic allows us to see that sometimes.

Chapter 6

POSTCOLONIALISM: A GIFT FROM THE SPONSOR OF WORLD MISSION

'Fear not, little flock; for your Father has chosen to give you the Kingdom.'

Despite expressions such as 'building the Kingdom' the unmistakable impression given by the New Testament is that the Kingdom is not something you build, but something you discover. Jesus and John the Baptist both called for repentance because the Kingdom of God was 'just around the corner'; it was about to emerge, and though it was necessary to ready oneself for its appearance, that was all that Jesus' disciples could do: get ready and watch it happen. And when it came it was a *gift*. After that it continued to have its own momentum. Luke, in describing the growth of the church in Acts, punctuates his account with phrases such as 'the word of God continued to grow and spread'. The word of God had a life of its own!

More recently there has been the discovery (or re-discovery in the light of the above) that mission which was thought to belong to the church, belongs to God. Missiologists have been talking for some time now about *missio Dei*, the mission of God, reminding us that God is at work in the world, and always has been, and that he invites us to join him in that work, rather than the other way round.

Postcolonialism, too, if we can think of it as a discourse and also as a historical development, is a gift from God. This statement may seem absurd and even dangerous. Why mention an aspect of twentieth century political theory and some recent events in world affairs in the same breath as the Kingdom of God and *missio Dei*? But this shows, once again, the dualism that characterises our thinking. We still find it difficult, do we not, to accept that God is at work in the world outside of the church and without the help of believing people. We can attribute something evil like fascism or colonialism to 'satanic forces', but we are not prepared to give God any credit for something good such as the anti-*apartheid* movement or the (at least partial) success of the Civil Rights movement in the United States.

What has God given us then, when we look at his world through a postcolonial lens? Here are some suggestions, based on the ideas in this book.

- New ways to resist and subvert the Empire
- A renewed concern for 'subalterns' and their place in history and society
- A new vision of the hybrid society, a 'third way' which challenges the 'us and them' of so much of our thinking including our thinking about mission
- A critique of the Enlightenment Project (rationalism, Development, 'progress')
- A better way of thinking about displaced peoples, those who are 'pilgrims and strangers'
- Some help with intractable social and economic problems such as 'urban drift'
- Some help with today's political conundrums such as the Israel-Palestine conflict and the nature of nationalism as an ideology
- A defence of the local, together with a concern for the survival of threatened communities
- A re-reckoning of the possibilities for mission in the twenty-first century in the light of the shifting centres of world Christianity
- New insights into 'the Great Economy'

All in all I would say that these aspects of postcolonialism are God-given tools. We need them to work with as we respond to God's mission in the world. They help us to 'see' the Kingdom of God in our own day.

Conclusion: Time to Wake Up

If you have come thus far, perhaps you are saying to yourself that the picture presented in this book is altogether too melodramatic and too dark. The author is obviously a gloomy apocalypsist, who gets a perverse pleasure in telling people that whatever the weather looks like now, it will certainly rain by nightfall. Yet the author is an optimist! I feel quite unafraid about the future, while quite sure that our civilisation cannot go on in the way that it is, and survive. Essentially, I am optimistic because I am a Christian. It is not that I am appealing to the traditional Christian belief in 'the hope of heaven', though that is something which does comfort me when I have time to think about it. No, it has to do with my belief that this world which we inhabit is God's creation and was, so to speak, his idea in the first place. Of course, our particular civilisation may be doomed. That seems to me quite possible, even probable. Also there may be ways in which we humans can 'destroy' the earth, though I think we have some way to go before that is likely to happen. What is indestructible is the idea. The idea, for example, of the walk I have just come back from – the winter sun, the pale blue sky, the wind sighing in the trees, the mist beginning to gather as the afternoon wears on, the chill in the air – is eternal. It is probably fixed forever in my memory – I am not sure about that – but it is certainly lodged eternally in the mind of God. All these terrible forces that we have been inspecting, real and powerful as they are, have no equivalent status. 'The domination system passes away' as John says in his letter.

If it is not the author's fault, perhaps we might say that the New Testament itself – especially the Book of Revelation – was written by the sort of people who, because of their tough experience of life, are never happy unless disaster threatens. Was Jesus himself one of these, making enemies of the Scribes and Pharisees, weeping over Jerusalem, always talking about death and crosses? Do we have to be like that? After all, there is much to enjoy in the twenty first century. Why not try a little harder to do so? Globalisation itself promises much. It is delivering people from the parochialism of village and small town life, from the confines of office and factory, from the tedium of a monocultural existence and a monodirectional job, from the tyranny of the patriarchal family. It is offering 'choice', and travel (or at least virtual travel) and connectedness, such as our forbears would never have imagined.

It sounds wonderful, but I am reminded of the oracle in Isaiah which asks, 'Why do you spend your money for what is not food, your earnings for what fails to satisfy?' (55:2) Are we really a *satisfied* society? How much solid enjoyment is going on? We have already identified some of the diseases of Empire. Well, there are plenty more. Nor is it possible to argue that these symptoms have always been around and that we cannot put them down to such recent developments as globalisation. The current crisis of human wellbeing has to do with precisely the remedies that we are prescribing for ourselves. It is not enough to reach back to some primordial causation such as 'original sin'. We know perfectly well that human beings are flawed and always have been, but that is not the point. It is not enough to say that sailors drown because they put out to sea. True enough, but the question we need to ask is why did they set out in a leaky boat? Humanity is a perilous condition, but we have added to that peril in our day by adopting systems of thought and action which are all but lethal.

If the effects of our present life-style are so dire, why do we not do something about them? Life under modern conditions is *not* some inexorable fate that twenty first century humanity cannot escape. Basically we are subject to a series of calculated, mostly economic, decisions which allow a small minority to prosper by means of the systematic exploitation of the majority. It is time, therefore, that we calculated how to undo the system. I admire George Monbiot for his work in this area. He refuses to say 'there is no alternative'. He proposes, for example, a form of democratic global governance. Everybody says that this is hopelessly utopian, but he is not daunted. What then, he asks, would people suggest? Abandon democracy? Accept the status quo? He is open to suggestions, but until they turn up he is getting on with building a new world. What is so depressing is that we Christians stand by wringing our hands, claiming that *we* have no alternative either. (Also, and this is worse than depressing, we, in the West, do not *want* there to be an alternative, because we are fearful that if there were, we might be the ones to lose out.)

So – is there no balm in Gilead, as the old song says? Is there no tree growing in the New Jerusalem for the healing of the nations? Is the Great Economy not so great after all?

Far from painting a darkly gloomy picture, filled with threats of apocalyptic disaster, I am saying that the good news of the rule of God is exactly what it says it is, and it is for precisely this reason that we do not have to live by the false promises of the Domination System. This is not a time for resignation and fear. Jesus and the New Testament writers, for example, living as they did in 'the last chance saloon' of an apocalyptic age, still strike an authentic note of joy.

> At that time Jesus exulted in the Holy Spirit and said, 'I thank you, Father, Lord of heaven and earth, for hiding these things from the learned and wise, and revealing them to the simple. Yes, Father, such was your choice.' (Luke 10:21)

Or, as the author of 3 John says: 'Nothing gives me greater joy than to hear that my children are living by the truth' (3 John 4). Real joy is no doubt an elusive experience, but the really big moments in my life have been when there has been a revelation of the truth, so that I, and the people who are sharing with me, see things with a new clarity. Perhaps I should go further and say not just a revelation, but a contagion of the truth, so that you know that there is also a new determination to live by it. The opposite side of the coin is the defeat of error. 'Shout, shout we're gaining ground, Satan's kingdom is tumbling down' as the Spiritual says. Babylon is fallen, is fallen. 'Let heaven exult over her; exult God's people, apostles and prophets' (Rev 18:20). Over how many freed slaves of the Domination System will we be able one day to rejoice? The labourers in our sweatshops, the poor farmers who cannot feed their children, the forest dwellers driven from their homes by some great 'development' scheme, the children who live on our streets, the AIDS patients who cannot afford unnecessarily expensive drugs – all set free from Babylon. They can all come out of their global prison, and the party can begin. 'Happy are those who are invited to the wedding party of the Lamb' (Rev 19:9). Frankly, I would like to challenge the readers of this book to join in the fun. Jesus lived the way he lived and died the way he died, not just because he loved us, but because it was the way that everything could end up joyfully (Hebrews 12:1).

The Bible, as we have suggested, will have nothing to do with a joyless existence. 'You have increased their joy, and given them great gladness; they rejoice in your presence as those who rejoice in harvest, as warriors exult when dividing the spoil.' Can we recapture the substance offered in these Biblical images? What does it *feel* like to get in a bumper harvest (just before the rain comes) and know that the job has been done? What does it *feel* like to be victorious in battle and to know that the rewards of victory are ours? What does it *feel* like to bring forth a child after hard labour? What does it *feel* like to have finished the marathon when fifty times during it we have wanted to give up? What does it *feel* like to be going up the aisle with the man or woman that we love when for years together everything seemed to conspire against us to make that day seem an almost impossible dream?

'It is high time that you woke up from your sleep', says the Apostle Paul, because our salvation is nearer now than when we first believed' (Romans 13:11). 'What should Christians do, as they 'wake up' to globalisation and the Domination System? I would like to conclude with some positive suggestions.

It is time that we read our Bibles more and read them more carefully. Perhaps we could try and get some serious help in thinking about the circumstances of those to whom the Biblical messages were addressed, the people of the Bible. They were people who lived in a country which was always liable to invasion by ruthless and powerful enemies. (The history of Israel might be better compared to that of Poland in modern times rather than that of Britain or the United States.) They were people in exile ('By the waters of Babylon, there we sat down and wept.'). They were living in a country side by side with a permanent occupying force as was true in Jesus' day. They belonged to a 'minority religious group' like the Christians in the Roman Empire. There is hardly a book in the Bible which is not coloured by these massive political realities. Some, like Daniel and the book of Revelation, were written precisely to confront them. So how do we read the Bible? As if it had nothing to say about invasion, exile, occupation and resistance, about injustice and the abuse of power. Even more worryingly, what if we can see no connection between the Bible and the arms industry, Third World poverty and debt, neo-colonialism, and the plight of refugees. What if we could not even *see* the imperialistic forces of today despite the fact that the Bible provides a magnifying glass which displays, even to the partially sighted, the text of the Domination System?

We need to ask ourselves 'upstream' questions. The idea of an 'upstream ministry' is based on a simple illustration which is recorded by Dona Schaper.

> The story is told of a missionary who spent every day down on the banks of the river, bandaging the wounded who came to her. Finally one day she had had enough and walked to the headwaters. There she found out who was hurting her people and camped, determined to stop them. (Meyers 1992, 35)

So we must stop living on the river bank, always dealing with victims, however faithfully, and start asking why things happen. Why are there so many poor people in the world? Is it just a fact of nature? Why are the churches in the West sinking towards the margins of life? Who exercises power in our world, and which of those powers are opposed to the gospel? Why are there so many depressed people in my church? Has the media got anything to do with it? Of course, there are hundreds of questions waiting to be asked, but remember – we are asleep. Sleepers ask no questions, never want to know the reason for anything.

We could visit the poor and marginalised, the ones who are only just surviving (they live round the corner or a cheap flight away) and try to understand what their lives are like. It is better not go as a tourist, or an expert or a benefactor, just to go to be with them and see what it does to us.

What about turning our churches (as if it were as easy as that!) into anti-imperialist zones. Under the general heading 'love your neighbour as yourself' we could introduce fair trade buying, or environment friendly policies, or special events for asylum seekers and refugees, or English classes for newly arrived international visitors, or finishing the morning service with a letter writing session protesting about the arms trade. After all the church is the *sign* of the Kingdom, the place where the rule of God is actually seen to be operating, or that is the theory. If people come into our churches and find that we are supportive of unfair methods of trade, careless of the environment, indifferent to 'strangers', or accepting of violence, what sign or signal are we giving?

We need to talk more. We know that the world, the domination system, is not right. Why are we so quiet about it? We talk about witnessing to the gospel as if this had nothing at all to do with our daily experience. The Domination System is not shy about its value system. It talks about it all the time and indeed glories in it. It pays highly intelligent and talented people to represent its case. We need to know what *our* case is and to make it. The liturgy that we intone together in church is meant to be public. 'Jesus Christ is Lord' is a slogan designed for the market place. Today's 'exorcisms' have to do with telling the truth that the world denies. 'We stand in need' says Bill Wylie Kellerman, 'of what the Bible calls exorcism, liturgies which engage the powers at the level of their mythic and psychic and spiritual claims on human beings and human cultures.' (1991, 102).[26] It is by no means insignificant that the first exorcism that Jesus did (at the synagogue in Capernaum, see Mark 1:21-28) was above all a demonstration of authoritative *teaching*.

We could be a whole lot louder! Sometimes it is time to get angry. In Acts 16 (see verses 16 -18) we read about Paul getting angry. I hope it was for the right reasons. He seems to have become annoyed because the slave girl kept on doing his preaching for him! What he should have been angry about was that this girl was a slave, treated like a sort of performing monkey, bringing profit to her (odious word in this context) owners. Are there any slaves in our world today bringing unjust profits to their owners? There certainly are. The question is when did we last get angry about it. Of course we know about slavery in the Sudan or even about slave-labour in the sweatshops of the world that make our sports garments, footballs and trainers; and we certainly should be making a fuss about that. But nearer home what about the millions of people in our Western world who are paid the minimum wage (and the tens of thousands who are paid less than the legal sum)? Frankly, almost whatever country you are talking about, it is simply not possible to live decently on the minimum wage, and we professional and comfortably-off people, are living off the back of these unfortunates. Our food and our services – the cleaning done for us in our offices, the attendance upon us in shops, the care given in nursing homes, are all subsidised by their meagre wages. All this may seem a long way from grand talk about 'the Domination System', but it is not. In truth the ideology of the Domination System today is based on an economic model which believes that it is *right* for employers to pay as little as possible to their employees. It's what they call 'market forces'.

Have we got enough information? Are we reading enough and watching the right TV programmes? 'You can't reach what you can't see' as Harvie Conn used to say. We have to be selective here and try to work out which newspapers and magazines are telling the news from an anti-imperialist stance. Of course we do not like to be told what newspapers and magazines we should be reading. Surely it is a matter of private (!) choice, or alternatively 'politics are my own affair'. But they are not. If I challenged you to stop watching late-night pornography on the TV, this might be considered sound Christian advice. Yet in these crucial areas of the Domination System we have to keep our advice

---

[26] The whole chapter which follows this comment – chapter 5 'Liturgical Direct Action' is enlightening.

to ourselves, apparently. It is another example of the woeful privatisation of Christian faith and practice in our world.

It is not as if we were helpless. We all have something we can use in the battle. We are familiar, no doubt, with the sermon based on the experience of Moses where he claims that if he goes to the Egyptians 'they will never believe me or listen to what I say?' And God says to Moses 'What is that in your hand?' (Exodus 4:1,2) So what have we got in our hands? Again, here are just a few suggestions. We have computer skills and we are internet literate. Much information is passed on the internet today and much opinion is expressed. We can even have our own website with the minimum of fuss. So the Domination System does not have a monopoly of the means of communication. Many of the protests against it such as Jubilee 2000 have been greatly assisted by the flexibility of internet communication. Again, something else we have 'in our hands' is influence. Christians in the Roman Empire probably had very little influence, but we are in a quite different situation. We all have an elected representative relatively nearby. I have seen mine on a couple of occasions recently. He was courteous, ready to listen and willing to do what he could, if and when he agreed with me! We may be part of a management team or part of a Trade Union, we may own shares in a company and be eligible to attend the Annual Meeting, we may have joined a political party (if not, why not?), we may work with an NGO, we may belong to a Residents' Association or a Neighbourhood Watch scheme. In each case we have *influence*. Always and everywhere in these situations, the influence of the Domination System can be detected, and we are in a position to expose that influence and resist it. Something else that most of us have 'in our hands' is friends, and in this case I am thinking particularly of Christian friends. The burden of confronting the Domination System and engaging with it can be considerable and we usually need 'a little help from our friends'. The synergy of a small group of like-minded people can be remarkable. Planning together is so much more fun than planning alone, and the same is true for praying. To go back to our original illustration, when Moses felt he could not do it all by himself, God gave him Aaron. Teams are also efficient. Management studies (see, for example, Belbin's Teams: these are well described in Handy 1993, 160-1) have demonstrated conclusively that the variety of skills and attitudes that a team provides can make a crucial difference in successfully completing a task.

Finally, we can 'think mission'. To take the highest possible example, when Jesus was setting out to confront the Domination System of his day, he openly acknowledged and claimed that he was impelled by the Spirit to do so. (Luke

4:18,19) He was sent (the mission word) to 'preach good news to the poor'. Later he said to his disciples, 'As the Father has sent me, so I am sending you' (John 20:21). We are not taking on the Domination System out of duty, or because we have a bad conscience, or because it is the sort of thing we are good at, or for any other such reason. We are doing it because God has sent us.

Appendix 1

Israel and the land

I shall begin with a consideration of Romans 9-11 and a definition of the term 'Israel'. It is *not* a term which denotes race alone, that is, physical descent. It never was. The descendants of Abraham – Ishmael and Esau (the latter was just as much in line in terms of physical descent as Jacob, which is the point that Paul makes in Romans 9:6-13) were not considered to be true Israelites. Descent from Abraham, in the Biblical sense, is a matter of living by the faith of Abraham (Romans 4:11b-12). In every age of post-Abraham history we have had to think of a *remnant* (Romans 9:27, 11:5). Further this remnant, those who are truly Israel, were often joined by those of other nations. Rahab was a Canaanite and Ruth came from Moab, and both are mentioned in the ancestry of the Messiah (Matthew 1:5). In Psalm 87 Philistines, Tyrians and Nubians are all admitted to citizenship in Zion. There are other examples. There was an exclusive *and* an inclusive element in reckoning the true descent from Abraham. The promise to Abraham is *exclusively* passed on to Isaac and then Jacob. Ishmael is rejected because he is the son of the handmaid (Genesis 16:2) and possibly also because his mother was an Egyptian (Genesis 16:3). Esau despises the blessing and is likewise rejected. His general life-style and his choice of wives may also have had something to do with it. Thereafter, however, the *inclusive* principle seems to take over. Two handmaids are admitted as wives, Bilhah and Zilpah, and they each produce two patriarchs, Dan and Naphtali and Gad and Asher respectively. Joseph marries an Egyptian and produces another pair, Manasseh and Ephraim. All receive the blessing. The importance of this is that exclusive and inclusive principles may both be at work in the story of Israel. The exclusive principle is worked out in the story of Abraham, Isaac and Jacob and thereafter the remnant, the inhabitants of Zion, the *ebed yahweh* and in the New Testament 'the people of God'. By contrast the inclusive principle is worked out in the sons of Israel, in the nation of Israel, in the 'earthly' Jerusalem, in the various experimental arrangements, such as the monarchy, that went beyond the original intention of the covenant, and finally, in our day, in 'the world'. God has an inclusive purpose as well as a much more obvious exclusive purpose which begins with Abraham. Ultimately the two link up. However exclusive and inclusive are not Jew and Gentile respectively, as we have seen.

The importance of Old Testament Israel (in terms of salvation history, that is) was not their racial heritage but that they were the vehicle that God used to create a spiritual heritage (see Romans 9:4,5). What matters is not natural descent but God's promise (Romans 9:8). In describing this heritage Paul does not mention 'the land'. As we know, the heritage was preserved even when the people lost their land and were exiled in Babylon. To centre the identity of the true Israelite either in race or in land is to miss the point.

What Paul is grappling with in Romans 9-11 is the situation now thoroughly familiar to us, but very strange to him, whereby Israel comprises a 'faithful remnant' in which there is a majority of Gentiles and a minority of Jews, the reverse of the situation in the Old Testament. Paul is at pains to say that this does *not* mean that God's patient work in the Old Testament has, so to speak, gone to waste. It remains part of God's plan to use the 'heritage' of the Old Testament (or rather the experience of God in Old Testament times), which is why we cannot dispense with that record. But to go back to where we began: the Old Testament never did bear witness to a people of God defined in terms of racial descent. The idea that this might be the key was disrupted right at the beginning of the story.

The new composition, in Paul's day, of the people of God – Gentile majority, Jewish minority – does not mean that this situation cannot be reversed. Paul speaks about the possibility of going back to the original arrangements (Romans 11:24). God's purpose is always to show mercy (Romans 11:32) and he does so indiscriminately. 'Everyone who calls on the name of the Lord will be saved' (Romans 10:13). In terms of spiritual heritage, a Jewish majority church would always be a more comfortable fit, as it is the Jews who have taken the courses on the menu in the right order (Romans 2:10).

In saying that race and land are excluded from this whole calculus, I am trying to emphasise something which I have called 'spiritual heritage'. Perhaps the widely used word 'culture' might also work. A 'covenant culture' was something that, from Abraham onwards, God was trying to establish. Ideas of race and land are the stock in trade of modern nationalist movements. (A certain well known German made this connection rather strongly when trying to define 'the true German' in the 1930s). Culture is a more flexible and friendly term. You can learn another culture, even if you cannot alter your racial heritage. Even if there is no question of defining yourself by a 'land' you can still be a sort of cultural diaspora (Hebrews 11:13-16, 1 Peter 1:1).

Two additional points. Romans 11:26 does not mean that the Jewish *race* will be universally saved. 'All Israel' (better 'Israel as a whole' – see Barrett) was not used in that sense in contemporary language. Perhaps the saying simply means that there will come a day when there will be a great influx of Jewish believers into the church, something to match the spectacular addition of Gentiles in Paul's day.

Also, I suspect that there is conditionality in all this. No individual (Esau) or generation ('the wilderness generation') or family (David and his descendants) or group of leaders (the tenants of the vineyard in Jesus' parable) can claim immunity from the rule that God's gracious choice must evoke a response of obedience and faith if the promises are to be secured. Dead wood will be removed. New branches may be grafted in.

Whether my exegesis of Romans 9-11 is correct or not, there is nothing that I can see in those chapters to do with 'the land' (though obviously a great deal to do with 'Israel'). Perhaps we can do better when we turn to the passages in the gospels (the so-called Little Apocalypse – Matthew 24, Mark 13, Luke 21,) which have been traditionally interpreted as having to do with the future of Israel. Some scholars, for example, have suggested that the parable of the fig tree (Matthew 24:32,3 and parallels) refers to the nation of Israel flourishing again in our day. Unfortunately for this line of interpretation the very next verse refers quite explicitly to the fact that 'all these things', of which the flowering of the fig tree is a parable, will happen within the lifetime of Jesus' hearers. As Tom Wright has pointed out (N. T. Wright, *Jesus and the Victory of God*, London: S.P.C.K., 1996 pp. 339-43) the language used to describe the destruction of Jerusalem in the Little Apocalypse is the same language as is used to describe the destruction of Babylon in the Old Testament. What this means in the context of Jesus' hearers is that Jerusalem is the second Babylon and that the exile there is coming to an end. The Little Apocalypse is not an apocalypse at all, and Matthew 24 and parallels need to be given a serious historical reading. When we do this we realise that the disciples had asked a specific question and were waiting for Jesus to give them an answer. What of course they were most interested in was the question as to when Jesus would be given his rightful place at the head of affairs, particularly in the light of the fact that Jesus has just warned them that the present arrangements (the temple-state) were about to be wound up. Jesus tells them to be patient but hopeful. Just as he is certain that the temple will be overthrown, so the vindication of 'the son of man' will certainly come to pass, indeed the two will be part of the same event. Like the destruction of the Temple, Jesus' vindication is also described in suitably apocalyptic language.

This interpretation allows us to see that these passages are speaking of the coming judgement on a rebellious people *and* the final rescue from judgement of the followers of Jesus. For them this was the final escape from exile (Babylon). Jesus is vindicated in at least three ways by these events. As a prophet who saw and foretold the doom that lay over Jerusalem and the Temple (Matthew 23:37-9); as the one who had the right to pronounce this doom, and as the one who would be the replacement for the Temple. (Jesus as a replacement for the Temple is a common theme in the New Testament e.g. Rev 21:22, John 2:19-21, Acts 7:48-50, Hebrews 9:11)

If this exegesis is correct there is no reference of any sort to the modern state of Israel in the Little Apocalypse and perhaps not to the second coming either. (Scholars disagree about this. Tom Wright would argue, as above, for no reference. F. F. Bruce and R. T. France to take a couple of examples, suggest Matthew and Luke (and Mark implicitly) make a distinction between the 'all these things' of Matthew 24: 34 (=the destruction of Jerusalem) and the 'that day' of Matthew 24:36 (= the second coming). (See e.g. F. F. Bruce, *The Hard Sayings of Jesus*, London: Hodder, 1983 pp. 225-30.) I agree with Wright.) It is also true, of course, as we have seen from Romans 9-11, that Paul does not even define 'Israel' as a physical or racial entity (rather as a spiritual tradition) let alone as a modern nation-state with a land of its own.

What about the book of Revelation? Are there not references in it to Jerusalem, to Armageddon (a place name in the Holy Land), to numerous specific end time events that can be put into the context of the Near East?

There is no doubt that the world of the author of the book of Revelation, John of Patmos, was what we would call today the Middle East. Patmos is an island in the Mediterranean, John directly addresses seven churches in Asia Minor (present day Turkey) and so on. So it would not be surprising if John also referred to Jerusalem; which of course he does, only he calls the city Sodom and Egypt (Revelation 11:8). At this point I think some doubts should begin to surface. Firstly, John does not always call a spade a spade. If he can call Jerusalem, Sodom, then perhaps he can call Rome, Babylon. Which of course he does (Revelation 11:9). Then secondly, if John is referring to the familiar geography and power structures of his own day, why do we need to look any further? Is it not possible that John is writing in cryptic language about events and places and people of his *own* day. Christians in Asia Minor were, it seems, fighting a life and death struggle with a persecuting, and at the same time seductive, imperial system. The struggle is described in apocalyptic language, the language of angels and stars and dragons and wars and cities. That does not mean that John does not have real, contemporary, situations and events in mind. It simply means that he has a powerful way of describing them. If this is all rather disappointing to some of us, it ought not to be. Real events in real history – Abraham's wanderings, Israel's exodus, the return of the captives from Babylon, the life, death and resurrection of Jesus, the travels of Paul – provide us with all the direction and instruction that we could ask for. It is a sad circumstance that serious Bible scholars today are devoting their time to the systematic wrenching of Scripture passages from their contexts to subject them to fanciful and irresponsible interpretations. It is bringing the Bible into disrepute and creating barriers to the proper understanding of Scripture.

But I digress. The book of Revelation is about Christian life and witness amid the persecutions and seductions of the Roman Empire. We can deduce nothing from it about Israel and 'the land'.

Notice that we have already disengaged from Old Testament prophecies. It is to secure this position that I began with Romans 9-11. There are certainly promises about the land in the Old Testament but they have been taken up and transformed into something better by means of a widening concept of the true people of God. This people, of course, is still partially defined by the Old Testament 'heritage', but has now entered into a much greater inheritance because of the work of Jesus. So covenant becomes new covenant; tabernacle and Temple become Jesus; Jerusalem becomes New Jerusalem, Jesus is our prophet, priest and king – why should we look for someone else? Finally, the land where we have our true citizenship is heaven. This is not, by the way, 'replacement' theology. The church does not replace Israel. That would be the sort of dispensationalism which I would reject. There is only one people of God (perhaps reduced to just one person in the Garden of Gethsemane) and they are the children of Abraham (everyone, Jew and gentile alike, who has faith) *not* the children of Israel.

We must face the fact that it is not possible to make out any 'special case' for the present day nation of Israel on the basis of Biblical exegesis. Of course God does have a purpose for the nation of Israel today, but not in any significant sense that is different from the fact that he has a purpose for, say, the nation of Nicaragua. This is vitally important. For one thing it makes a just settlement in Palestine a realistic goal. Why is this? Because God has a purpose for the Palestinian people too. We can deny this, but in the absence of any Biblical 'special pleading' then to do so would be to reveal ourselves as unjust and prejudiced. This should warn us of something even more serious. It is our use of the Bible which is *making* us unjust. As Michael Prior says: 'Biblical scholars have the most serious obligation to prevent outrages being perpetrated in the name of fidelity to the biblical covenant.' (Michael Prior, *The Bible and Colonialism: A Moral Critique*, Sheffield: Sheffield Academic Press, 1997 p. 292) And this is not simply prevention. It has happened throughout history. The Puritan fathers referred to the indigenous populations of North America as Amalekites and Canaanites with predictable results (Prior, 263, 282). The white South Africans invoked similar ideas, believing themselves to be the chosen people before whom the people of the land, inferior races one and all, must give way on Biblical warrant.

Much of this racially motivated colonialism and its supposed Biblical sanction, has been recognised and repudiated. The one exception tends to be militant Zionism. There are a number of reasons for this.

1. The state of Israel seems to be directly connected with Scripture in a way that other claims for Scriptural authentication do not seem to possess.
2. There is much guilt still in the west over the holocaust and related events.
3. There is a tendency to believe that Zionists speak for Judaism as a whole. Any attack on Zionism is therefore construed as an attack on the Jewish people as such (anti-Semitism).
4. The history of the occupation of Palestine by Jewish settlers has largely been told only from the Jewish point of view. (This is changing. Recently there have been path breaking attempts by Jewish historians such as Benny Morris to tell the story in a more even handed way.) Morris summarises the significant myths as follows:
    - Zionism was an inevitable result of Gentile pressures and persecution
    - The Zionists intended no harm to the indigenous population and did not intend to displace them. (Morris might have added the myth that the land was empty; a typical colonial myth. In

1897 when the settlement was first proposed the population of Palestine was 95 per cent Arab and they owned 99 per cent of the land (Prior, 187). As late as 1948 Jews owned only 6.6 per cent of the land and were about one third of the population (Prior, 133).)

- The local population and the neighbouring Arab states simply rejected sincere Zionist attempts at compromise and conciliation. They made an unprovoked attack in 1947-8.
- The Arabs, aided by the British, were stronger both politically and militarily in 1948 but lost the war anyway.
- The Arab leaders called upon the Palestinian Arabs to quit their homes both to clear the way for Arab armies and so that they could falsely accuse the Israelis of expulsion tactics. It was thus, so the story went, that the refugee problem arose. (Cited by Prior, 186)

5. Perhaps the most important point is that there are many Christians today who might be described as Christian Zionists. Their dispensational (pre-millennial) approach to Scripture tends to mean that they give unqualified support to the Israeli government and its expansionist policies. Most of these Christians are in the United States. Some have reckoned that as many as 10-15 million of the 29-30 million evangelical Christians who nominally support the Republicans 'think that it is contrary to God's will to put pressure on the Israeli government' (Victoria Clark, 'The Christian Zionists' in *Prospect* July 2003, p. 43). In 1998 televangelist John Hagee justified his collection of $1 million to help sustain West bank settlements with a simple appeal to 'higher authority'. 'I am a Bible scholar and a theologian and from my perspective the law of God transcends the law of the US government' (Clark, 44). While Jewish Zionists are suspicious of the motives of Christian Zionists, they are happy to accept the political and economic support they provide.

It is also significant and worrying that American (and not only American) dispensationalism seems to be able to link end time scenarios not just with the nation of Israel but also with a polemic against Islam. I am looking at a book by Arno Froese (the executive director of Midnight Call Ministry) titled *Terror Over America*, which is a response to the events of September 11, 2001. It does its best to link these events with 'Biblical prophecy' but has difficulty in that New York is not in the Middle East! However, what it does not find difficult is to finish up with a couple of chapters on Islam with such headings as 'Koran: Key to Terror' and 'Muslim Terrorist States'. For those Christians involved with Muslims, this sort of careless talk and the prejudice that lies behind it, are deeply damaging.

What of the situation today? A lethal stalemate seems the order of the day. Many crucial questions remain unanswered including perhaps the biggest one as to whether the United States has the political will to lean hard enough on Israel. The history of past negotiation does not suggest optimism. Well informed commentators are already saying that the present round of negotiations will not work, if only because they are based on a now defunct two state solution. The alternative – a truly democratic state for all the inhabitants of the area rather than partition – seems utopian.

I think two responses on our part are crucial.

Firstly we need to be clear what is actually going on. We have allowed ourselves to live with myths for far too long. Take the Oslo negotiations for example. I have heard this described more than once as a golden opportunity for peace which Yasser Arafat and the Arabs passed up. In fact if you look at it carefully it handed back no more than 18 per cent of the Occupied Territories to the Palestinians, and that on highly unfavourable terms. The Israelis were left in charge of security, borders and water, for example.

Secondly, we must refuse to allow the debate to be 'theologised'. Only thus, as I have already said, can we come to some sort of just settlement. If we are prepared to give the modern state of Israel some sort of Biblical sanction, then the argument ends at that point. Who wants to argue with God? If the Bible teaches that God has planted today's nation of Israel in the Holy Land, then that is that. But my contention is that the whole idea of modern day Israel being the inheritors of 'the promised land' is simply unsupportable in terms of the Biblical evidence. I am not saying, of course, that we should not think biblically about the whole situation. In every human theatre God is concerned with issues of justice and human flourishing and with the spread of the gospel. That having been said, Israeli expansion at the expense of the Palestinians is a perfectly recognisable form of colonial occupation typical of expanding (usually) European nations in the modern era. Zionism is an offspring of an aggressive European nationalism and it is not surprising that it arose when European imperialism was at its zenith. Colonialism continues to be the key to what is going on in the Middle East. One reason why the US (and Britain) are so supportive of Israel is that they continue to be colonial (or neo-colonial) powers with regard to the Middle East. Israel is a useful strategic bridgehead in the war against terror, in the 'clash of civilisations', and in the search for secure energy supplies.

Appendix 2

Eschatology and mission

One of my concerns is that there should be a renewal of our thinking about eschatology. At the same time I am aware that this is a particularly contentious realm, that a vast amount of speculation has gathered round such topics as the Second Coming, the end of the world, the defeat of Satan, and God's purpose for the state of Israel. Suffice it to say that I am not intending to add to that speculation. I do have something to say about eschatology, indeed I want to take another look at the book of Revelation, at the apocalyptic passages in the gospels and at the whole idea of 'the day of the Lord', but I do so, not because I think that I have new insights into eschatological patterns (pre-post-a-millennialist) or into what contemporary events tell us about the timing of the end of history. Rather, I think that we have misunderstood many of the apocalyptic passages in Scripture, particularly by referring them to a single event at the end of time. Better Biblical exegesis will 'pull back' most of these references and reveal that they have to do instead with events contemporary with the Biblical authors. This will make these passages, paradoxically, more relevant to our situation today, removing them from the realm of unanchored speculation.

In every age, including our own, there are patterns of human corporate behaviour which sharpen the conflict between the rule of God and the evil Empire. This conflict is not static or circular but tends towards an end, which could be, but we must not assume is, *the* end. This end can be described as 'the coming of the Son of Man' for us and our generation. Like all of God's interventions it will comprise both mercy and judgement. The news can be good or bad or even both. (One thinks of the people of Amos's day who thought that the 'day of the Lord' was going to be good news – deliverance from their enemies and the like – but were warned by the prophet that it would be 'darkness and not light'.) Notice that I am saying something a little different from the familiar 'now but not yet' thesis. I am saying rather that history consists of a series of crises which invite God's intervention as the crisis builds. We are called upon to try and understand this process and respond to it. We do need to read 'the signs of the times' as Jesus said. In Luke 12:54-6, Jesus condemned his hearers because they could interpret the weather, but were not ready to apply the same shrewdness to the indicators provided by contemporary events ('the present time', as the NRSV has it). The hypocrisy of which he accused them was not so much an inability to understand what was going on but an unwillingness. Notice also that there is no hint in this passage of delay. This is not future telling but being alert to what is presently happening.

We also need to know what our particular tasks are in the present crisis. Each day has its issue. Not yesterday's issues or my neighbour's task. For each one of us this is the eye of the needle, the narrow road, holiness itself. To turn aside from this task is the double-mindedness of which James speaks (James 4:8), it is the lame excuse of the man who hid the talent, it is the worship of the beast. If, as I am going to suggest, today's economic arrangements – resulting in massive poverty, environmental degradation and unstoppable postcolonial migrations – are the ultimate threat to our civilisation, then that defines our task. It helps us to understand how we should be 'ready', that injunction which otherwise seems rather bland and without specific content.

No two crises are the same, but there are always similarities, which is why the teaching of Scripture is so helpful. The behaviour of Empires in ever age is in one sense predictable. If we read about the life and death struggle of the churches in Asia Minor in the first century, a struggle to resist the power and fascination of the Roman Empire, we will not be entirely taken by surprise at the behaviour of the forces that confront us in the twenty first century. The apocalyptic passages in Scripture do not provide a timetable for the end of the world. They are much more like a handbook for faithful people in times of crisis. People stop reading the book of Daniel or Jesus' teaching about the destruction of the Temple, or the book of Revelation (to select a few passages from many) at their peril. The Empire may already have its hands round their throats and they may not even have noticed!

We can take as an example the Christians in the Third Reich. It is obvious what was *their* battle. But, I suspect, it was not necessarily obvious to them (except for a few, such as Bonhöffer and Barth). Was this because they were particularly wicked? I doubt it. But they were trapped in a culture bound Christianity, unable to hear what was being said to 'the angel of the church in Germany'. The true nature of the battle in which they were involved was hidden from them. For them 'the coming of the Son of Man' (Matthew 25:31) was encapsulated in the saying ' just as you did it not for your Jewish neighbours, you did it not for me'.

Let me try to back up this approach to eschatology with a little further meditation on Scripture and history. Firstly, I find the key to interpreting the apocalyptic passages in the Gospels in Jesus' saying about 'this generation not passing away until all these things are accomplished' (Mark 13:30 and parallels). Mark's sermon as a whole was addressed to Jesus' generation and this should remind us that it was *their* crisis he is primarily talking about, not ours. As many commentators have pointed out, the language ('the sun will be darkened and the moon will not give its light' and so on) does not have to be construed as referring to cosmic events at the end of history. Apocalyptic language rather refers to contemporary political events, only in cryptic style. Perhaps Jesus (in Mark 13) was referring to his own death (so Myers) when he spoke about 'the coming of the Son of Man' (Myers, *Binding the Strong Man* p. 343). Perhaps the whole sermon is about the destruction of the Temple in 70 C.E. (so N.T.Wright), an event which will finally vindicate the Messiahship of Jesus. (Wright, *Jesus and the Victory of God* pp. 510-9).

The most powerful clue that we need a new approach to the way we look at 'the end' is found in the book of Revelation. Here 'the end' is not essentially an event but a person. It is Jesus who is the *ho eschatos*. Whenever he comes there is 'an end' (and also a beginning). Then there is the pattern of the book of Revelation which leads us through what has been called a series of 'cancelled conclusions'. While we seem, in the book, always to be approaching the end, we do not easily get there. No sooner have we completed (or almost completed) one series of apparently terminal disasters than we set out on another. What John is portraying is not a chronological series of events, nor the same events described in different ways (as in, say, the four gospels) but a pattern or paradigm. This pattern, a mounting crisis leading to a finale, is both a repeated design (as in a carpet) and also the overall design in that we can expect it to lead finally to *the* end. Each crisis has features which are almost interchangeable with all other crises but also unique characteristics. So (in the book of Revelation) the disasters associated with the seals, trumpets and bowls are often similar, but each sequence also contains new features. (For further discussion on the structure of the book of Revelation see Caird, *The Revelation of St John the Divine* pp. 104-6.)

If I am claiming that there is a pattern, what is that pattern? Is any crisis and its resolution 'the coming of the Son of Man'? Are natural disasters, such as famines or earthquakes, occasions for his coming? Does it take a war, and if so how big a one?

I think there is something to be said for a fairly subjective approach to this question. The author of the oracle that begins Isaiah 64 ('O that you would tear the heavens open and come down'), for example, clearly felt that he needed his own 'day of the Lord'. Individuals, communities, nations, tend to know when the crisis is at hand. The author of *The Battle Hymn of the Republic* ('Mine eyes have seen the glory of the coming of the Lord') believed that she had seen 'the coming of the Lord' in her day in the events of the American Civil War and the abolition of slavery.

However, I do have some guidelines. The end ('the day of the Lord') will, I suggest, usually fulfil at least one of these criteria.

- The Powers (in the sense that Walter Wink uses the word) are significantly challenged and forced into the open. The supreme example is the crucifixion and we have a description of this process in John 12:31,32 and Revelation 12:7-9. Twentieth century examples might be the challenge to British imperialism mounted by Gandhi (the British could no longer pretend to be benefactors), and the Civil Rights movement in the United States (white supremacists were revealed as entrenched behind racially motivated laws).
- There is an exceptional manifestation of evil, such as in the Third Reich or in the *apartheid* system.
- There is a *combination* of forces; economic, political and cultural (religious) forces working together as in the Roman Empire, or indeed any great imperialistic system, such as economic globalisation.
- There is a clear 'end of an era' with a definite moment of fulfilment, completion and subsequent change. Perhaps the early church saw the preaching of the gospel to all nations (throughout the Roman Empire, that is) as that sort of 'end' (compare Matthew 24:14).
- There is a sense that God has intervened, or is intervening, powerfully. The events of Pentecost are described in this way by the early church. Peter calls Pentecost 'the Lord's great and glorious day' (Acts 2:20).
- A moment of 'pause' after a period of particularly intense activity might

be another example. 'Silence in heaven for about half an hour' as in Revelation 8:1 marks both an end and a beginning. Similarly, Siegfried Sassoon's poem 'Suddenly everybody burst out singing' when the armistice was declared at the end of the First World War, marks such an occasion.
- There is a sudden burst of creativity. The early years of the twentieth century, for example, marked no great historical events in terms of wars and the like, but in the culture of the West at least there was an amazing flowering of human talent.

Inevitably if we are able to identify times of crisis and climax, then we must also accept that there will be times, equally recognisable, when nothing much is happening. There is clearly a rhythm in our individual lives which allows for this, and I think we can say the same about communities and nations. The Restoration in England (1660 onwards) sounds to me like a period when the experience of the mercy and judgement of God was signally absent. The eighties of the twentieth century (Thatcher, Reagan) have a similar feel to them. However, with the fall of communism in the nineties, the rise of a globalised world system, the hegemony of the United States and the spread of international terrorism, we begin to build again towards crisis and our own particular 'end time'.

This may seem too speculative, the very thing I promised to avoid. I would base my analysis, however, on the extrapolation of trends, on likely outcomes, and I think this is different from speculation. Of course, trends may not be fulfilled. Nothing is certain. But it is foolish to overlook them all the same. If my business, according to all the indicators, is failing – fewer customers, workers laid off, debt increasing – my response might be to believe that there will be some 'miraculous' change for the good. This is not impossible, but it is no basis on which to try and understand the likely outcomes.

So what trends do I see? There are a number and I list them here.

- Economic globalisation in its present form will find itself *unable* to step back from a philosophy of 'growth at all costs'. The desirability of accepting limits will be acknowledged, but will not prove to be practical politics.
- The earth's resources (water in particular) will become dangerously stretched.
- Technology will be the saviour which cannot save itself.
- The growing disparity between rich and poor will result in increasing violence and invasion (migration).

- Continuing world poverty will lead to uncontrollable disease, as in the case of the AIDS epidemic.
- The word-wide arms industry will do further huge harm to our civilisation.
- Nationalism, ethnic particularity and religious hatred (think of Israel and Palestine, Sri Lanka, Ruanda and the former Yugoslavia) will not be 'healed' by modern secularist thought and the goodwill of peacemakers. Religious fundamentalism will be regarded increasingly as a *refuge*.

I see much more, but this will do for the time being! What is certain is that we are coming to an end, or, as we say, we cannot go on in the way that we are going. The day of the Lord is near, or, to speak more accurately, *a* day of the Lord is near. If we have eyes to see we will perceive that Babylon is (potentially) fallen and that new manifestations of New Jerusalem are about to appear.

Bibliography

Achebe 2001	Achebe, C. *Anthills of the Savannah* London: Penguin Classics
Allen & Thomas 1992	Allen T. and Thomas A. eds.*Poverty and Development in the 1990s* Oxford: Oxford University Press
Anderson 1993	Anderson, B. *The Imagined Community* London: Verso
Anderson 1998	Anderson, B. *The Spectre of Comparisons* London: Verso
Ashcroft 2001	Ashcroft, B. *Post-colonial Transformation* London: Routledge
Bartolovich 2003	Bartolovich, C. 'The Eleventh September of George Bush, Fortress US and the Global Politics of Consumption' in *Interventions* 5/2, 2003 pp. 177-99
Bauman 1993	Bauman, Z. *Postmodern Ethics* Oxford: Blackwells
Bauman 1995	Bauman, Z. *Life in Fragments* Oxford: Blackwells
Bauman 2003	Bauman, Z. *Liquid Love* Cambridge: Polity
Beeby 1994	Beeby, D. 'A White Man's Burden' *International Bulletin of Missionary Research* 18/1 pp. 6-8
Beilharz 2000	Beilharz, P. *Zygmunt Bauman, Dialectic of Modernity*, London: Sage
Benjamin 1999	Benjamin, W. *Illuminations* London: Pimlico
Berry 1981	Berry, W. *Recollected Essays*, San Francisco, North Point Press
Berry 1987	Berry, W. *Home Economics* San Francisco: North Point

	Press
Berry 1993	Berry, W. *Sex, Economy, Freedom and Community* New York: Pantheon
Berry 2002	Berry W. 'The Agrarian Standard' in *Orion* Summer 2002 edition
Bhabha 1990	Bhabha, H. *Nation and Narration* London: Routledge
Bhabha 1994	Bhabha, H. *The Location of Culture* London: Routledge
Bronner 1994	Bronner, S. *On Critical Theory And Its Theorists* Oxford: Blackwell
Brown 2001	Brown, C. *The Death of Christian Britain* London: Routledge
Brittain 2004	Brittain, V. *Testament of Youth* London: Virago
Brueggemann 1977	Brueggemann, W. *The Land: Place as Gift, Promise and Challenge in Biblical Faith* Philadelphia: Fortress Press
Brueggemann 1993	Brueggemann, W. *The Bible and the Modern Postmodern Imagination* London: SCM
Caird 1966	Caird, G.B. *The Revelation of St John the Divine*, London: A & C Black
Callil 2006	Callil, C. *Bad Faith* London: Vintage
Carter 2000	Carter, W. *Matthew and the Margins* Maryknoll: Orbis
Castells 1998	Castells, M. *The End of the Millennium* Oxford: Blackwell
Castells 2000	Castells, M. *The Rise of the Network Society* (Second edition), Oxford: Blackwell
Castells 2004	Castells, M. *The Power of Identity* (Second edition) Oxford: Blackwell
Chambers 2005	Chambers, R. *Ideas for Development* London: Earthscan
Chatterjee 1986	Chatterjee, P. *Nationalist Thought and the Colonial World, A Derivated Discourse?* London: Verso
Chatterjee 1993	Chatterjee, P. *The Nation and its Fragments* Princeton: Princeton University Press
Cohen & Kennedy 2000	Cohen R. & Kennedy P. *Global Sociology* London: Macmillan
Collier & Estaban 1998	Collier J. & Esteban R. *From Complicity to Encounter, The Church and the Culture of Economism* Harrisburg, Pa.: Trinity Press
Crossan 1975	Crossan, J.D. *The Dark Interval, Towards a Theology of*

	Story Niles, Ill.: Argus
Curtis 2001	Curtis, M. *Trade for Life: Making Trade Work for Poor People* London; Christian Aid
Curtis 2003	Curtis, M. *Web of Deceit* London: Vintage
Davis 2001	Davis, M. *Late Victorian Holocausts* London: Verso
Davis 2006	Davis, M. *Planet of Slums* London: Verso
Dempster 1999	Dempster, M., Klaus, B.D., Peterson, D. eds. *The Globalization of Pentecostalism: A Religion Made to Travel* Oxford: Regnum
De Zengotita 2006	De Zengotita, T. *Mediated* London: Bloomsbury
Dirlik 2003	Dirlik, A. '*EMPIRE?* Some Thoughts on Colonialism, Culture, and Class in the Making of Global Crisis and War in Perpetuity' in *Interventions* 5/2, 2003 pp. 207-17
Drown 2002	Drown, F. & M. *Mission to the Headhunters* Ross-shire: Christian Focus
Ehrenreich 2002	Ehrenreich, B. *Nickel and Dimed* London: Granta Books
Elliott 1995	Elliott, N. *Liberating Paul* Sheffield: Sheffield Academic Press
Ellwood 2001	Ellwood, W. *The No-Nonsense Guide to Globalization* London: Verso
Evans 1989	Evans, C. *To See And Not Perceive* Sheffield: JSOT Press
Ford 1999	Ford, D. *Theology, A Very Short Introduction* Oxford: Oxford University Press
Freedman 2002	Freedland, J. 'Situating Hybridity, The Positional Logic of a Discourse' pp. 125-47 in Chew, S.C. & Knottnerus, J.D. *Structure, Culture and History, Recent Issues in Social Theory* Lanham: Rowman & Littlefield
France 1990	France, R. *Divine Government* London: SPCK
Fraser 2005	Fraser, G. 'Rebuff this mad, bad clique with a bullying version of the Gospel' in *Guradian* Nov 19
Freire 1996	Freire, P. *Pedagogy of the Oppressed* Revised Edition, Harmondsworth: Penguin
Gandhi 1997	Gandhi, M. *Hind Swaraj* Cambridge, Cambridge

	University Press
Giddens 1999	Giddens, A. *Runaway World* London: Profile Books
Gillis 1994	Gillis, J.R. ed., *Commemorations: The Politics of National Identity* Princeton: Princeton University Press
Gilmour 2003	Gilmour, D. *The Long Recessional, The Imperial Life of Rudyard Kipling* London: Pimlico
Goldberg 2002	Goldberg, D. & Quayson, A. eds. *Relocating Postcolonialism*, Oxford: Blackwell
Goldsmith 2001	Goldsmith, E. & Mander, J. eds. *The Case Against the Global Economy* London: Earthscan
Gorringe 2000	Gorringe, T. 'The Shape of the Human Home: Cities, Global Capital and Ec-clesia' *Political Theology*, 3, Nov 2000 pp. 80-94
Gorringe 2002	Gorringe, T. *A Theology of the Built Environment*, Cambridge: Cambridge University Press
Gray 2002	Gray, J. 'Why Terrorism is Unbeatable', *New Statesman* 25 February 2002
Handy 1993	Handy, C. *Understanding Organizations* Harmondsworth: Penguin
Hardt & Negri 2000	Hardt, M. and Negri, A. *Empire*, London: Harvard University Press
Harvey 1989	Harvey, D. *The Condition of Postmodernity* Oxford: Blackwell
Harvey 1996	Harvey, D. *Justice, Nature and the Geography of Difference* Oxford: Blackwell
Harvey 2000	Harvey, D. *Spaces of Hope* Edinburgh: Edinburgh University Presss
Held & McGrew 1999	Held, D. & McGrew, A. et al. *Global Transformations* Cambridge: Polity
Held & McGrew 2000	Held, D. & McGrew, A. (eds.) *Global Transformations Reader*, Cambridge: Polity
Held & McGrew 2002	Held, D. & McGrew, A. *Globalization/Anti-Globalization*, Cambridge: Polity
Herzog 1994	Herzog II, W. *Parables as Subversive Speech* Louisville: Westminster John Knox Press
Heslem 2002	Heslem, P. *Globalization, Unravelling the New Capitalism* Cambridge: Grove Books
Hesse 2000	Hesse, B *Un/settled Multiculturalisms* London: Zed Books

Hiebert 1987	Hiebert P. 'Critical Contextualization' *International Bulletin of Missionary Research* 11/3 pp. 104-12
Hirst 2001	Hirst, P. *War and Power in the 21st Century*, Polity, Cambridge
Hollwenger 1986	Hollwenger, J.W. 'After Twenty Years of Research in Pentecostalism', *International Review of Mission* 75, 297
Horsley 2000	Horsley R. ed. *Paul and Politics*, Harrisburg: Trinity Press
Howard-Brook & Gwyther 1999	Howard-Brook, W. & Gwyther, A. *Unveiling Empire, Reading Revelation Then and Now*, Maryknoll, N.Y.: Orbis
Huddart 2006	Huddart, D. *Homi K. Bhabha* London: Routledge
Hughes 2002	Hughes, D, 'Ethnicity and Globalisation', part of an unpublished paper given at a Global Connections Conference on Globalisation and the Kingdom of God, July 2002
Hutchinson 1999	Hutchinson, M. *What's Wrong With Globalisation Anyway?* Cambridge: Currents in World Christianity Position Paper Number 125
Inda 2002	Inda, J.R. & Rosaldo, R. eds *The Anthropology of Gloibalization, A Reader* Oxford: Blackwell
Ingleby 1997	Ingleby, J.'Trickling Down or Shaking the Foundations: Is Contextualization Neutral?' in *Missiology* XXV, No.2 April 1997
Ingleby 2000	Ingleby, J.C. *Missionaries, Education and India* Delhi: Indian Society for Promoting Christian Knowledge
Ingleby 2007	Ingleby, J. 'Small Communities and the Impact of Modernity: a Meditation on Mario Vargas Llosa's *El Hablador* and its Meaning for Mission Today' in *Transformation* 24/1 January 2007
Jameson 2000	Jameson, F. 'Globalisation and Political Strategy' in *New Left Review* 4 July/August 2000 pp. 49-68
Jeater 1992	Jeater, D. 'Roast Beef and Reggae Music' in *New Formations: Hybridity* Winter, 1992
Jenkins 2002	Jenkins, P. *The Next Christendom* Oxford: OUP
Kellermann 1991	Kellermann, B.W. *Seasons of Faith and Conscience*, Maryknoll: Orbis

Kelly 1999	Kelly, G. *Get a Grip on the Future without Losing Your Hold on the Past* London: Monarch
Kenrick 1962	Kenrick B., *Come out the Wilderness* (Harper and Row, New York
Khor 2001	Khor, M. *Rethinking Globalization*, London, Zed Books
Kingsolver 1999	Kingsolver, B. *The Poisonwood Bible* London: Faber
Kirk 1999	Kirk, A. *What is Mission?* London: DLT
Klein 2002	Klein, N. *Fences and Windows* London: Flamingo
Kovel 2002	Kovel, J. *The Enemy of Nature* London: Zed Books
Kramer 2006	Kramer, M. *Dispossessed, Life in our World's Urban Slums* Maryknoll: OrbisLechner & Boli Lechner F. & Boli, J. *The Globalization Reader* Oxford: Blackwell
Levi 1987	Levi, P. *If This Is A Man* London: Abacus
Lewis 1955	Lewis, C.S. *The Magician's Nephew* London: The Bodley Head
Lyon 2000	Lyon, D. *Jesus in Disneyland: Religion in Postmodern Times*, Cambridge: Polity Press
MacCarthy 1994	MacCarthy, F. *William Morris* London: Faber & Faber
McConville 2006	McConville, J.G. *God and Earthly Power, An Old Testament Political Theology* London: T & T. Clark
McLeod 2000	McLeod, J. *Beginning Postcolonialism*, Manchester: Manchester University Press
Maier 2000	Maier, K. *This House Has Fallen* London: Penguin Books
Martin 2006	Martin, D. 'Global expansion and radical primitive Christianity' in *Princeton Seminary Bulletin* 26/1
Meyer 1998	Meyer, B. ' "Make a Complete Break with the Past": Memory and Postcolonial Modernity in Ghanaian Pentecostal Discourse' chapter 7 in Richard Werbner, ed., *Memory and the Postcolony*, London: Zed Books
Meyers 1992	Meyers, E.S. *Envisioning the New City* Louisville: Westminster/John Knox Press
Morris 1984	Morris, W. *William Morris: News from Nowhere and Selected Writings and Designs* Harmondsworth: Penguin
Morrisy 2004	Morrisy, A. *Journeying Out* London: Moorhouse

Myers 1988	Myers, C. *Binding the Strong Man* Maryknoll: Orbis
Myers 1994	Myers, C. *Who Will Roll Away the Stone?* Maryknoll: Orbis
Myers 2001	Myers, C. *The Biblical Vision of Sabbath Economics* Washington DC: Tell the Word
Nandy 1990	Nandy, M. *At the Edge of Psychology* New Delhi: Oxford University Press
Niebuhr 1951	Niebuhr, H.R. *Christ and Cultue*, New York: Harper and Row
Oakeshott 1960	Oakeshott, M. ed. *Thomas Hobbes, Leviathan* Oxford: Blackwell
O'Riordan 2001	O'Riordan T. ed., *Globalism, Localism and Identity*, London: Earthscan
Pirouet 1999	Pirouet L. 'The Legacy of Johann Ludwig Krapf' in *International Bulletin of Missionary Research* 32/2 April 1999
Porter 1997	Porter, A. ' "Cultural Imperialism" and Protestant Missionary Enterprise, 1780-1914' *Journal of Imperial and Commonwealth History* vol 25 no 2, Seprtember 1997
Powers 1997	Powers, C.T. *In the Memory of the Forest* London: Anchor
Pugh 1988	Pugh, M. *Lloyd George* London, Longman
Puttnam 2000	Puttnam, R., Phatt S. and Dalton, R., *What is Troubling the Mature Democracies?*, Princeton: Princeton University Press
Robert 2002	Robert, D. 'The First Globalization: The Internationalization of the Protestant Missionary Movement Between the World Wars' *International Bulletin of Missionary Research* 26/2 pp. 50-66
Rochenko 2005	Smokewriting/Blog Archive/Philosophy as Radical Thought: a Tribute to Gillian Rose http://ccgi.bluesmokedesign.plus.com/?p=34
Rogers 2002	Rogers, P. *Losing Control: Global Survival in the Twenty-first Century*, Second Edition, London: Pluto Press
Rogers 1997	Rogers R. *Cities for a Small Planet* London: Faber

Rose 1992	Rose, G. *The Broken Middle* Oxford: Blackwells
Rose 2005	Rose, J. *The Question of Zion* Princeton: Princeton Univesity Press
Rose 2007	Rose J. *The Last Resistance* London: Verso
Roy 2002	Roy, A. *The Algebra of Infinite Justice* London: Flamingo
Rushdie 1991	Rushdie, S. *Haroun and the Sea of Stories* London; Granta
Ruskin 1862	Ruskin J., *Sesame and Lilies* and *Unto This Last* London: Gresham, 1862
Rutherford 1990	Rutherford J. *Identity* London: Lawrence and Wishart
Sachs 2002	Sachs, J. *The Dignity of Difference*, London: Continuum
Said 2003a	Said, E. *Orientalism* (New Edition) London: Penguin
Said 2003b	Said, E. *Freud and the Non-European* London: Verso
Sanneh 1989	Sanneh, L. *Translating the Message* Maryknoll: Orbis
Sardar & Davies 2002	Sardar, Z. and Davies, W.M. *Why Do People Hate America?* Cambridge: Icon Books
Schaeffer 2003	Schaeffer, R. *Understanding Globalization* (Second Edition), Lanham: Rowman & Littlefield
Schaper 1992	Schaper, D. 'Bricks Without Straw: Ministry in the City' in Meyers E.S. *Envisioning the New City* Louisville: Westminster
Schluter 1994	Schluter, M. *The Rise and Fall of Nations: How Far Can Christians Interpret History?*, Cambridge Paper 3/3, Cambridge: The Jubilee Centre
Schuurman 2001	Schuurman, F. ed. *Globalization and Development Studies* London: Sage
Seabrook 1996	Seabrook, J. *In the Cities of the South* London:Verso
Sen 1999	Sen, A. *Development as Freedom* Oxford: Oxford University Press
Sinclair 1980	Sinclair, M. *Green Finger of God* Exeter: Paternoster Press
Sine 1981	Sine, T. 'Development: Its Secular Past and Its Uncertain Future' in Sider, R. ed. *Towards a Theology of Social Change* Exeter: Paternoster Press
Sine 1999	Sine T. *Mustard Seed versus McWorld* London: Monarch
Singer 2003	Singer, P. *Pushing Time Away* London: Granta Books
Skidelsky 1992	Sidelsky, R. *John Maynard Keynes, The Economist as

	Saviour 1920-37 London: Macmillan
Smith A. 1995	Smith, A.D. *Nations and Nationalism in a Global Era*, Cambridge: Polity Press
Smith D. 2003	Smith, D. *Mission After Christendom*, London: Dartman, Longman & Todd
Smith N. 2003	Neil Smith, 'After the American *Lebensraum*' in *Interventions* 5/2, 2003
Spivak 1988	Spivak, G. 'Can the Subaltern Speak?' in Nelson, C. and Grossberg, L. editors *Marxism and the Interpretation of Culture* London: Palgrave
Stackhouse 2000	Stackhouse J., *Out of Poverty and Into Something More Comfortable*, Random House Canada
Steger 2003	Steger, M. *Globalisation, A Very Short Introduction*, Oxford: Oxford University Press
Stanley 1990	Stanley, B. *The Bible and the* Flag Leicester: Apollos
Stiglitz 2002	Stiglitz, J. *Globalization and its Discontents* London: Penguin
Stoll 1982	Stoll, D. *Fishers of Men or Founders of Empire?, The Wycliffe Bible Translators in Latin America* London: Zed Press
Stott 1992	Stott, J. *The Contemporary Christian* Leicester: IVP
Sweetnam 2006	Sweetnam, M. 'Dan Crawford, *Thinking Black*, and the Challenge of a Missionary Canon' in *Journal of Ecclesiastical History* Vol 57 No.4, October 2006
Thistleton 1992	Thistleton, A. *New Horizons in Hermeneutics* London: Harper/Collins
Toynbee 2003	Toynbee, P. *Hard Work* London: Bloomsbury
UNSRID 2000	United Nations Research Institute for Social Development, *Visible Hands, Taking Responsibility for Social Developments*, Switzerland: UNSRID
Van Dijk 1998	Van Dijk, R. 'Pentecostalism, Cultural Memory and the State: Contested Representations of Time in Postcolonial Malawi' in Richard Werbner, ed. *Memory and the Postcolony*, London: Zed Books
Vargas Llosa 1991	Vargas Llosa, M. *The Storyteller* London: Faber
Volf 1996	Volf, M. *Exclusion and Embrace* Nashville TN: Abingdon
Walls 2002	Walls, A. *The Cross-Cultural Process in Christian History*

	Maryknoll: Orbis
Walsh & Keesmaat 2004	Walsh, B. & Keesmaat, S. *Colossians Remixed* Carlisle: Paternoster
Weil 2001	Weil, S. *Oppression and Liberty* London: Routledge
Weil 2002	Weil, S. *The Need for Roots* London: Routledge
Werbner 1998	Werbner R. (ed.) *Memory and the Postcolony* London: Zed Books
Werbner 2002	Werbner R. (ed.) *Postcolonial Subjectivities in Africa*, London: Zed Books
Werbner & Ranger 1996	Werbner, R. & Ranger, T. (eds.) *Postcolonial Identities in Africa*. London: Zed Books
Williams 1958	Williams, C. *The Image of the City and Other Essays* Oxford: OUP
Williams 1988	Williams, R., *Border Country*, London: Hogarth Press
Wink 1984	Wink, W. *Naming the Powers* Minneapolis: Fortress Press
Wink 1992	Wink, W. *Engaging the Powers* Minneapolis: Fortress Press
Wright 1991	Wright, N.T. 'How Can the Bible Be Authoritative?' *Vox Evangelica* 21 pp. 7-32
Wright 1996	Wright, N.T. *Jesus and the Victory of God* London: SPCK
Wright 2000	Wright, N.T. 'Paul's Gospel and Caesar's Empire' in Richard A. Horsley ed., *Paul and Politics*, Harrisburg, Pa.: Trinity Press
Young 2001	Young, R. *Postcolonialism, An Historical Introduction* Oxford: Blackwell
Young 2004	Young, R. *White Mythologies* (Second Edition) London: Routledge

INDEX

Index

Symbols

9/11 **10, 152**
10/40 window **169**
2012 Olympics **140**

A

Aaron **234**
Aborigines **129, 130**
Abraham **108, 110, 236, 238, 240**
Achebe, Chinua **132, 174**
Adam **210, 212, 213**
Adorno, Theodore **222**
Aesop's fables **123**
Afghanistan **10, 154, 170**
African Independent Churches **187**
Ahab, King **87**
Ahaz, King **98**
AIDS **20, 128, 230, 249**
Akinola, Archbishop **186**
Algerian war of resistance **47**
Al Jazeera **11**
Al Qaeda **10, 23, 33**
Amazon **132**
American revolution **89, 198**
Amnesty International **203**
Amsterdam **52**
Anabaptists **31, 38, 175**
ANC **47**
Ancient Near East **212**
Anderson, Benedict **53, 126, 250**
Anderson, Laurie **107**
Andrews, C.F. **184**
Angola **126**
Anschluss **148**
Antioch **28**
anti-semitism **144, 149**
apartheid **129, 227, 247**
apocalyptic **12, 18, 30, 37, 97, 215, 216, 217, 218, 219, 220, 221, 222, 223,**

224, 230, 239, 240, 244, 245, 246
Arafat, Yasser **243**
archaeology **52, 53, 61**
Arendt, Hannah **145**
Argentinean Chacko **126**
Argentinean Chako **206, 207**
Aristides **114**
Armageddon **239**
Armistice Day **219**
Armstrong, Karen **172**
Arnott, F.S. **126**
Ashcroft, Bill **44, 48, 50, 250**
Asher **236**
Asia Minor **25, 216, 239, 245**
Assyrians **17, 98**
Augustine of Hippo **112**
Au Revoir Les Enfants **148**
Australasia **40**
Australia **116, 129**
Austria **147, 148**
Avnery, Uri **150**
Azariah, Bishop **92**

B

Babel **17, 85**
Babylon **13, 17, 27, 30, 39, 94, 136, 218, 221, 230, 231, 237, 238, 239, 240, 249**
Bach, Johann Sebastian **41**
Badaga **105**
Bader-Meinhof **47**
Balkans **82**
Bangkok **75, 76**
Barker, Pat **219**
Barmen Declaration **38**
Barth, Karl **38, 246**
Battle Hymn of the Republic **247**
Bauman **3, 101, 102, 160, 161, 250**
BBC **24, 153, 154**
Beast **18, 19, 26, 97**
Bede, the Venerable **181**
Beeby, Dan **79, 250**
Belbin's Teams **234**
Bellow, Saul **107**
Bengal **6**

Benjamin, Walter 57, 58, 118, 142, 143, 145, 221, 222, 250
Benn, Tony 24
Bentinck, William 165
Berry, Wendell xviii, 41, 73, 76, 77, 86, 109, 114, 136, 250, 251
Bhabha, Homi 44, 45, 50, 51, 53, 102, 103, 122, 159, 161, 251, 254
Big Pharma 223
Bilhah 236
Blade Runner 119, 120
BNP 152
Boers 33
Bonhöffer, Dietrich 31, 38, 246
Bretton Woods 63, 89, 90
Britain xviii, 11, 17, 32, 34, 36, 39, 56, 58, 67, 117, 118, 125, 139, 140, 144, 145, 152, 153, 158, 172, 185, 186, 187, 193, 194, 196, 202, 231, 243, 251
British Museum 169
Brittain, Vera 219, 220
Britten, Benjamin 218, 219
Broadbent, E.H. 38
Broadbent, Peter 169
Bronner, Stephen 221, 251
Brown, Callum 172, 251
Bruce, F.F. 206, 239
Bruderhof 202
Brueggemann, Walter 10, 251
Buber, Martin 221
Buena Vista Social Club. 41, 52
Burnett, David 127
Bush, G.W. 152, 250
Buxton, Derbyshire 220

C

Caesar 17, 25, 30, 155, 216, 259
Calcutta (Kolkota) 6
Calill, Carmen 144
Callil, Carmen 148
Cameroons 128
Campaign Against the Arms Trade 196
Canada 81, 116, 258
capitalism 32, 38, 62, 63, 78, 89, 90, 166, 172, 196, 197, 214
Carey, William 81
Carlyon, H.C. 167
Carter, Warren 28, 114, 251
Castells, Manuel 11, 63, 66, 106, 110, 183, 251
Chambers, Robert 80, 81, 251

Chatterjee, Partha **126, 251**
China 59, 66, 139, 222
Christian Association of Nigeria **186**
Christian Peoples Alliance **12**
Christian Social Union **190**
Christian Zionists **242**
Church **xvii**, 38, 40, 50, 176, 181, 187, 251
church planting 2, 81, 105
city 21, 134, 138, 141, 167, 218, 240
CMS **185**
Coca Cola 50, 65, 188
Cohen, Leonard 108, 189, 251
Cold War 89, 149
colonialism **xvii, xviii, xix**, 6, 8, 13, 14, 28, 40, 43, 44, 46, 47, 48, 52, 54, 56, 83, 89, 91, 100, 111, 116, 125, 135, 137, 139, 140, 143, 145, 146, 147, 149, 168, 169, 170, 173, 182, 188, 227, 231, 241, 243, 252
colonial transaction **44**
Colossians, letter to 15, 16, 113, 213, 259
coming of the Son of Man 29, 245, 246, 247
Commonwealth 146, 256
communications industry **20**
Communism **xviii**, 168
conquistadores 174, 185
Constantinianism 155, 175, 189
Cooder, Ry 41, 52
Courtine-Denamy, Sylvie **145**
covenant **96**
Coventry Cathedral **219**
Crawford, Dan 126, 258
Crossan, Dominic **119**
Crusades **43**
Cuba 41, 52

D

Dan **236**
Daniel, book of 29, 71, 210, 215, 231, 245
Danish cartoons **152**
Dante **119**
Darquier, Louis 144, 148
David, King 59, 95, 190, 238
Davies W.M. **56**
Davis, Mike 7, 136, 137, 252
Davos forum 22, 183
Dawkins,Richard **159**

D Day 25
debt 18, 28, 35, 86, 207, 231, 248
Decca 219
Delhi 139, 254, 256
democracy 19, 22, 33, 41, 62, 89, 152, 175, 194, 211, 229
Derrida, Jacques 56
destruction of Jerusalem 4, 238, 239
Deuteronomy, book of 87, 95, 195, 203, 210, 211
De Zengotita, Brian 124, 252
diaspora 43, 103, 104, 109, 115, 117, 118, 121, 122, 123, 124, 125, 127, 141, 147, 149, 238
disarmament 90
dispensationalism 240, 242
Disraeli, Benjamin 144
Domination System 14, 17, 18, 27, 37, 98, 125, 134, 192, 216, 217, 218, 223, 230, 231, 232, 233, 234
Drown, Frank 132, 133, 252
Duff, Alexander 165
DuPont 29

E

East Harlem 206
East India Company 7
ebed yahweh 237
Economist 34, 64, 257
Edge of Darkness 217, 223
Edict of Nantes 176
Edinburgh 2010 183
Edinburgh Conference 1910 59, 92
Egypt 210, 240
Ehrenreich, Barbara 113, 114, 252
Elliott, Neil 30, 31, 252
Empire 15, 17, 18, 19, 25, 27, 28, 30, 31, 32, 34, 36, 37, 40, 52, 64, 87, 93, 97, 99, 103, 113, 114, 115, 136, 139, 146, 150, 158, 165, 167, 169, 172, 173, 175, 176, 183, 213, 216, 217, 218, 221, 223, 227, 229, 231, 234, 240, 244, 245, 247, 253, 254, 258, 259
Enlightenment xviii, xix, 8, 37, 39, 52, 53, 54, 79, 92, 93, 109, 133, 139, 140, 160, 165, 166, 168, 170, 176, 191, 221, 222, 227
Enlightenment Project xviii, 133, 227
environmentalism 80, 90
Ephesus 55
Ephraim 236
Esau 236, 238
eschatology 15, 141, 171, 244, 246

essentialism **104**
ETA **23**
European Union **80**
Evangelical Revival **172**
Evangelicals **26, 53, 81, 151, 158, 242**
exorcism **28, 114, 233**
Ezra **190**

F

Fanon, Frantz **47**
Fascism **xviii**
Faulk, Sebastian **219**
feminism **90, 176**
Fortune 100 **26**
Foucault, Michel **48**
France **47, 68, 69, 117, 144, 146, 147, 176**
France, R.T. **111, 239, 252**
Francis of Assisi **38**
Fraser, Giles **186, 252**
Freire, Paolo **88, 162**
French revolution **198**
Freud. Sigmund **9, 53, 145, 146, 147, 257**
Froese, Arno **242**
Fuller Theological Seminary **183**

G

G20 **197**
Gad **236**
Galatia **103**
Gamsk **128**
Gandhi, Mohandas **16, 22, 31, 41, 44, 47, 126, 247, 252**
Garden of Eden **212**
Garden of Gethsemane **240**
Garton Ash, Timothy **80**
GCHQ **24**
Genoa **21**
German Confessing Church **38**
Germany **23, 38, 47, 147, 246**
Gilead **230**
Gillis, John R. **120, 253**
Gilroy, Paul **104, 118**
globalisation **10, 34, 37, 62, 63, 64, 65, 66, 67, 69, 70, 71, 74, 76, 77, 79, 80,**

81, 82, 83, 84, 89, 91, 94, 104, 110, 111, 117, 118, 122, 126, 127, 152, 158, 171, 183, 196, 207, 229, 231, 247, 248, 254, 258
Global South 35, 44, 45, 46, 48, 89, 91, 92, 108, 117, 130, 137, 140, 142, 146, 158, 168, 172, 173, 174, 183, 186, 187, 188
globfrag 80
glocalisation 66, 67, 68, 78
Gloucester 73, 76, 80
Gloucestershire Network Against the War 12, 24
Gramsci, Antonio 21, 22, 48
Grant, Charles 165
Great Economy 84, 114, 192, 193, 195, 196, 210, 213, 215, 227, 230
Great War 56, 218, 219, 220
Greenpeace 203
Guardian 80, 104
Guevara, Che 47
gunboat diplomacy 33

H

Hagee 242
Hall, Stuart 105
Hamas 23
Hardt, Michael 19, 20, 116, 253
Harvey, David 6, 66, 84, 138, 161
Hawthorne, Nathaniel 31, 119
Hebrews, book of 28, 121, 150, 230, 238, 239
hegemony 12, 19, 21, 22, 48, 49, 248
Heslam, Peter 70
Hiebert, Paul 82, 105, 127, 254
historicism 144
Hitler, Adolf 31
Hobbes, Thomas 8, 153, 256
Holland 117, 176
Holland, Henry Scott 166
Holocaust Day 31
Holy Land 239, 243
Hong Kong 139
Horsley, Richard 37, 254, 259
Huddart, David 53, 254
Hughes, Dewi 77, 81, 82, 254

Huguenots 176
Hutchinson, Mark 79, 254
Hutus 180
hybridity 43, 44, 46, 66, 80, 83, 101, 102, 103, 104, 108, 130, 135

I

IMF 26, 34, 35
imperialism 12, 14, 18, 19, 20, 26, 27, 31, 32, 33, 34, 35, 36, 37, 39, 40, 55, 56, 73, 79, 83, 125, 133, 136, 139, 146, 165, 166, 167, 170, 171, 172, 173, 178, 243, 247
Independent 172, 205
India 7, 16, 32, 34, 42, 43, 51, 66, 85, 94, 103, 105, 125, 139, 147, 165, 166, 168, 175, 187, 254
Indian Christian Theology 184
Indian Civil Service 42
Indonesia 186
Iniciativa Cristiana 84, 126, 206, 207
Integral 88
interpolation 44, 48
IRA 23
Iran 152
Iraq 10, 19, 24, 33, 34, 154
Iroquois 56
Isaac 108, 236
Isaiah, book of 29, 30, 87, 96, 98, 113, 114, 169, 190, 208, 213, 214, 229, 247
Islam 5, 10, 11, 67, 93, 151, 153, 158, 159, 185, 242
Israel 10, 17, 30, 43, 86, 87, 95, 107, 110, 115, 144, 145, 146, 149, 150, 152, 171, 190, 194, 227, 231, 236, 237, 238, 239, 240, 241, 242, 243, 244, 249
Italy 21, 47, 147, 149, 152

J

Jenkins, Philip 181, 254
Jerry Springer – The Opera 153
Jerry Springer –The Opera 154
Jerusalem 17, 27, 28, 96, 138, 142, 169, 195, 202, 213, 218, 229, 237, 238, 239, 240
Jesus 2, 4, 5, 12, 13, 15, 16, 17, 18, 22, 25, 27, 29, 30, 31, 37, 47, 49, 50, 57, 59, 73, 80, 85, 87, 88, 96, 105, 110, 111, 112, 113, 114, 115, 125, 133, 136, 143, 150, 155, 156, 163, 166, 168, 171, 177, 186, 190, 192, 195, 196, 201, 208, 213, 215, 222, 224, 226, 229, 230, 231, 232, 234, 238, 239, 240, 245, 246, 255, 259
Jezebel 87

Joffe, Joseph 22
John of Patmos 14, 17, 27, 97, 215, 216, 217, 218, 220, 221, 223, 239, 240, 246, 247, 251
Johnson, Lionel 225
Johnson, Samuel 49
John the Baptist 27, 226
Jones, Martin Lloyd 59
Joseph 236
Jubilee 86, 90, 234, 257
Judea 142

K

Karambola 129
Käsemann, Ernst 222
Kashmiri separatists 23
Keesmaat, Sylvia 113, 114, 259
Kellerman, Bill Wylie 233
Kelmscott Manor 194
Kenrick, Bruce 206
Kenya 139
Keswick Convention 110
Kew Gardens 218
Keynes 8, 89, 90, 257
Khoi 126
Kingdom of God xvii, 4, 5, 12, 70, 88, 96, 108, 111, 114, 121, 122, 150, 151, 163, 179, 192, 213, 226, 227, 254
Kingdom Of God 189
King, Martin Luther 22, 31, 47, 59
Kingsolver, Barbara 38
Kipling, Rudyard 32, 33, 253
Klein, Naomi 21
Klong Toey 75, 76
Koran 242
Kovel, Joel 78, 202, 255
Koyama, Kosuke 184
Kraft, Charles 82
Krapf, Ludwig 185, 256
Kyoto agreement 34

L

Lambeth Conference 1999 176
Last Supper 224

Latin America **45, 116, 164, 165, 170, 174, 184, 185, 258**
Lausanne **183**
Le Carré, John **223**
Leigh, Mike **120**
Lemuel, King **202**
Lenin, V.I. **89**
Lennon, John **211**
Leviathan **8, 256**
Levi, Primo **144, 149, 255**
Lewis, C.S. **59, 255**
Liberal Party **34**
Liberation Theology **3, 82, 184, 222**
Little Apocalypse **238, 239**
Livingstone, David **182**
Llosa, Mario Vargas **41, 254, 258**
London **8, 104, 110, 140, 141, 169, 190, 197, 218, 238, 239, 253**
Lord of the Rings **43, 218**
Luddites **86**

M

Macaulay, Lord **51, 165**
MacCarthy, Fiona **193, 194, 255**
Macedonia **1**
Machiguengas **41, 133, 136**
Madagascar **129**
magic realism **47, 52, 53, 54**
Malawi **127, 135, 258**
Malle, Louis **144**
Manasseh **236**
Manchester United **75, 78**
Mandela, Nelson **22, 47, 102**
Manila **36, 183**
Mann, Thomas **8**
MARC publications **88**
Martin, David **184, 255**
Martin, Troy Kennedy **217**
Marxism **9, 121, 221, 222, 258**
Marx, Karl **9, 221**
Massinger, Philip **183**
Matthew, gospel of **4, 16, 27, 28, 50, 59, 87, 110, 111, 114, 150, 190, 195, 196, 202, 208, 213, 236, 238, 239, 246, 247, 251**
Maugham, Somerset **222, 223**
Mbang, Sunday **186**
Mbarara **50**

Mbiti, John **184**
McCarthyism **37**
McConville, Gordon **210**, **255**
Medicin sans Frontières **203**
Mendelssohn, Felix **41**
Methodism **172**
Micah Network **88**
Micaiah **98**
Microsoft **29**
Middle ages **32**
Middle East **10**, **31**, **33**, **95**, **144**, **145**, **147**, **149**, **150**, **239**, **242**, **243**
Midnight Call Ministry **242**
mimicry **44**, **47**, **50**, **51**, **52**, **61**
minjung **82**
Mision Chaquena **207**
missio Dei **226**, **227**
missiology **4**, **57**, **116**, **124**, **125**, **126**, **127**, **130**, **142**, **162**, **163**, **187**
mission **xvii**, **xix**, **1**, **2**, **5**, **9**, **10**, **11**, **16**, **17**, **30**, **44**, **45**, **46**, **58**, **78**, **80**, **81**, **88**, **92**, **100**, **103**, **107**, **108**, **109**, **114**, **115**, **116**, **122**, **126**, **127**, **131**, **132**, **133**, **135**, **141**, **142**, **148**, **150**, **158**, **163**, **164**, **165**, **168**, **169**, **170**, **171**, **173**, **177**, **179**, **183**, **184**, **189**, **191**, **195**, **213**, **226**, **227**, **234**, **244**
Mizoram **103**
Mohammed **155**
Mokades, Raphael **104**
Moldova **87**
Monbiot, George **229**
More, Thomas **8**, **106**, **153**, **165**, **250**, **256**
Morris, Benny **241**
Morris, William **41**, **193**, **194**, **211**, **255**
Morrisy, Ann **106**, **107**, **255**
Moses **234**
MTV **77**
Mugabe, Robert **36**
multiculturalism **100**, **102**, **116**
Mumbai **36**, **139**
Munich Conference on Security Policy **22**
Murdoch, Rupert **80**
Myers, Ched **xviii**, **28**, **41**, **70**, **71**, **87**, **119**, **131**, **132**, **222**, **246**, **256**
Mysore **139**
myth of redemptive violence **20**

N

Naboth **87**
Naipaul V.S. **50**

Nairobi 139
Nandy 6, 256
Naphtali 236
Narnia 225
National Health Service 118
nationalism 48, 249, 258
nations 17, 30, 31, 32, 103, 114, 136, 140, 147, 159, 195, 208, 217, 230, 243
Native Americans 56
Nazis 38, 47, 130, 145, 147
Negri, Antonio 19, 20, 116, 253
Nehemiah 190
Nehru 43
Neighbourhood Watch 204, 234
Neocons 152
New Hampshire 186
New Jerusalem 5, 17, 27, 94, 114, 136, 195, 208, 213, 216, 217, 218, 225, 230, 240, 249
New Statesman 146, 253
New Testament xviii, 5, 6, 12, 14, 15, 17, 30, 37, 42, 85, 105, 109, 141, 144, 150, 175, 193, 201, 223, 226, 228, 230, 237, 239
New York 22, 52, 63, 206, 242
NGOs 20, 200, 203
Nigeria 186, 187
Nike 29
Nilgiri Hills 42, 105
non-aligned movement 89
Norberg-Hodge, Helena 204
Notting Hill Carnival 110
Nuba 128
Nubians 236

O

Oakeshott, Michael 8, 256
Obama, Barak 34
Occupied Territories 243
Oceania 164
Old Testament prophets 22, 37, 98, 113
Ongoni delta 13
Ootacamund 85, 105
opium trade 165
Oppenheim, David 148
Orientalism 44, 48, 55, 257
Osama Bin Laden 10, 23
Oslo negotiations 243

Ott, Martin **127**
Owen, Wilfred **218, 219**
Oxfam **203**
Oxford **40, 104, 220**
Oxfordshire **193, 194**

P

Pakistan **10, 117, 147**
Palestine **6, 10, 43, 105, 145, 190, 241, 242**
Palestinians **43, 46, 147, 149, 243**
palimpsest **54, 55, 61**
Palmer, Christopher **219**
Participatory Rural Appraisal **81**
patriarchalism **49, 166**
patriarchy **174, 176, 229**
Paul, Apostle **1, 2, 15, 25, 29, 30, 31, 46, 55, 84, 85, 103, 106, 110, 113, 115, 163, 206, 231, 233, 236, 237, 238, 239, 240, 252, 254, 259**
Pax Americana **15**
Pax Britannica **15**
Pax Romana **15**
Peck, Bob **217**
Pentecost **85, 247**
Pentecostals **53, 185, 255**
people groups **169, 171**
Peru **133**
Peter, Apostle **2, 114, 238, 247**
Philip, John **126**
Philippines **32**
Philip the Evangelist **115**
Philistines **95, 97, 236**
Pilate **31**
Plymouth Brethren **38**
Poland **147, 231**
pornography **180, 233**
Porter, Andrew **83, 256**
Portugal **117, 185**
postcolonialism **xvii, xix, 1, 2, 5, 6, 11, 40, 43, 44, 45, 52, 54, 55, 56, 61, 112, 122, 145, 151, 158, 164, 173, 174, 188, 213, 227**
powers **1, 15, 16, 31, 63, 93, 116, 233**
Powers, Charles **119**
premillennialism **171**
Prior, Michael **241, 242**
Prodigal Son, parable of **190**
Prospect **242**

prosperity gospel **186, 188**
prosperity teaching **177**
Puddleglum **224, 225**
Pullman, Philip **215**
Puritan revolution **212**
Puritans **119, 212, 241**
Putin, Vladimir **152**

Q

Quakers **31**

R

Rabbit Proof Fence **129, 130**
racism **8, 31, 36, 68, 90, 91, 175**
Radical Reformers **22**
Rahab **236**
Raj, British **36, 64**
Reagan, Ronald **90, 248**
Red Brigades **47**
Reformation **31, 38, 58, 175, 176**
Remembrance Day **56**
representation **55, 199**
Restoration in England **248**
Revelation, Book of **13, 14, 16, 17, 18, 19, 25, 26, 27, 37, 38, 94, 97, 134, 136, 138, 151, 208, 213, 215, 217, 218, 220, 221, 223, 228, 231, 239, 240, 244, 245, 246, 247, 248, 251, 254**
Ricardo, David **41, 86**
Richard the Lionheart **43**
Ricoeur, Paul **161**
Ridley, Scott **119**
Rogers, Richard **138, 141, 256**
Rohak district **167**
Romans 9-11 **236, 237, 238, 239, 240**
Rome **17, 29, 30, 32, 65, 66, 84, 113, 114, 115, 183, 216, 240**
Roosevelt, Teddy **32**
Rose, Gillian **107, 108, 109, 140, 160, 256, 257**
Rose, Jacqueline **145, 146, 147, 160**
Royal Shakespeare Company **183**
Roy, Arundhati **2, 3, 131, 257**
Rushdie, Salman **104, 162**
Ruskin, John **41, 257**
Russia **26, 152**

Ruth, book of **87, 236**
Rwanda **180**

S

Sabbath Economics **131, 256**
Sachs, Jonathan **63, 257**
Saddam Hussein **19, 33**
Said, Edward **43, 44, 48, 55, 145, 146, 147, 149, 257**
Salvation Army **190**
Samaria **142**
Sanders, J.A. **159**
Sanneh, Lamin **49, 81**
Sardar, Z. **56, 146, 257**
Sartre, Jean Paul **47**
Sassoon Siegfried **248**
Satan **18, 28, 218, 230, 244**
satyagraha **47**
Saudi Arabia **10**
Schaper, Dona **231, 257**
Schluter, Michael **116, 257**
Seabrook, Jeremy **75, 137**
Sebald, W.G. **144**
Second Boer War **33, 34**
Second Coming **244**
Second Gulf war **20**
Second World War **23, 56, 89, 219**
secularism **xviii, 79, 127, 173, 176, 190**
security **2, 22, 23, 24, 25, 29, 114, 138, 153, 197, 198, 199, 200, 201, 214, 217, 243**
Selene **28**
Seleucid empire **29**
September 11 **10, 19, 22, 25, 75, 242**
Sermon on the Mount **49, 111**
Servants For Asia's Urban Poor **142**
Seth, Vikram **144**
Shanghai **139**
Sharpeville Massacre **47**
Shell **13**
short term mission **171**
Shuar **132**
signs of the times **17, 245**
Simpson, John **24**
Sinclair, Maurice **84, 88, 126, 206, 257**
Sine, Tom **73, 86, 88, 257**

Singer, Peter **144, 148**
Skidelsky, Robert **8, 9, 90, 257**
slavery **xvii, 1, 28, 132, 143, 168, 233, 247**
Smith **71, 258**
Smith, Adam **86**
sociology **3, 79, 127, 160**
Sodom **13, 240**
Solomon, King **95, 212**
Song of Songs **211, 212, 213**
South Africa **33, 47, 126, 135, 241**
South Asian Concern **124, 125**
South Sea Islands **165**
Spain **176, 185**
Spivak, Gayatri **48, 258**
Spring Harvest **110**
Spurgeon, C.H. **59, 190**
Sri Lanka **91, 93, 249**
Stein, Edith **145**
St Francis **22**
Stott, John **3, 258**
street children **2, 9, 10, 11, 114, 139**
structural adjustment **26**
Subaltern Studies **38**
Sub-Saharan Africa **8, 164, 185**
Sudan **128, 233**
Suez War **56**
Sugden, Chris **105**
Swan, C.A. **126**
Synoptic gospels **215**
Synoptic Gospels **4**

T

Taliban **23**
Talmud **160**
Tamil **23, 81, 105**
Tamil Tigers **23**
TEAR Fund **88**
terrorism **158, 253**
terrorists **11, 20, 22, 23, 171**
Thackeray, Jake **212**
Thatcher, Margaret **90, 95, 248**
The Constant Gardener **223, 224**
The Painted Veil **222, 223**
Theresienstadt **148**

The Story of the Weeping Camel **134**
the System **23, 26, 29**
Third Reich **112, 144, 216, 246, 247**
Third Space **100, 101, 102, 104, 107**
Third World **35, 37, 231**
Thoreau, Henry David **31**
TIME magazine **22**
TNCs **203**
Tobin Tax **200**
Toffler, Alvin **157**
torah **210**
Transvaal **33**
tribe **18, 85, 87, 132, 133, 136, 210**
tricontinentalism **89**
Trinity **160, 259**
Trojan war **43**
Truman Doctrine **90**
Truman Show **20**
tsunami **91**
Tutsis **180**
Tutu, Archbishop Desmond **40**
Tyrians **236**

U

Uganda **128**
Ulysses **43**
umma **10**
uncanny **53**
United States **19, 31, 32, 33, 34, 41, 59, 62, 71, 89, 116, 144, 145, 147, 185, 188, 190, 227, 231, 242, 243, 247, 248**
University of Gloucestershire **210**
US State Department **33**

V

Van Gogh, Theo **152**
V Day **25**
Venceer, Jun **81**
Vespasian **28**
Vietnam War **37**
Volf, Miroslav **109, 258**

W

Wal-Mart **113**
Walsh, Brian **113**, **114**, **259**
war against Iraq **24**
Warfield, Benjamin **59**
War Requiem **218**, **219**
Washington Consensus **90**
Waterworld **119**
weapons of mass destruction **33**
Weil, Simone **32**, **71**, **76**, **119**, **145**, **259**
Werbner, Richard **128**, **255**, **258**, **259**
West Indies **xix**
Willams, Raymond **72**
Williams, Rowan **108**
Wink, Walter **14**, **15**, **47**, **49**, **93**, **247**, **259**
World Bank **34**, **89**, **93**
World Cup (2006) **75**
World Development Movement **12**
World Vision **88**, **203**
Wright, N.T. **4**, **30**, **111**, **190**, **193**, **238**, **239**, **246**, **259**
WTO **34**, **35**

Y

Yugoslavia **127**, **249**

Z

Zambia **126**
Zilpah **236**
Zimbabwe **36**
Zionism **11**, **147**, **241**, **243**